Rethinking

Children and

Inclusive

Education

Rethinking Children and Inclusive Education

Sue Pearson

New Childhoods series
Series Editor: Phil Jones

Bloomsbury Academic
An imprint of Bloomsbury Publishing Plc

B L O O M S B U R Y
LONDON · OXFORD · NEW YORK · NEW DELHI · SYDNEY

Bloomsbury Academic

An imprint of Bloomsbury Publishing Plc

50 Bedford Square	1385 Broadway
London	New York
WC1B 3DP	NY 10018
UK	USA

www.bloomsbury.com

BLOOMSBURY and the Diana logo are trademarks of Bloomsbury Publishing Plc

First published 2016

© Sue Pearson, 2016

British Library Cataloguing-in-Publication Data

A catalogue record for this book is available from the British Library.

ISBN:	HB:	978-1-4725-6837-3
	PB:	978-1-4725-6836-6
	ePDF:	978-1-4725-6838-0
	ePub:	978-1-4725-6839-7

Library of Congress Cataloging-in-Publication Data

A catalog record for this book is available from the Library of Congress.

Series: New Childhoods

Typeset by Fakenham Prepress Solutions, Fakenham, Norfolk NR21 8NN
Printed and bound in India

Contents

Part III Implications for Children's Lives:
Using Children's Perspectives to Inform
Inclusive Education

List of Tables

List of Illustrations

Acknowledgements

I would like to thank the Series Editor, Prof. Phil Jones, for suggesting the original idea and for his generous support throughout. I am extremely grateful to Karen Atkinson for her assistance with the preparation of the manuscript. The encouragement from my friends including their willingness to read drafts has been invaluable.

My final thanks are to all the children I have met during my career. They helped to shape my views and values.

Introduction to New Childhoods Series

The amount of current attention given to children and to childhood is unprecedented. Recent years have seen the agreement of new international conventions, national bodies established and waves of regional and local initiatives all concerning children.

This rapid pace has been set by many things. From children themselves, from adults working with children, from governments and global bodies: injustice, dissatisfaction, new ideas and raw needs are fuelling change. Within and, often, leading the movement is research. From the work of multinational corporations designed to reach into the minds of children and the pockets of parents, through to charity driven initiatives aiming to challenge the forces that situate children in extreme poverty, a massive amount of energy is expended in research relating to children and their lives. This attention is not all benign. Research can be seen as original investigation undertaken in order to gain knowledge and understanding through a systematic and rigorous process of critical enquiry examining 'even the most commonplace assumption' (Kellett, 2005, 9). However, as Kellett has pointed out, the findings can be used by the media to saturate and accost, rather than support, under-12s who are obese, for example, or to stigmatize young people by the use of statistics. However, research can also play a role in investigating, enquiring, communicating and understanding. Recent years have seen innovations in the focus of research, as political moves that challenge the ways in which children have been silenced and excluded result in previously unseen pictures of children's experiences of poverty, family life and community. The attitudes, opinions and lived experiences of children are being given air, and one of the themes within this book concerns the opportunities and challenges this is creating. As this book will reveal, research is being used to set new agendas, to challenge ways of living and working that oppress, harm or limit children. It is also being used to test preconceptions and long held beliefs about children's lived experiences, the actual effects rather than the adult's opinions of the way parents see and relate to their children or the actual impact of services and their ways of working with children.

In addition to the focus of research, innovations are being made in the way research is conceived and carried out. Its role in children's lives is changing. In the past much research treated children as objects, research was done on them, with the agenda and framework set purely by adults. New work is emerging where children create the way research is conceived and carried out. Children act as researchers, researchers work with questions formulated by children or work with children.

This series aims to offer access to some of the challenges, discoveries and work-in-progress of contemporary research. The terms 'child' and 'childhood' are used within the series in line with Article 1 of the United Nations Convention on the Rights of the Child which defines 'children' as persons up to the age of eighteen. The books offer opportunities to engage with emerging ideas, questions and practices. They will help those studying childhood, or living and working with children, to become familiar with challenging work, to engage with findings and to reflect on their own ideas, experiences and ways of working.

Phil Jones
UCL Institute of Education, University College London

Part I

Debates, Dilemmas and Challenges: The Background to Inclusive Education, Children's Participation and Inclusive Research

1

Introduction to *Rethinking Children and Inclusive Education*

Introduction and key questions

This book explores three complex developments in education and the interactions between them. These developments are inclusive education, children's participation and inclusive research. Each of them is a social phenomenon, and each is linked to a wide range of research, policy and practice. Both individually and collectively, the themes are complex and dynamic, and to a greater or lesser degree are contested. Therefore the book does not attempt to provide simplistic accounts or solutions. The intention is to promote a critical response to each of the ideas and to explore established and potential links. An underpinning value of the book is that children should be stakeholders in education, and have both views and agency. Like other volumes in the New Childhoods series, the terms 'child' and 'childhood' are used in line with Article 1 of the United Nations Convention on the Rights of the Child, which defines children as persons up to the age of eighteen.

The literature in each of the three areas is extensive and includes policy documents, research, scholarly writing and media coverage. There is a historical dimension to it, as views about inclusive education, childhood and involvement of children in research have evolved over time. There is also an international dimension, as each of the themes has a global significance. The stance adopted is that all children – whatever their characteristics or circumstances – have an equal right to be heard and listened to, and can contribute to shaping education and, by extension, society. This book explicitly places in the foreground the perspectives and contributions of children who are (potentially) vulnerable and marginalized – those who might be 'accidentally' overlooked.

The issues in the book are important to children themselves, to their families and to the wide range of professionals who work with children. It is mainly for the latter group that this book has been written; the ambitions of inclusive education will only be fulfilled if professionals are alert to the potential of thinking afresh, of challenging stereotypes and of seeing education through different lenses.

The book has the following aims;

- to review recent thinking and research about inclusive education;
- to consider the implications of viewing children as stakeholders;
- to illustrate how children, especially those who are potentially marginalized, can be involved in research; and
- to consider the insights offered by children and the implications for inclusive education.

By the end of the book, you will have started to explore these issues – the Further Reading at the end of each chapter will help you to take your thinking further. There aren't simple answers; there are complex interactions which are dynamic and context-related. If this book had been written ten years ago, the emphasis may have been slightly different. Looking to the future, without doubt thinking will have moved on again. The aim is therefore to prompt you to review critically the material that is available and to develop your approach so that it can be applied to materials that become available.

You should be alert to some characteristics of the text. As noted above, the three themes (inclusive education, children as stakeholders and research involving children) are internationally relevant, and that will be evident in the examples that are provided. You will also notice that education is not treated as a silo but rather as part of a complex set of experiences for children and the adults who live and work with them. Therefore there is an interdisciplinary approach with references to other aspects of children's experience. Equally, education is not seen as synonymous with school. The children who are marginalized are very diverse, so that the evidence from or relating to one group may not easily transfer to another group. However, accessing children's perspectives is illuminating, and the data collected through doing so should be used as evidence in research, policy and practice. Examples of research that illustrate the points above appear throughout the text.

Terms such as 'inclusive education' have become buzzwords used by many stakeholders. However, what is meant by this particular term is both complex and contested. The growing recognition that children are stakeholders in education raises questions about how their views are gathered, whose views are gathered, how the findings of research based upon these views are disseminated and the influence they can exert. As preparation for the subsequent chapters, this introduction considers each of the three themes.

This introductory chapter aims to address the following questions:

- What does the term 'inclusive education' mean?
- What does it mean to think of children as stakeholders?
- How can inclusive education, children as stakeholders and research all be related to each other?

The chapters and in particular the examples of research illustrate the potential of that relationship. The examples are connected with the implications for specific issues but collectively they also illustrate the value of rethinking the relationship between inclusive education and children.

What does the term 'inclusive education' mean?

An approach to this question is to refer to the *Salamanca Statement and Framework for Action on Special Needs Education* (UNESCO, 1994) which is often cited as being a pivotal moment in the history of inclusive education. How the statement was developed provides useful insights. It involved ninety-two governments and twenty-five international organizations, representatives of which met in Salamanca, Spain from 7 to 10 June 1994 and reached a consensus. The document acknowledged that there were variations in the contexts to which it would be applied. In other words, the principles are universal but the context needs to be taken into account.

The opening section of the document set it within the wider agenda of *Education for All* (EfA) and a world conference on this was held in 1990. This produced a World Declaration and Framework on *Education for All* (UNESCO, 1990). Thus, whilst the focus of the *Salamanca Statement* was on children, youth and adults with special educational needs, it was set within a broader debate about universal access to quality education. The second section of the Salamanca statement reads:

> We believe and proclaim that:
> - every child has a fundamental right to education, and must be given the opportunity to achieve and maintain an acceptable level of learning,
> - every child has unique characteristics, interests, abilities and learning needs,
> - education systems should be designed and educational programmes implemented to take into account the wide diversity of these character-istics and needs,
> - those with special educational needs must have access to regular school which should accommodate them within a child-centred pedagogy capable of meeting these needs,
> - regular schools with this inclusive orientation are the most effective means of combating discriminatory attitudes, creating welcoming communities, building an inclusive society and achieving education for all; moreover, they provide an effective education to the majority of children and improve the efficiency and ultimately the cost-effectiveness of the entire education system.
>
> (UNESCO, 1994, viii–ix)

Whilst the title of the statement referred to 'special needs education' a guiding principle was that schools should 'accommodate *all children* regardless of their physical, intellectual, social, emotional, linguistic or other condi-tions' (UNESCO, 1994, 6). The term 'inclusive education' has been applied more widely to other groups who may be marginalized or vulnerable. For example, the UNESCO website related to inclusive education (http://www.unesco.org/new/en/education/themes/strengthening-education-systems/inclusive-education) currently refers to Roma children, street children, child workers, people with disabilities, indigenous people and rural people.

Whilst there are proponents of inclusive education and a plethora of policies, statements, research and commentaries, there are also critics and opponents. In relation to education, countries have to balance priorities – sometimes competing priorities – in terms of resources or aims. There may be systemic inequalities which extend beyond the school. For instance, Hickling-Hudson, writing about country-wide curriculum reform in Jamaica, stated:

> They [the pupils] will still face the material hardships of coming from extremely poor families unsubsidized by welfare payments, and therefore will be less able to access a full range of opportunities in schools. These inequalities show in the differential qualifications of teachers (those in the poorest schools are almost invariably not university or college graduates), and in the differential chances of processing to grade ten to thirteen … It is more than likely, therefore, that in spite of ROSE [the abbreviation for the reform of secondary education], the majority of Jamaica's school students do not have a hope of accessing equal educational opportunity, or of achieving a similar level of academic performance levels, at their peers in elite schools.
> (2000, 180)

The situation described is not unique to Jamaica. However, the quotation makes no reference to another common factor, attitudinal barriers. There may be depressed expectations of the potential of individuals or groups. Teachers may feel underprepared to work with some pupils and have concerns about appropriate approaches.

The *Salamanca Statement* called for 'child-centred pedagogy', yet the emphasis was on planning *for* children not planning *with* children. It called for governments to 'establish decentralized and participatory mechanisms for planning, monitoring and evaluating educational provision for children and adults with special educational needs' (UNESCO, 1994, ix).

The role of parents was recognized, including reference to them forming associations whose 'representatives could be involved in the design and implementation of programmes intended to enhance the education of their children' (UNESCO, 1994, 38). The same was suggested for organizations of people with disabilities. However, the value of the authentic view of children was not explicitly referred to.

This section has highlighted the international dimensions of inclusive education, has acknowledged both a narrow definition referring only to those with special educational needs and a wider interpretation, has identified the prevailing view in the 1990s of groups and organizations able to contribute to the promotion of inclusive education and has noted the lack of reference to the views of children. Later chapters will illustrate how the principles of the *Salamanca Statement* are apparent in different countries and settings and how conceptualizations have evolved.

What does it mean to think of children as stakeholders?

Historically there was a view that, over a period of time, children needed to gain the capacities to think and act for themselves. Children were viewed as dependent, in need of protection and requiring systems to provide that protection. The *Salamanca Statement* referred to states, governments, the community and voluntary organizations and parents and disabled people working at an organizational level. Children were not identified as stakeholders. Indeed, as noted above, the tone was about doing *to* children not doing *with* children.

This emphasis and apparent muting of children within the *Salamanca Statement* is curious, given that 1989 saw the publication of the United Nations' *Convention on the Rights of the Child* (UNCRC). This human rights instrument defines and ensures children's right to participate in matters that impact on their lives. Without question, education impacts on children's lives; indeed, some would argue that they are the chief stakeholders. However, there has been a tendency towards under-representation of the views of children, and the same tendency for certain other groups in society (such as people in poverty, people from certain ethnic groups and disabled people). Thus, children who are also members of groups such as these are doubly disadvantaged in terms of under-representation.

More recently, phrases such as 'pupil participation', 'voice of the child', 'children's right to be heard' and 'the voice of pupils' have entered the lexicon of education. Their use is often linked to the UNCRC, and they appear in research, policy documents and practical guidance.

Although the terms are in common usage, they need to be treated with some caution. Lundy (2007) argued that whilst these terms are convenient, 'each has the potential to diminish its [Article 12] impact as they convey an imperfect summary of what it requires'. Lundy analyzed Article 12, which states that:

> (1) State Parties shall assure to the child who is capable of forming his or her own views the right to express those views freely in all matters affecting the child, the views of the child being given due weight in accordance with the age and maturity of the child.

> (2) For this purpose, the child shall in particular be provided the opportunity to be heard in any judicial and administration proceedings affecting

the child, either directly, or through a representative or an appropriate body, in a manner consistent with the procedural rules of national law.

After analyzing this Article in the context of other Articles of the UNCRC (UN, 1989), Lundy argued that Article 12 can only be understood fully when 'it is considered in the light of other relevant UNCRC provisions' (2007, 933). For example, Article 13 refers to the right to information. Children's participation isn't simply about hearing their views and giving them due weight. The children also need access to information.

This book accepts that line of argument but takes it further by considering the implications of other policies and statements, specifically those related to inclusive education. For example, if schools are trying to develop more inclusive practices, is there input and monitoring by the pupils? Where a school provides extracurricular activities, are they accessible to all pupils? This book therefore questions which voices are dominant and which are still either rarely heard or unheard. It challenges the assumptions that some children may not (through age, abilities or circumstances) have views to express or have been afforded the right to express them.

Two large national projects illustrate that children can and have expressed views about education. In 1997 and 2001, children in the UK were invited to design or describe 'The school I'd like'. In 2001, this attracted thousands of responses 'from over 1,500 schools and hundreds of individuals' (Burke and Grosvenor, 2003, xii). The children came from diverse backgrounds, were aged between five and eighteen and completed the activity in different circumstances (for example, some completed it for school homework; others completed it independently). The introduction to Burke and Grosvenor's book is subtitled 'Neglected Voices' and argues that children have yet to be convinced that their right to be heard has been established. The open-ended invitation extended to children gave them the opportunity to be heard and to express their dissatisfaction with a system that they feel doesn't listen. Burke and Grosvenor's introduction concludes with quotations from the children, an approach which in their view is consistent with the production of a book about the voices of children and young people. In a similar way, this section concludes with quotations from children drawn from the work of Burke and Grosvenor. They have been selected because of their relevance to the themes of this book.

> In my ideal school it would be made clear to all pupils that they would all be treated as equal citizens. No-one would be turned away because they were

black or because they lived in a caravan. This is deeply unfair and, I feel, cruel.

Elizabeth, lower secondary, Leiston

What I would change about the atmosphere is that no-one should be picked on or slagged off just because they are different from everyone else, or if they wear different clothes. Everyone should treat other people the way they would like to be treated, and if someone didn't like someone else they shouldn't call them names or slag them, they should just say nothing.

Lindsay, lower secondary, Renfrew

(Burke and Grosvenor, 2003, 100)

The second piece of research which illustrates, in a way that is relevant to inclusive education, the potential of children's views is entitled *Improving Learning through Consulting Pupils* (Rudduck and MacIntyre, 2007). They argued that '[c]onsultation can be a Pandora's box: opening it reveals issues that teachers may not have the time to, or be ready to, address. One of them is recognizing possible prejudices in their feelings about some of the pupils they teach' (Ruddock and McIntyre, 2007, 159).

Rudduck and McIntyre's book was based on research undertaken in secondary schools which are complex organizations. Their book did not underestimate the challenges involved, the need for a sustained commitment or the competing demands on schools. The closing remarks cited the work of McQuillan (2005) who claimed that 'the most promising strategy for reversing (the) long-standing failings of our educational system would be to make student empowerment – in all its dimensions – our top educational priority' (2005, 665). Inclusive education has arisen because of dissatisfaction with the existing system and therefore it is worth exploring whether pupil voice can contribute to addressing the perceived failings in the status quo.

In their book, Rudduck and McIntyre acknowledged that in the consultation process less successful pupils can feel marginalized; that the process can 'affirm rather than challenge the existing dividing processes in the school and the regimes which lead to some pupils being valued above others' (2007, 165).

This section has made the case for seeing children not as recipients of education but as stakeholders. It has further argued that they have views about education and the right to have them heard. This would be advantageous to the educational provision and also an educational process in its own right for the children.

How can inclusive education, children as stakeholders and research be related to each other?

In the contexts of inclusive education and pupil participation, some common themes about the value of individuals and groups, empowerment, challenging stereotypes and evolving systems are already emerging. These are also reflected in the ways in which some research has been developing; increasingly it has become more inclusive. There is evidence that some researchers see children as competent to express views. For instance, researchers may pose questions to children in interviews or design questionnaires specifically for children. There are multiple examples, some of which appear in later chapters, which show that this approach can be used with all children, whatever their characteristics or whatever the context. A smaller number exemplify how children can be involved in the research process itself by, for example, suggesting topics to research, assisting in the analysis of the data or engaging in disseminating the results. Again, there are examples throughout this book. This shift in the positioning of children in the research process from being respondents to adult-generated questions towards being co-researchers can be thought of as them moving from being passive to taking a more active role.

In terms of active involvement, a way to think about this is in terms of a continuum.

A particularly strong position taken by some activists is that research that doesn't include children or marginalized groups isn't valid. This book accepts that there is a need for some research that doesn't draw on data gathered directly from children. For instance, the next chapter presents data on children's access to education. However, the emphasis will be on research in which children are participants or are actively involved. A framework which expands on the roles of children within research appears in Chapter 3.

It is important to note that this book isn't based on an assumption that children have a single, useful set of insights. The data from them is messy, potentially idiosyncratic and complex. Partly it is presented to show that the traditional power balances between the researcher and the researched can be challenged. Additionally, in line with the two examples presented above, the argument is that children provide useful insights which may not be accessible to adults or which are overlooked by them. We need to

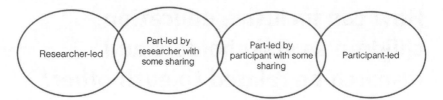

Figure 1.1 Continuum of overlapping approaches. *Source: Based on Nind, 2014a, 11*

question how research that doesn't involve children can fully comment on inclusive education; being included/excluded is a subjective experience and educational provision which is solely perceived from an adult standpoint lacks those insights.

The process of selecting examples of research for inclusion in this book gave attention to who was involved and the methodologies that were used. The book gives precedence to children who are often overlooked or silenced. In the context of disabled children in the global south, Wickenden and Kembhavi suggest four reasons why disabled children may not be evident in research:

- 'they are simply forgotten as potential participants'
- 'they may be invisible in communities because of their absence from school or community activities, and thus hard to recruit'
- 'the adult gatekeepers may assume they have nothing to say or are incapable of having or expressing views'
- 'the researchers judge that including them is methodologically difficult and expensive'

(2014, 403–4).

Each of the above scenarios of non-inclusion denies the children their rights under the UNCRC, and the examples of research selected here will challenge the perspectives which create these situations. This section has illustrated how children's views can positively influence education and emphasized the point that the views of all children need to be heard and listened to. Their perspectives have implications for inclusive education as is evident in the text.

The structure of the book

The three themes (inclusive education, participation and inclusive research) have shared roots and are interrelated. Each domain sees children as being competent and having agency; each is dynamic and socially situated; both individually and collectively the themes offer challenges and opportunities. Individually and collectively, they each contest the status quo.

The book is structured in three parts. The first is entitled 'Debates, Dilemmas and Challenges: The Background to Inclusive Education'. The second part is entitled 'An Interdisciplinary Overview of Recent Research and Scholarship'. The final part is 'Implications for Children's Lives: Using Children's Perspectives to Inform Inclusive Education'.

Part I 'Debates, Dilemmas and Challenges: The Background to Inclusive Education', this part (comprised of Chapter 1 only) introduces and discusses the key aims of the book and its major concepts and themes.

Part II 'An Interdisciplinary Overview of Recent Research and Scholarship', this part has three chapters. The first (Chapter 2) considers current perspectives on inclusive education. The second (Chapter 3) considers children's participation. The third (Chapter 4) considers inclusive research.

Part III 'Implications for Children's Lives: Using Children's Perspectives to Inform Inclusive Education' presents and considers the evidence from research, predominantly that which is inclusive/participatory. It includes chapters focusing on children having access to the places and spaces of education (Chapter 5), developing an inclusive curriculum informed by children's perceptions (Chapter 6) and children's sense of belonging (Chapter 7). It also includes a synoptic chapter which identifies some of the recurrent themes within the book (Chapter 8). The concluding chapter (Chapter 9) draws together the themes of the book and further reading.

The following key themes emerge during the course of the book:

- The topics are complex and contested.
- There is international and interdisciplinary interest in the themes.
- All children, including those who are sometimes marginalized, have valuable insights which should be given attention.
- Researchers need to think creatively about the roles of children in all aspects of research.
- Research findings should influence policy and practice, and that may have implications for how findings are disseminated.

This is an ambitious book, and throughout your reading of it you should adopt a critical approach and interrogate the material presented. Here are some questions which could help you to do that:

- The book is based on some values associated with inclusive education, children as active agents and the linking of policy, research and practice. Are these values evident to you? How might they have influenced the selection of themes and materials?
- Research and scholarly writing are produced for various purposes. Within the limits of this book, only some examples have been selected. In your view, are some sources more convincing than others? If so, why?
- In your view, did the selection of material result in any gaps in coverage?
- It has been noted that inclusive education is complex and contentious. Can you identify instances where cited writers disagree with each other or offer alternative perspectives? (How did you deal with these instances?) How do you understand the reasons for these disagreements or alternatives?
- Inclusive education and understandings of childhood are both evolving fields. How does the content link to your experiences? Are you convinced by the argument that international and interdisciplinary research of these topics is relevant and important?

Remember that there is no right or wrong answers to these questions. There will be a reminder in the concluding chapter to reflect on them.

Part II

An Interdisciplinary Overview of Recent Research and Scholarship

2

Current Perspectives on Inclusive Education

Chapter outline

Introduction and key questions

The preceding chapter illustrated some of the complexities and tensions involved in inclusive education and challenged you to reflect on your own current views. That is not to suggest that your ideas are 'wrong' or 'deficient'. Rather it is to help you broaden your understanding, explore alternative perspectives and ensure your views are evidence-based. This is important since:

> the meaning of 'inclusion' is by no means clear and perhaps conveniently blurs the edges of social policy with a feel-good rhetoric that no one could be opposed to. What does it really mean to have an education system that is

'inclusive'? Who is thought to be in need of inclusion and why? If education should be inclusive, then what practices is it contesting, what common values is it advocating and by what criteria should its successes be judged?

(Armstrong et al., 2010, 4)

This chapter will guide you away from the 'feel-good rhetoric' towards a more critical understanding of some of the complexities and tensions involved. The following questions will be addressed:

- What are the contexts in which inclusive education has developed?
- Who defines inclusive education?
- Are children's views about inclusion valued?
- What are the implications of having multiples definitions of inclusion?
- Is progress being made towards more inclusive education?

What are the contexts in which inclusive education has developed?

Historically, education was not universal but limited to some members of society. For instance, if we go back in English history, only the royal family, the Church and other valued members of society had access to education. For many years, there was a strong bias towards men being educated whilst the provision for women lagged behind. In the twenty-first century, such scenarios may seem remote and irrelevant. However, they link to perceptions of children, inclusive education and the global commitment to *Education for All* (UNESCO, 1990). With regard to the latter, in 2000, 194 countries agreed on *The Dakar Framework for Action* (UNESCO, 2000), which committed to providing good-quality, basic education for all by 2015. Later, they set out six goals to achieve this and systems to track progress.

The latest figures published in *Education for All 2000–2015: Achievements and Challenges* (UNESCO, 2015) drew attention to the progress that has been made, but some of the findings are stark. They include:

- 'In 2012, nearly 58 million children of primary school age (typically between 6–11) were not enrolled in schools' (77).
- '[E]fforts to address the issues of quality, age-appropriate entry and schooling costs have not matched needs. As a result, significant problems persist with dropout, progression and completion levels' (78).

- '[O]nly 13 of the 106 countries are likely to have at least 97% of children entering schools and reaching the last grade' (84).
- 'A major challenge in improving education for children with disabilities is that cultural discrimination can exacerbate undercounting of disabled children, their lack of access to education and other opportunities to lead fulfilling lives' (103).
- 'Emergency situations exacerbate marginalization, as poverty, social exclusion, conflict, natural disasters and climate change interact to compound vulnerability' (103).
- [In relation to gender equality] 'there is no consistent global trend. In some countries, respondents in recent years were more likely to reveal positive attitudes towards gender equality … But in other countries, there was no change and in still others attitudes towards gender equality deteriorated' (123).

The emphasis in this data is on formal education. That is unquestionably important but the contribution of informal education should not be overlooked. It provides educational opportunities and can prompt reflection about formal education. With regard to the first of these, Dawson (2014) acknowledges the role of schools and mass media in science education but also highlights the role of Informal Science Education (ISE) (e.g. science museums, zoos and science centres). She argues that access to ISE is unequal with some individuals marginalized. She does not view this as inevitable and her article ends on an optimistic note:

> ISE has vast potential for disrupting the reproduction of social disadvantages rather than reproducing them. In placing concepts of social justice, critical pedagogy and empowerment at the heart of ISE, the affordances and benefits of participation in ISE may become more available to more people. I have argued that it is important to recognize how, where, when and for whom ISE practices reproduce social disadvantages by being inaccessible and/or inequitable. By doing so ISE policies, practitioners and researchers can begin to acknowledge where change is needed, to explore how to make those changes and, through developing more inclusive practices, may be able to shift community acceptance on the part of 'non-visitors' and, ultimately, change the current patterns of infrastructure access.
>
> (Dawson, 2014, 239)

With regard to the second point, research undertaken by Sumida Huaman and Valdiviezo in Peru considered formal and informal education. They argue that although formal and community-based education are usually researched independently individuals 'continuously encounter both' (2014, 65).

In relation to formal education, they adopted the term 'aggressive educational practices'. They did so not to 'devalue formal schooling, but [to] recognize[s] that such systems can be linked to colonial and oppressive race and class-based hierarchies' (Dawson, 2014, 66). In contrast, they argued that community-based education 'exhibits a structure that is culturally inclusive, intergenerational and values-driven, and rigorous and complex' (2014, 65). They suggest that a detailed knowledge of indigenous education could transform how we think about education and knowledge.

The UNESCO report contains statistical data with an accompanying commentary. Faced with the need to make the data presented 'real' to the readers, the World Bank Report 2006, *Equity and Development*, used an additional approach. The report's initial overview included vignettes, as considered below. These extracts from the report were selected to illustrate that it is not only the data but also the medium by which it is disseminated that need to be considered. How the data is presented may influence how it is perceived.

Example of research: Disseminating the research

The World Bank produces a report annually, and in 2006 the title was *Equity and Development*. The report opens with a narrative account of three fictitious children (Nthabiseng, Pieter and Sven), whose stories were developed to exemplify the findings of the report:

> Consider two South African children born on the same day in 2000. Nthabiseng is black, born to a poor family in a rural area of the Eastern Cape Province, about 700 km from Cape Town. Her mother had no formal schooling. Pieter is white, born to a wealthy family in Cape Town. His mother completed a college education at the nearby prestigious Stellenbosch University.

> On the day of their birth, Nthabiseng and Pieter could hardly be held responsible for their family circumstances: their race, their parents' income and education, their urban or rural location, or indeed their sex. Yet, statistics suggest that those predetermined background variables will make a major

difference in the lives they lead. Nthabiseng has a 7.2 per cent chance of dying in the first year of her life, more than twice Pieter's 3 per cent chance.

Pieter can look forward to 68 years of life, Nthabiseng to 50. Pieter can expect to complete 12 years of formal schooling, Nthabiseng less than 1 year. Nthabiseng is likely to be considerably poorer than Pieter throughout her life. Growing up, she is less likely to have access to clean water and sanitation, or to good schools. So, the opportunities these two children will face to reach their full potential are vastly different from the outset – through no fault of their own.

(2006, 1)

The report then provides an account of aspects of their later lives, before introducing a new character, Sven, who was:

born on the same day to an average Swedish household. His chances of dying in the first year of life are very small (0.3 per cent) and he can expect to live to the age of 80 – 12 years longer than Pieter and 30 years more than Nthabiseng. He is likely to complete 11.4 years of schooling – 5 more than the average South African. These differences will be compounded by differences in quality: in the eighth grade, Sven can expect to obtain a score of 500 on an internationally comparable math test, while the average South African student will score only 264 – more than two standard deviations below the median of countries that are in the Organization for Economic Cooperation and Development (OECD). Nthabiseng, most likely, will not reach that grade and so will not take the test.

(2006, 1–2)

Reflections on the research

The report's overview asserts that there are links between equity and long-term prosperity. The report defines equity as meaning 'that individuals should have equal opportunities to pursue a life of their choosing and be spared from extreme deprivation in outcomes' (2006, 2).

They also comment that 'at the global level, when developing countries have little or no voice in global governance, the rules can be inappropriate and costly for poorer countries' (2006, 2). They adopt the term 'inequality trap' to refer to the cycles that perpetuate the existing inequalities.

The examples illustrate both inclusion and inclusive education by drawing attention to the dynamics of (sustained) access to education, access to good-quality education, the importance of qualifications and the consequences of these in adulthood in terms of employment, opportunities and life expectancy.

Activity 1

In this chapter, your attention has been drawn to how organizations can present evidence in different ways, e.g. through statistics with commentaries and vignettes. What do you consider to be the relative strengths of the two approaches? What, in your view, are the implications for the dissemination of research data?

Activity 2

The examples in the vignettes came from rather different countries, South Africa and Sweden. In your view, can such differences arise within broadly comparable countries/districts/states? (Hint: think about the countries in Europe or areas of a single country.)

Activity 3

To write the vignettes, the author needed to make decisions about which factors were significant. For instance, information was included about life expectancy. Analyse the three vignettes in terms of the variables (factors) that are included in them.

Activity 4

The World Bank has collected and presented this data. It reflected the World Bank's view of poverty, how to eradicate it and therefore the bank's goals. (You can find information about the World Bank at http://www.worldbank.org/en/about/what-we-do)

The work of the World Bank is not uncontroversial. As the World Bank prepared to discuss 'A common vision for the World Bank group', based on some leaked documents, an article in the *Guardian* (http://www.theguardian.com/global-development/2013/mar/21/world-bank-vision-poverty-unambitious) included these comments:

> Nuria Molina, policy director at Save the Children UK, said the targets were *'very unambitious'. 'The narrative is right, the terminology is right, but the devil is always in the details,'* she said. To address inequality you must also rein in growth at the top, she argued. *'You need to have a meaningful measure, and just looking at the bottom is not sufficient. It's very important to look at the gaps.'*

David Woodward … said the documents showed the bank is still subordinating development goals to an overall economic growth agenda. *'What we've still got is a global version of trickle-down economics,'* he said. *'We should not be designing policies promoting growth on the assumption that this will deliver everything else.'*

Think about these observations and the question that they raise about how to make progress in areas such as development and addressing inequalities. In particular, consider the role that (inclusive) education can and should play. (Hint: Woodward is questioning whether economic growth is sufficient and Molina uses the terms 'top' and 'bottom'.)

Terms such as 'marginalized' and 'vulnerability' are used, with some documents making reference to specific groups. The vignettes gave information about several variables, including mother's education, length of education, rural/urban location. Whilst the contrasts in the vignettes have an international dimension, national policy documents may identify children who may require enhanced attention. Which children are referred to and how they are grouped will indicate a perception of diversity within that country and thereby the chosen priorities. For instance, the National Curriculum Framework in England contains a section on inclusion which states that: 'Teachers should take account of their duties under equal opportunities legislation that covers race, disability, sex, religion or belief, sexual orientation, pregnancy and maternity, and gender reassignment' (DfE, 2013, Section 4.2).

Links are apparent, in England, between the national curriculum and legislation related to equalities. The statement about teachers and equal opportunities legislation was designed for a particular context but may not be suited to other circumstances. Internationally UNESCO, which is an agency of the United Nations, adopts a broad definition of inclusive education which may be more universally applicable. Their website has resources structured around Roma children, street children, child workers, people with disabilities, indigenous people and rural people. It can be viewed at: http://www.unesco.org/new/en/education/themes/strengthening-education-systems/inclusive-education.

Education for All 2000–2015: Achievements and Challenges provided a reminder that contextual factors (such as conflict, droughts or poverty) can exacerbate the vulnerabilities of children or specific groups of children.

What are the long-term ramifications of the Syrian crisis? Some believe the crisis will lead to a 'lost generation' with the majority of Syrian children lacking fundamental necessities and unable to gain an education.

Girls have additional vulnerabilities in conflict situations: more than 200 Nigerian schoolgirls were kidnapped in April 2014 just because they were at school.

(UNESCO, 2015, 104)

Chapter 1 commented on how views about who should access education have changed and there have been increases in the spending on it. Progress from education being the prerogative of a minority to national educations systems has both benefits and costs. The international picture is complex.

Many countries have increased their spending on education. Between 1999 and 2012, 38 countries increased their spending by 1 percentage point or more of the national income.

Education is not a priority in many national budgets. As a share of government spending, expenditure on education has changed little since 1999 and at 13.7% in 2012, falls short of the recommended 15% to 20% target.

Governments and donors have neglected to fund EFA goals outside primary education. As a result, pre-primary and adult literacy, in particular, remain underfunded.

(UNESCO, 2015, xiv)

Even where more established systems exist and at least some priority is given to resourcing education, access may not be universal. In Europe, countries have established education systems. Yet, as the UNESCO report *Inclusion from the Start: Guidelines on Inclusive Early Childhood Care and Education for Roma Children* notes:

as many as 50% of Roma children in Europe fail to complete primary education; no more than 20–25% attend secondary schools, with the vast majority enrolled in vocation courses; and less than 1% complete tertiary education. When young Roma children do enter school, they often feel unwelcome and undervalued by their teachers and the non-Roma peers. Far too high a proportion of Roma children are placed in special classes within the public sector, or they are routed to special schools with children with disabilities. Sadly, exclusion, discriminations, segregation, poverty and disempowerment are the norm for many Roma children.

(2014, 7)

This quotation links to the idea introduced earlier that inclusive education is not an end in itself but is linked to processes at work within society more broadly. The final sentence alerts the reader to the consequences experienced long after the individual Roma child becomes an adult. It echoes the theme of the earlier research example which made links between education and life chances. Additionally, the case has been made that inclusive education is also about the nature of society. In circumstances such as those experienced by Roma children and their peers, there are lost opportunities for all children to interact and get to know each other rather than forming judgements based on stereotypes.

Another identified source of inequality is disability. Globally, there are around a billion people with disabilities. Of these, around 93 million are children (UNICEF, 2013, 3). They are more likely than their peers to have no access to education. They account for a third of the children who are out of school. In other words, they are disproportionately excluded from education with the likelihood that this will impact on their life chances (e.g. employment, family life, housing).

In 2000, the Dakar World Education Forum summarized the challenges, stating that: '[e]ducation systems must be inclusive, actively seeking out children who are not enrolled, and responding flexibly to the circumstances and needs of all learners …' (UNESCO, 2000, para. 33). Data about access to education and continued engagement in education is increasingly available. It has already been argued that although inclusive education is a global concern, there are local differences in the challenges and opportunities. The information provides a basis upon which to develop plans and monitor progress towards *Education for All*. It also allows for patterns of provision and innovation to be tracked so that case studies about the countries that are making accelerated progress can be disseminated.

Those promoting *Education for All* emphasize human rights and equality: education should be available to all, and furthermore the quality of the education should be 'good'. Schools can be viewed as a microcosm of wider society, and as such provide a context in which exclusion and marginalization can and should be challenged. It is argued that if stereotypes and negative views remain uncontested, then marginalization will be perpetuated; this is the 'inequality trap'. Education is seen as a way to challenge discrimination, thereby influencing society now and in the future. Thus, promoters of inclusive education argue that in addition to the rights of individuals, it is about improving both schools and wider society.

Societal changes in how differences are viewed can be illustrated by considering disability. Historically, disability has been viewed as an individual tragedy – as a deficit within the child, who was viewed as in need of a cure or normalization. This conceptualization is often referred to as the 'medical model'. This doesn't denote that medical staff are necessarily involved, although they may be. Rather, it is about the locus of the difficulties and consequentially the focus of the response. The medical model locates the difficulties within the child and therefore places the emphasis on diagnosis, labelling and treatment. This approach has been criticized by those who highlight that society creates barriers (e.g. linguistic, physical, attitudinal) for those with impairments (i.e. a problem in body function or structure). The 'social model' shifts the focus towards the barriers that society creates. The view is that disability is created by the organization and values of society rather than by the impairment itself. The social model has challenged earlier thinking and moved the thinking from wanting to 'fix the individual' towards altering society.

These two perspectives, the medical model and the social model, are often presented as the two alternative perspectives. However, there are other models that contribute to our understandings. The ecological model recognizes individual differences, the importance of the social context and the interaction between these two sets of variables – they are not independent of each other. An example illustrates this point. Assuming you have good eyesight and you move into a room with very low or no light, then you can't see adequately. Most of us will have stumbled as we enter a darker environment – or put out a hand to use another sense. You are disabled by the environment. If you look at the moon you can't see any detail. If you are provided with a strong enough telescope then you can, you have gained an ability. The changes in your environment interact with your abilities.

It is possible to consider the interactions between the resources of the individual, the available resources and the task, and in so doing avoid seeing any 'difficulties' as a result of shortcomings in the individual.

Understandings of differences are not universal. Currently it is possible to find examples of policy and research that adopt each of these models (medical, social, ecological). However the emergence of models that offer alternatives to characterizing any 'difficulties' as a deficit in the individual or a deficiency that distinguishes a group means that the focus of research also needs to shift. There has been a shift away from objectifying individuals who have different resources to seeing them in context and also seeing all individuals (including children) as able to engage in research in ways that include – but extend beyond – providing data. The theme of participation is developed in the next chapter and the following chapter outlines some of the inclusive/participatory developments in research.

For the present, we will return to the environment and specifically what UNESCO referred to as 'cultural discrimination' (UNESCO, 2015, 103). This can be illustrated by how characteristics of individuals in films are associated with 'goodies' and 'baddies'. If there were no stereotypes or preconceptions, the characteristics would not be associated with the qualities of 'good' and 'bad'.

Example of research: 'Goodies' and 'baddies' in films

In 2012, YouGov surveyed 1,741 people (male 846, female 895) in the UK about the associations they make between characteristics and 'good' or 'bad' characters. Table 2.1 shows the composition of the sample in terms of age.

Table 2.1 Participants in the research on 'goodies' and 'baddies' in films

18–24	25–39	40–59	60+
211	444	595	491

Source: Based on YouGov, 2012

Table 2.2. shows the responses of interviewees to the question, 'For each of the following, do you think they usually play good or evil characters?'

Table 2.2 Data from the research into 'goodies' and 'baddies' in films

Characteristic	Good character	Same equally	Bad character
People with marks/scars/ disfigurements	5	35	48
People from ethnic minorities	7	70	13
People with physical disabilities	38	43	6
Men	2	84	5
Women	20	72	0
Gay, lesbian and bisexual people	21	59	4
Fat people	14	61	14
Thin people	13	70	6
People with bad teeth	1	19	66
People with blonde hair	29	57	3
Bald people	2	57	30
People with moustaches	3	54	29
People with English accents	15	61	15
Young people	13	72	6
Old people	30	59	2

Source: Based on YouGov, 2012

The responses from each of the age groups can be found in the full report, which also analyses the responses by gender, social grade and location (London, rest of the South, Midlands/Wales, North, Scotland).

Reflections on the research
Reference is made to this survey on the website of Changing Faces, a charity for 'people, and families who are living with conditions, marks or scars that affect their appearance' (https://www.changingfaces.org.uk/About-Us). They comment:

> What concerns us is this type of shorthand is used without
> any thought as to how it might affect the lives of real people:

people who are living with scars, burns, marks or conditions that affect their appearance. As part of the audience you know how to respond, with fear, horror or revulsion. The problem is that how people react in the cinema spills over into real life.

(https://www.changingfaces.org.uk/Face-Equality/face-equality-on-film)

Activity 1
Review the findings and think about your own responses to the listed characteristics. What associations would you make?

Activity 2
Whilst the data makes interesting reading, how do you think attitudes are formed? Do you think it matters what associations are made? To what extent do you think they reflect and/or influence society? (Hint: look at the quotation from the Changing Faces website.)

These associations – or perhaps, more properly, evaluations – were made on the basis of visible/audible characteristics. Young people were rarely seen as 'baddies' (6 per cent) but there are deeper ways in which children can be viewed and childhood understood. These have been shifting. Historically, children have been viewed as passive objects who can be researched as such. They were the objects of research. There has been a shift towards a recognition of their agency, and of their abilities to hold and express views, to be active in research processes and to be interested in research in terms of process and findings.

In summary, there has been unequal access to education which impacts on the life chances of individuals and also on their societies. We have considered the 'inequality trap' that impacts on individuals and also on wider society. The evidence suggests that we, as a society, do stereotype people by their characteristics. The next section moves on to think about how challenging stereotypes can be linked to education. This will be done through the lens of inclusive education, although that is only one of the possible lenses. It will consider what is meant by the term and the different definitions that exist.

Who defines 'inclusive education'?

Chapter 1 has already acknowledged that a consensus about the definition of inclusive education has proved elusive. This is further complicated by the concurrent use of a range of terminology including (but not restricted to) inclusion, partial inclusion, responsible inclusion and reverse inclusion.

Activity 1

Copy the structure of the table below and make a list of recent occasions when you have heard any of the terms above (or similar terms). Add the terms to the left-hand column, the first two have been done. Then complete the boxes in each row. You can add more rows if necessary.

Table 2.3 Usage of terms related to inclusion

Term	Who used it?	In what context?
Inclusion		
Reverse inclusion		

What do you notice about how people use the term(s)? Are there connections or differences with your own understandings?

Now compare these answers with some that are evident in the literature, including the examples cited below. Some people approach the task of defining inclusive education by saying what it is *and* what it isn't (inclusionary and exclusionary criteria), whilst others just say what it is.

> An inclusive education culture celebrates and embraces uniqueness, has appropriate supports and resources, and provides equitable access to lifelong learning.
> (Inclusion BC [formerly the British Columbia Association for Community Living])

Available at http://www.inclusionbc.org/our-priority-areas/inclusive-education

> Inclusion is a process by which schools, local education

---

authorities and others develop their cultures, policies and practices to include pupils.

(Department for Education and Skills, 2001, 2)

Inclusive education provides a fundamentally different pedagogical approach to one rooted in deviance or difference. In other words, it stresses:

- the open learning potential of each student, rather than a hierarchy of cognitive skills.

- reform of the curriculum and a cross-cutting pedagogy, rather than a need to focus on student deficiencies.

- active participation of students in the learning process, rather than an emphasis on specialized discipline knowledge as key to teachers' expertise.

- a common curriculum for all, based upon differentiated and/or individualized instruction, rather than an alternative curriculum being developed for low achievers.

- teachers who include, rather than exclude.

(UNICEF, 2012, 12)

Activity 2

Now return to the first part of Activity 1 and think about the connections between these definitions, those you have heard and your own ideas. Are there similarities and differences? If so, how would you account for them?

It would not be surprising if you've found that different people have used different terms which are sometimes linked to the same ideas, or conversely have used the same terms to describe different things. This isn't a situation unique to the terminology in this area, but the lack of clarity about the meaning of inclusion/inclusive education is problematic. We will return to that theme in the next section, since the lack of consensus may be an obstacle to implementation.

There is a further difficulty in that you will have been involved in the process of interpretation. It is unlikely that you'll actually have stopped the person and asked for a definition. So there is a complication in that it is not just how terms are expressed that counts, but also how they are received:

However well we define the word, the ways in which it is understood by others is also partly determined by how they choose to use it themselves. This is not just a matter of wordplay. The concept of inclusion continues to be shaped like past interpretations and in particular their association with the notion of physical presence and absence of students in mainstream schools.

(Black-Hawkins et al., 2007, 48)

There have been concerted efforts to reach a consensus about the definition of and practices associated with inclusive education. A notable example amongst these is the UNESCO *Salamanca Statement*. This was agreed in 1994 by representatives of ninety-two governments and twenty-five international organizations. This statement is important because it has exerted a global influence on laws, policy and guidance. Part 2 of the statement reads:

We believe and proclaim that:
- every child has a fundamental right to education and must be given the opportunity to achieve and maintain an acceptable level of learning,
- every child has unique characteristics, interests, abilities and learning needs,
- education systems should be designed and educational programs implemented to take into account the wide diversity of these characteristics and needs,
- those with special educational needs must have access to regular schools which should accommodate them within a child-centred pedagogy capable of meeting these needs,
- regular schools with this inclusive orientation are the most effective means of combating discriminatory attitudes, creating welcoming communities, building an inclusive society and achieving education for all; moreover, they provide an effective education to the majority of children and improve the efficiency and ultimately the cost-effectiveness of the entire education system.

(UNESCO, 1994, viii–ix)

UNESCO (2015), in a quotation related to gender, illustrates that inclusive education is associated with attitudes. You will remember that in some countries attitudes towards girls' education have become more positive, in some it has remained stable and in others it has deteriorated. Teachers have a specific role to play in promoting and implementing inclusive education and therefore their attitudes have received particular attention. This is not unproblematic since understandings of inclusive education vary. Additionally, researchers have given attention to particular aspects, for example the role of head teachers, teacher preparation, the variables that impact on their attitudes, variations in attitudes across different groups of children, the significance of contact with diverse groups of children and/or adults. The European Agency for Development in Special Needs Education, working across twenty-five countries, has produced a document entitled *Teacher Education for Inclusion: Profile of Inclusive Teachers* (2012), which focuses on teacher preparation.

Example of research: Profile of inclusive teachers

This group, in the context of special educational needs, responded to a request from a European Agency representative for 'concrete information on the necessary competences, attitudes, knowledge and skills required of all teachers working in inclusive settings' (European Agency for Development in Special Needs Education, 2012, 8).

The objectives of the profile are to:

1 Identify a framework of core values and areas of competence that are applicable to any initial teacher education (ITE) programme;
2 Highlight the essential core values and areas of competence necessary for preparing all teachers to work in inclusive education considering all forms of diversity;
3 Highlight key factors supporting the implementation of the proposed core values and areas of competence for inclusive education within all ITE programmes;
4 Reinforce the argument made within the TE4I (Teacher Education for Inclusion) project that inclusion is the responsibility of all teachers and that preparing all teachers for work in inclusive settings is the responsibility of all teacher educators working across ITE programmes.

Given the subject matter of this chapter, focused attention is given to what this document says about conceptions of inclusive education. In the document, this is divided into three sections: attitudes and beliefs, essential knowledge and understanding and crucial skills and abilities. Quotations from the first and third of these are presented below.

The attitudes and beliefs underpinning this area of competence are that …

education is based on a belief in quality, human rights and democracy for all learners;
inclusion is about societal reform and is non-negotiable;
inclusive education and quality education cannot be viewed as separate issues;
access to mainstream education alone is not enough;
participation means that all learners are engaged in learning activities that are meaningful to them.

(2012, 11)

The crucial skills and abilities to be developed within this area of competence include:

… critically examining one's own beliefs and attitudes and the impact these have on actions;
… engaging in ethical practices at all times and respecting confidentiality;
… the ability to deconstruct educational history to understand situations and contexts;
… coping strategies that prepare teachers to challenge non-inclusive attitudes and to work in segregated settings;
… being empathetic to the diverse needs of learners;
… modelling respect in social relationships and using appropriate language with all learners and stakeholders in education.

(2012, 12)

Activity 1
Return to the examples you wrote down about who used which terms and in what context. Use this alongside the definitions provided to consider the meaning(s) of 'inclusive education'. In your view are 'inclusive education' and 'inclusion' synonyms? If not, what are the differences?

Activity 2
There is an emphasis on inclusion being a matter for *all* teachers. The focus of this European Agency document is on initial teacher education. What do you think the implications are for those who have already entered the profession?

Activity 3
The last crucial skill and ability refers to 'all learners and stakeholders in education'. This could be read as distinguishing between two

distinct groups, learners and stakeholders. Who do you view as stake-holders in education? (Hint: in reference to who had been involved in the overall project, there were nominated country experts and 'over 400 other stakeholders including student teachers, teachers and school leaders, local area administrators, representatives from voluntary organisations, policy makers, learners, their parents and families' [2012, 5].)

The role of stakeholders is important, and they will each have their own views about inclusive education. These are unlikely to be uniform, but there may be trends. Think back to the research example of how stereotypes influence how we link characteristics to 'good' or 'bad' characters in films. There was evidence of trends in the associations made between characteristics and character, but these were not uniform across the sample. There was an analysis about voting intentions, vote in 2010, gender, age, social grade and regions (London, rest of the South, Midlands/Wales, North, Scotland). There are some variations although it is not clear whether these are statistically significant.

We have seen a policy perspective on inclusive education, and the next example draws on a different source. The following extract comes from a report by Her Majesty's Inspectors (HMI) who inspect education and care providers in England, challenge them to improve and help them get the support they need.

Example of research: Inclusive schools and parents

Between September 2009 and March 2010, HMI visited forty-seven schools to evaluate how effectively the partnership between parents and schools had developed. The schools varied in size, geographical location and socio-economic circumstances. Inspectors also drew on other sources of information, including organizations working with parents, parents' groups and evidence that the Office for Standards in Education (OfSTED) already held (such as data from parents' panels and school inspections). This quotation comes from a section on 'Parents and Inclusion':

In each of the schools visited, Inspectors evaluated how effectively the school's work with parents made it more inclusive for all pupils. In eight of the forty-seven schools (four primary, three secondary and one special), this judgment was more positive than the judgment for the school's overall effectiveness of its work with parents. In no school was a judgment on inclusion less positive than the judgment on the school's overall effectiveness of its work with parents.

The most effective examples showed that such work helps to narrow gaps between the attainment of underachieving pupils and their peers. It was very common for the schools, in their different ways, to reach out to families and pupils who were potentially vulnerable or at risk of underachievement or becoming marginalized. The following cases illustrate some of the aspects of inclusion seen during the visits:

- An infant child needed surgery. While she was off school, staff visited her home to provide work and talk to her and her parents about what was happening at school, so she was included as much as possible.
- One of the primary schools visited had a significant and rapid intake of children from Poland. It quickly appointed a bilingual teaching assistant to ensure that the families felt welcomed and were helped with many practical concerns. The school offered English classes for newly arrived parents and pupils, led in part by other parents. The new families learnt much about the locality, its values and customs. At the same time, all the pupils in school were given taster sessions in Polish language and culture. This enabled the two cultures to mix successfully.
- A secondary school decided that students whose truancy or behaviour showed that they were at risk of not being in education, employment or training once they were 16 would be helped and brought back on track. Once the students were identified, school staff visited their homes, involved external agencies and offered further suitable curriculum revisions and options. The school drew on its already good relationships with students and their families. In the most recent cohort, 14 of the 18 students who

had been identified as being at risk went on to further education, employment or training.

(OfSTED, 2011, 25–6)

Activity 1

Based on the examples that they selected, how do you think OfSTED was defining inclusion? For instance, which groups of pupils are represented in the quotations above? What are the implications for inclusive education of the way in which OfSTED seemed to approach the topic?

Activity 2

The emphasis in the Profile for Inclusive Teachers was on *all* children, *all* teachers and *all* teacher educators. This report by OfSTED compared work with parents specifically in relation to inclusion and work with parents overall. Thus there may be difference in views: is inclusion about some children or all children? What is your view on this? (Hint: this will be evident in the research cited within this book where sometimes the focus is on a discrete group of children and sometimes on all children.)

The views that have been presented have been predominantly adult-centric, but we have also questioned whether children can/should be seen as stakeholders in education. The next section considers whether children have views about inclusion.

Are children's views about inclusion valued?

This section raises a fundamental question about who defines inclusive education and who decides whether someone is included or how they are included. Toni Morrison in *Beloved* provided an extreme example: 'Schoolteacher beat him [Sixo] anyway to show him that definitions belong with the definers – not with the defined' (Morrison, 1987, 199).

But do those in power have a monopoly on defining others? Alternative views would be that definitions could come from the potentially marginalized people themselves, or could be an outcome of the negotiation between different levels of society. In the context of inclusive education, she argued that differences are socially constructed and not simply created by the definers. The following two examples indicate that although children may not have the terms 'inclusion' or 'inclusive education' in their vocabulary, they hold and can express views.

Example of research: Young children's views of segregation/inclusion

Koller and San Juan (2015), based in Canada, undertook a preliminary qualitative study of children's perspectives on inclusion. They held play-based interviews with twelve typically developing children aged between three and a half and eight years of age. The children were from different ethnic backgrounds but had all been born in Canada. Eight were from an early years childcare centre which provided full-day care to pre-school-age and early-school-age children. Four were from a family resource centre providing a drop-in service and after-school care for comparable children. Both settings included typically developing children, those with visible disabilities and some with non-visible disabilities. Those with disabilities comprised about 15 per cent of the cohort in each setting.

The interviews addressed five questions, although these were not presented in a specific order. The topics were:

1 the participant's favourite activities,
2 knowledge of disability,
3 perspective of inclusion vs. segregation,
4 descriptions of peer relationships, and
5 recommendations for their centre.

(2015, 617)

This account focuses on the third topic. The authors stated: 'Two dolls (one with a physical disability and one without) were physically separated and placed in two different play schools alongside similar dolls' (2015, 621). The children were then prompted to 'explore the topic of segregation' (2015, 621), using prompts such as: 'Do you think that kids like this, who are in wheelchairs, should come to the same school as you or a different school?' (2015, 621). Nine of the children endorsed the idea that it should be the same school. The cited quotations included: 'They should play all together, otherwise they may "feel left out" in a segregated environment'; and 'They can play with each other' (2015, 621).

Two examples were provided that indicated reasons for segregation. The first related to the availability of assistance for the child with a disability because 'they will all be busy playing'. The second was that disability might be caught, like a disease (2015, 622).

Reflections on the research
A strength of this piece of research is that it considers the inclusion of prospective members of an educational setting. Some research, including examples cited in this book, focuses on the experiences of those currently attending an educational setting. However that overlooks those children who might attend that setting if the circumstances were changed. Consider whether some schools will appear so uninviting that children and their families don't approach them.

Activity 1
Reread the Salamanca Statement. What parallels and differences, if any, do you see between that and the views of these young children?

Activity 2
It has been argued that attitudes to difference are learnt. These children had all attended inclusive settings. If children don't attend an inclusive setting, how would they develop ideas about differences? In your view, do you think children from non-inclusive settings would have held different views?

Drawing on Morrison's terminology, this section has considered whether the 'defined' have views about being perceived in particular ways and whether they are able, with or without support, to convey them. It rejects the view that definitions belong solely to adults; children are also definers.

What are the implications of having multiple definitions of inclusion?

The first comment to make is that it is important to acknowledge the range of terminology in use, including (but not limited to) 'inclusion', 'inclusive education', 'social inclusion' and 'responsible inclusion'. Some definitions have already been provided, and below are some further examples:

An educationally inclusive school is one in which the teaching and learning, achievements, attitudes and well-being of every young person matters. Effective schools are educationally inclusive schools. This shows, not only in their performance, but also in their ethos and their willingness to offer new opportunities to pupils who may have experienced previous difficulties ... The most effective schools do not take educational inclusion for granted. They constantly monitor and evaluate the progress each pupil makes. They identify any pupils who may be missing out, difficult to engage, or feeling in some way apart from what the school seeks to provide.

(OfSTED, 2000, 7)

Inclusion involves change. It is an unending process of increasing learning and participation for all students. It is an ideal to which schools can aspire but which is never fully reached. But inclusion happens as soon as the process of increasing participation is started.

(Booth et al., 2002, 3)

Points to ponder include the basis of these definitions, the extent to which they differ and the reasons for any discrepancies. Ainscow et al. provided a useful typography of different approaches evident in English policy:

- Inclusion as concerned with disabled students and others categorized as 'having special educational needs'.
- Inclusion as a response to disciplinary exclusion.
- Inclusion in relation to all groups seen as being vulnerable to exclusion.
- Inclusion as developing the school for all.
- Inclusion as 'Education for All'.
- Inclusion as a principled approach to education and society.

(2006, 15)

The complexity of definitions and approaches is a currently unavoidable characteristic of the research, scholarly writing, policies and advice on practices. It can prove to be highly emotive with individuals and groups defending strongly held views. However, there are real challenges including: 'How can it be possible for government policies to be made in the name of a concept for which there is no agreed definition? In the circumstances what is the basis for believing that such policies will be successful?' (Cooper and Jacobs, 2011, 2).

Emerging themes from the examples presented include access/placement and participation. There have also been links to 'good' education. A framework that has been used in a range of contexts is to consider: *Placement/Access, Participation* and *Progress/Achievement.*

This framework has the appeal of accommodating multiple factors and perspectives, having global relevance and being applicable in varied contexts linked to inclusion/inclusive education. For example, it was used to consider how best to meet the needs of children who cannot be reunited with their parents (Biehal et al., 2009).

A commonality across the definitions presented thus far has been the assumption that inclusion is necessarily 'good'. Some problematize that idea and allow for the fact that some may not wish to be included. As Edwards et al. observed:

> There can be no sense of difference in a condition of homogeneity in the same way as it makes no sense to talk about equality without inequality, normal behaviour without deviance, or being educated without a sense of what it is to be uneducated. Moreover, seeking to promote social inclusion heightens awareness of difference and social exclusion. In this sense, we need to understand that non-exclusion is not the same as inclusion, and that we must avoid taking away the freedom of those who choose not to be included.
>
> (2001, 426)

Perhaps the crucial point here is that we need to be clear that we can't take it for granted that all children will want to be included in all aspects all of the time. That may depend on factors including (but not limited to) the context, the nature of the invitation to engage and the perceived benefits of engagement. It is not as simple as saying 'education is good'; the nature and quality of the education need to be considered alongside the sense of welcome/belonging. Those themes will be developed in subsequent chapters.

This chapter should have given you a sense of existing debates about the reform of education, including its emphasis on inclusion. That raises a question about whether progress is being made.

Is progress being made towards more inclusive education?

Given the complexity of the issues outlined, it is unsurprising that the answer to this question is far from clear-cut. The first challenge is determining what is meant by 'progress'. When reviewing special educational needs in the twenty-first century, Dyson distinguished between:

- scientific progress in the understanding of children's difficulties;
- technical progress in developing effective educational responses to those difficulties;

- moral progress in terms of changes in prevailing attitudes to difficulty;
- political progress to implement change.

(2001, 24)

Additionally, there are multiple variables which affect progress, some of which are listed below.

- *Location.* The data about *Education for All* illustrated geographical variation in access to education and, by extension, to inclusive education. You can extend your thinking in this area by visiting the World Inequality Database on Education (available at http://www.education-inequalities.org). Even within a single country there are variations. In England, we refer to the 'postcode lottery'. The postcode indicates where someone lives and provision is a lottery in the sense that although there are national policies there is also local interpretation.
- *Characteristics of the pupil.* The 'challenges' associated with including particular groups of children are not universal. They may be linked to prejudices, views and experiences. For example, in England, the group viewed as most challenging to include are those with 'social, emotional and behavioural difficulties'. Yet in Ghana, including that group of children was seen by teachers as less problematic than including children with sensory impairments (Gyimah et al., 2008).
- *Perspectives.* Whilst teachers may feel that the pace of change towards inclusive education has been rapid, parents may be frustrated by the slow progress.
- *Superficial change.* Questions have been asked (e.g. Slee, 2011) as to whether there have been changes in practice or simply changes in language; thus merely a rebranding of existing practices. The 'elastic' use of language is exemplified by Slee:

  > Special education departments in Faculties of Education have undergone rebranding exercises so that they are now Departments or Schools of Special and Inclusive Education, offering special education courses to teachers so that they will become more inclusive in their classrooms

  (Slee, 2013, 896).

- *Tensions between conceptual models.* Earlier in the chapter, the ideas of the medical and the social models of disability were introduced. Mintz makes the point that 'teachers are faced with the inherent tension involved in the political and cultural imperative of looking at children's needs as part of the social model of disability whilst at the same time having often to rely on a medical concept of diagnosis' (2014, 43).

Given the complexity of inclusive education and the multiple dimensions of progress, it is unsurprising that views are contested. This can be illustrated by a commentary on Michael Oliver's keynote speech at the International Special Education Congress 2000. Allan and Slee noted that whilst Oliver 'announced he was "dancing on the grave of special education", others were clear that special education had a more formidable and continuing presence and saw themselves as either working to maintain it or accommodate it' (Allan and Slee, 2008, 36).

Strands of dissatisfaction with the current understanding of inclusion have emerged. For instance, Slee (2011) argues that we need a better understanding of exclusion if we are to progress towards inclusion. He also urges the readers to be alert to the role of language: 'Language sanitizes and it shields us from the recognition of the enormity of events and from our complicity' (2011, 61).

The notion of 'complicity' is important in developing our personal approaches to diversity/inclusion/stereotyping. Do we unthinkingly speak about children in particular ways that are excluding? Are we complicit in lowering our expectations of individuals or groups without understanding their potential? If either of these traits is evident, are they more pronounced with some children who we, without evidence, view as less capable?

Further, a book by Cooper and Jacobs entitled *From Inclusion to Engagement* uses the term 'educational engagement' to refer to 'the ways in which a learner is involved with the social and academic aspects of learning' (2011, 21). The focus of the book is on children with social, emotional and behavioural difficulties and, in that context, 'exclusion' can refer to processes which result in pupils not being present in the school.

> Exclusion from school, be it formal or informal, is always an admission of a school's failure to meet the needs of the excluded. After all, the minimum purpose of schooling must be to promote positive social and educational engagement within a particular setting, meaning that at the very least students have to be at the very least present in that setting.
>
> (2011, 6)

You will see the shift from placing the responsibility on the pupil to the shortcomings of the school. The notion of presence, in the sense of being in the school, is emphasized.

In summary, the lack of consensus about the definitions of terms such as inclusion and inclusive education is long-standing. Views about progress are contentious. This may present a rather pessimistic account, but there are grounds for optimism. Messiou argues that 'listening to children in relation to inclusion is, in itself, a manifestation of being inclusive' (2012, 130). Earlier in the chapter, the suggestion has been made that children are stakeholders in education. Inclusion has been linked to participation, and children have rights based on the United Nations Convention on the Rights of the Child. Children can make a unique contribution based on their lived experiences; this is a key value of this book.

Chapter activities

The following activities have been designed to help you reflect on some of the concerns of this chapter.

Activity 1
Inclusive education has been portrayed as being a global concern and the problem of local interpretation has been highlighted. In what ways might this make comparisons between different contexts both valid and problematic?

Activity 2
A range of definitions of inclusive education have been provided. These have drawn on the views of both adults and children. Cooper and Jacobs (2001) linked definitions to the success of policies.

1 Who do you think should be involved in defining and informing inclusive practices?
2 How would you justify your view?
3 What are the implications for how the success of policies related to inclusion are evaluated?

Activity 3
This chapter has raised issues about stereotyping. For example, the research about 'goodies' and 'baddies' in films showed some association between physical characteristics and character. The *Salamanca Statement* asserts that 'regular schools with this inclusive orientation are the most effective means of combating discriminatory attitudes' (UNESCO, 1994, ix).

1 What do you understand by the term 'regular schools'?

2 Where do you think stereotypes are developed?

3 In your view, do schools ever stereotype children? If so, how can they also combat discriminatory attitudes?

Summary

This chapter has:

- linked inclusive education to the wider agenda of *Education for All*
- illustrated that characteristics of people in films may be linked to stereotypes and questioned whether such views may influence perceptions in everyday life
- questioned who is involved in defining inclusive education
- considered the implications of the existence of multiple definitions of 'inclusion' and 'inclusive education'.

Further reading

Hodkinson, A. and P. Vickerman (2009). *Key Issues in Special Educational Needs and Inclusion*. London: Sage.

This is a very accessible text that provides an introduction to the topic. It includes case studies, points for reflection, student activities and suggestions for further reading.

Messiou, K. (2012). *Confronting Marginalisation in Education: A Framework for Promoting Inclusion*. London and New York: Routledge.

This provides a four-step approach to addressing marginalization. It is replete with data from children and ways in which to engage them in the process.

Rix, J., M. Nind, K. Sheehy, K. Simmons and C. Walsh (eds) (2010). *Equality, Participation and Inclusion 1: Diverse Perspectives*. London: Routledge.

Rix, J., M. Nind, K. Sheehy, K. Simmons, J. Parry and R. Kumrai (eds) (2010). *Equality, Participation and Inclusion 2: Diverse Contexts*. London: Routledge.

These linked volumes draw on a range of perspectives including academics, professionals, children and young people and those who have experienced exclusion.

Research details

Disseminating the research

This is a co-publication between the World Bank and Oxford University Press. It is the twenty-eighth report in the annual series. It was underpinned by two basic principles. 'The first is equal opportunities: that a person's life achievements should be determined primarily by his or her talents, rather than by predetermined circumstances such as race, gender, social or family background. The second principle is the avoidance of deprivation in outcomes, particularly health, education and consumption levels' (2006, xi).

World Bank (2006). *Equity and Development*. Washington, DC: World Bank Institute.

'Goodies' and 'baddies' in films

Changing Faces is a UK charity that supports, represents and campaigns for people who have disfigurement of the face or body. They commissioned a YouGov survey of how films portray 'goodies' and 'baddies'.

YouGov UK (2012). 'Goodies and Baddies'. Available online: https://yougov. co.uk/news/2012/04/16/do-bad-teeth-equal-bad-character (accessed 20 February 2016).

Profile of inclusive teachers

The European Agency has developed a range of materials associated with inclusive education. The focus of this document is on Initial Teacher Education.

European Agency for Development in Special Needs Education (2012). *Teacher Education for Inclusion: Profile of Inclusive Teachers*. Odense, Denmark: European Agency for Development in Special Needs Education.

Inclusive schools and parents

OfSTED's publication, *School and Parents*, published in April 2001, reported on the outcomes of its visits to forty-seven primary, secondary and special schools and pupil referral units.

OfSTED (2001). 'Schools and Parents'. Available online: https://www.gov.uk/government/uploads/system/uploads/attachment_data/file/413696/Schools_and_parents.pdf (accessed 7 April 2016).

Young children's views of segregation/inclusion

This research was undertaken in Canada and is one of the few papers which analyses the views of inclusion held by young children. It involved twelve typically developing children who attended inclusive settings.

Koller, D. and V. San Juan (2015). 'Play-Based Interview Methods for Exploring Young Children's Perspectives on Inclusion'. *International Journal of Qualitative Studies in Education 28* (5): 610–31.

3

Children's Participation

Introduction and key questions

Chapters 1 and 2 both referred to 'participation' and this chapter will deepen your understanding of that concept. As with several of the concepts in this book, there is no universally agreed definition, and practices vary. The following questions will be addressed in this chapter:

- How is 'participation' defined?
- Why do the perspectives of children matter?
- What are the links between the UNCRC and education?
- Can Article 12 of the UNCRC be understood in isolation?

- What are the links between Article 12 and inclusive education?
- From the perspective of teachers, what are the assets and barriers to participation in (inclusive) education?
- What forms can participation take and what are the implications for how adults act?

How is 'participation' defined?

There is no single agreed definition of participation. Different authors and researchers emphasize different aspects, and definitions are designed for specific audiences. This is demonstrated by the following examples:

> The terms empowerment and participation are central to the discussion [in their book]. They are to some extent interchangeable, though empowerment is more assertive and implicitly invokes power relationships. The most constructive means of defining these two terms is to consider participation as the process and empowerment as the outcome.
>
> (Treseder, 1997, 4)

> Participation means that it is my right to be involved in making decisions, planning and reviewing an action that might affect me. Having a voice, having a choice.
>
> (cited in Welsh Government, 2011)

(The definition above, including the sound bite 'Having a voice, having a choice', was the winning entry to a competition for children run by the Welsh Assembly in 2004.)

> [Participation is] the process of sharing decisions which affect one's life and the life of the community in which one lives. It is the means by which a democracy is built and it is a standard against which democracies should be measured. Participation is the fundamental right of citizenship.
>
> (Hart, 1992, 5)

To help you critique these definitions and engage with the concept of participation, the next section considers why the perspectives of children are important.

Why do the perspectives of children matter?

Historically, there has been a binary view of children/adults. Children were seen as needing to gain, over a period of time, the capacities to think and act for themselves. They were seen as 'less than adults' and in need of care and protection. In recent years, this view has been challenged. The new perspective argues that children – all children – can be protagonists for themselves. There are no age limitations and the rights apply equally to all children, including those who are marginalized or potentially marginalized. (For a fuller discussion of this, see Jones, 2009.) There is therefore a moral reason for taking into account the views of children, which is sometimes expressed as 'children are human beings'. It follows from this that they therefore have human rights – a fact often left unspoken and perhaps unaccepted by some. Indeed, there are notable examples where the views of children are being given greater weight. In September 2014, there was a referendum in Scotland to decide whether the nation should become independent from the rest of the UK. For this, the voting age was lowered to sixteen rather than eighteen.

The Electoral Commission Report on the Referendum (2014) stated that:

> This referendum showed that for young people, indeed for all voters, when they perceive an issue to be important and are inspired by it, they will both participate in the debate and show up on polling day. This is borne out by the figures. 109,593 16 and 17 year olds were included on the registers by the registration deadline and 75% of those we spoke to claimed to have voted. Importantly, 97% of those 16–17 year olds who reported having voted said that they would vote again in future elections and referendums. The voting process worked for them and thanks to the professionalism of electoral staff across Scotland their experience was positive.
>
> (Electoral Commission, 2014, 1)

Key ideas in this commentary include 'important to them', 'inspired', 'debate', 'professionalism' and 'positive experiences'. Further, the Electoral Commission embedded the change of voting age within the context of political literacy initiatives. An aspiration was that early experience of voting will have a long-term impact on young people in terms of voting in the future.

In other contexts, participation as a human right is also associated with anticipated benefits, examples of which include:

- *Effectiveness of change.* The case is made that a child right-based approach is a very effective way in which to bring about change in all areas, including health and welfare, leisure and culture and education. The following bullet points relate specifically to education.
- *Enhancing educational provision.* The work of Flutter and Rudduck (2004) demonstrated that the views of children can enhance educational provision.
- *Being a citizen and learning about citizenship.* Education is linked to citizenship and whilst pupils can be taught its theoretical side, schools can also provide children with experiences of citizenship (see Hart's definition above).
- *Benefiting from synergies between initiatives.* Schools have experienced a stream of policy initiatives and innovations. A way in which to make sense of these is to look for the synergies between them. Pupil voice is a recurrent theme across many of the recent developments.

Beyond the moral and practical rationales for taking into account the views of children, there are also legal and policy factors. International agreements are an expression of how children and childhood are conceptualized at that point in time; we have already commented on these have evolved. They are also a touchstone for policies and practices. The *United Nations Convention on the Rights of the Child* (UNCRC) (United Nations, 1989) was the first treaty to address the rights of children. It has been ratified by all countries in the world except the USA. The African Union developed a similar document, the *African Charter on the Rights and Welfare of the Child* (African Union, 1990), which protects the rights of children and addresses their needs and also emphasizes the responsibilities of the children. Both the Convention and the Charter are supported by guidance, workshops and international discussions; they are regularly monitored and reported upon.

We noted above that children can be viewed in different ways. In the view of United National Children's Emergency Fund, the UNCRC 'changed the way children are viewed and treated – in other words, as human beings with a distinct set of rights instead of as passive objects of care and charity' (UNICEF, http://www.unicef.org.uk/UNICEFs-Work/UN-Convention). Given the significance of education (including formal schooling) to children, the next section considers the UNCRC in that context.

What are the links between the UNCRC and education?

There is an expectation that education has a key role in implementing the UNCRC through research, policies and practices. Terms such as 'pupil participation', 'voice of the child', 'children's right to be heard' and 'the voice of pupils' have entered the lexicon of education. They are often explicitly associated with the UNCRC and appear in educational policy, research and practical guidance. The influence of the UNCRC is evident in schools, e.g through annual consultations about the expectations within classrooms, or through the work of school councils (http://www.schoolcouncils.org).

In educational materials, there is often an explicit link between the terms above and Article 12 of UNCRC which is summarized as 'respect for the views of children'. However, Lundy argues that whilst such terms are convenient, 'each has the potential to diminish its [Article 12's] impact as they convey an imperfect summary of what it requires' (Lundy 2007, 930). A comprehensive understanding needs to be based on the full text of Article 12, which reads:

> (1) States Parties shall assure to the child who is capable of forming his or her own views the right to express those views freely in all matters affecting the child, the views of the child being given due weight in accordance with the age and maturity of the child.

> (2) For this purpose, the child shall in particular be provided the opportunity to be heard in any judicial and administration proceedings affecting the child, either directly, or through a representative or an appropriate body, in a manner consistent with the procedural rules of national law.

The assumption of this book is that education affects the child and that children's views should be given due weight. It adopts an optimistic approach and presumes that *all* children have these rights regardless of age or circumstances. Restrictions on universal participation may be created by:

- limitations in the local adoption of the UNCRC;
- a superficial reading of Article 12, including a lack of attention to other Articles within the UNCRC;
- dealing with Article 12 in a discrete manner without adequate attention to other conventions or policies. For example, the United Nations also has also produced a Convention on the Rights of Persons with Disabilities (UN, 2006) which includes an Article related to children.

The survey cited below provides an insight into some of the issues related to limitations in local adoption. The research involved local authorities (LAs), which are administrative bodies in local government in the UK, and which therefore have a role in promoting and implementing the UNCRC.

Example of research: Beyond Article 12

A survey was undertaken by the Children's Rights Alliance for England (CRAE) in 2007 of the implementation of the UNCRC at local level in England with a report, *Beyond Article 12: The local implementation of the UN Convention on the Rights of the Child*. Of a total of 150 LAs, 140 responded to the survey. It found that:

- 55 per cent of LAs had 'adopted' the UNCRC, while 45 per cent had yet to do so;
- 77 per cent of LAs did not explicitly reference the UNCRC in their Children and Young People's Plan;
- only one LA referenced the UNCRC in its job description for the Director of Children's Services;
- 19 per cent of LAs did not have a designated person in charge of implementing the UNCRC at a strategic level.

The researchers emphasized that the percentages were illustrative and should not be taken as absolute values.

In response to a question about local barriers to implementation, 26 per cent of LAs either didn't answer this question or stated there were no barriers. Those that did respond identified four major local limitations:

- funding;
- lack of knowledge;
- difficulty of achieving meaningful participation;
- negative public attitudes towards children's rights.

In terms of frequency of response, inadequate knowledge of the UNCRC was identified as the second major barrier to the fulfilment of children's rights: 'Local authorities that identified a need for training on the UNCRC and how its provisions can be applied noted that a lack of understanding about the UNCRC often led to resistance from staff at all levels to the concept of children's rights, and a fear that such rights come at the expense of parental rights (CRAE, 2009, 19). Of those LAs who had received training on children's rights and adopted the UNCRC, only 14 per cent felt they had an 'excellent' awareness and understanding of children's rights. The LAs had adopted three approaches to dissemination:

- an approach which focused on Article 12, e.g. 'It is explicitly part of the [name of local authority] Youth Engagement Strategy' (2009, 7);
- a 'holistic' approach linked to the children's rights, e.g. 'This local authority has adopted the Rights Respecting Schools Award as part of its Raising Achievement Plan/Children and Young People's Plan. This is based on the UNCRC. Both the DCC and the Children's Trust have adopted Hear By Right in support of the agenda' (2009, 7);
- an approach based on the presence of the UNCRC in strategies and legislation (e.g. the UNCRC was ratified by the government on 16 December 1991). This is a national government issue and national government is responsible for compliance. The council complies with all associated duties on local authorities' (2009, 8).

Reflections on the research

This research provides an example of how LAs implemented the UNCRC. It indicates that practices and implementation are not uniform and that progress is 'patchy'. As you read this book, you will notice that a wide range of organizations have taken a role in promoting the UNCRC, with many benefitting from the insights and activities of children.

Activity 1

Three approaches to disseminating information about the UNCRC were evident with the first being the most common. What, in your view, are the strengths and limitations of each of them?

Activity 2

The research report asserted that 'Engaging children in decision-making can be tokenistic, and championing Article 12 is not the same as embedding the provisions of the UNCRC within all services for children and young people' (CRAE, 2009, 3). Can you suggest any potential long-term consequences of adopting a tokenistic approach?

The second most common barrier identified in this research was 'inadequate knowledge of the UNCRC' (CRAE, 2009, 19). In the light of this data, we will commence by focusing on developing a more adequate understanding of Article 12. Lundy proposed a new model for understanding Article 12. She argues that there are four elements involved, namely:

Space: Children must be given the opportunity to express a view.
Voice: Children must be facilitated to express their views.
Audience: The view must be listened to.
Influence: The view must be acted upon, as appropriate.

(Lundy, 2007, 931)

Lundy acknowledges that there are overlaps between space/voice and influence/audience. Further, she argues and diagrammatically portrays Article 12 as an iterative process rather than a static state. Some of these factors will be illustrated in the next example of research.

In the introduction to this book, reference was made to research by Burke and Grosvenor entitled *The School I'd Like: Children and Young People's Reflections on an Education for the 21st Century* (2003). The researchers created the opportunity for children to express a view, or in Lundy's terms a 'space'. It is arguable that whilst this data collection method was 'open'-ended, some children would have found it difficult to exercise

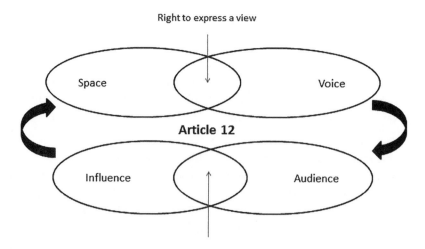

Figure 3.1 Four elements of Article 12 of the UNCRC. *Source: Based on Lundy, 2007, 932*

their right to express a view or in Lunt's terminology to have a 'voice' in the research. The following research example focused on a comparable area – that of designing 'the best school in the world'. It was planned to encourage a particular group of pupils to participate.

Example of research: 'Today's learning objective is to have a party'

This project was undertaken 'with five students in a special needs unit of a secondary school in a deprived community in England' (Greenstein, 2014, 71). It was part of a PhD study aimed at 'theorising "good education" from the perspective of disability' (2014, 72). In discussing the methodology, Greenstein argues that '[p]lay, as an activity occurring in an actual social reality yet not totally governed by its rules, offers an interesting starting point for researchers interested not only in describing the existing but also in imagining viable alternatives' (2014, 71).

The part of her doctorate reported in this article was a series of five creative and playful workshops completed by five students who were in Years 8 and 9 (i.e. 12–14 years old) and who attended an innovative special needs unit (SNU). The themes of each workshop were as follows.

Workshop 1: Teasing out the students' ideas
Two dice were provided. One was marked with a series of school-related nouns (subjects, roles, equipment, places, rules and activities). The second was marked with a list of adjectives (important, interesting, boring, fair/unfair, annoying and fun). The students took turns to roll the dice and then make a statement. For example, a student who rolled 'unfair' and 'places' said: 'The library, because you have to be quiet and you can't speak – even if you sneeze, they shush you'.

Workshop 2: The best teacher, the best student, the best friends
In this session, life-sized models were made which represented the students' ideas of each of the above.

Workshop 3: Sorting out the rules
The students were provided with thirty 'rules'. They were asked to sort these into the following categories: rules that must be in the best school in the world; rules that should never be in the best school in the world; and rules they didn't care about. They also had

to rank the best and worst rules. A further analysis involved catego-
rizing the rules as: those similar to the current rules (e.g. no smoking
in school); those that opposed existing rules (e.g. you can wear what
you want); and 'weird rules' (e.g. coming to school naked).

Workshop 4: Improvisation
The students performed improvised scenes from both the best
school in the world and the school from hell. These were videoed
and the researcher turned them into a strip cartoon.

Workshop 5: Building a model
During the final session, a cardboard model of the school was built
and the project was summarized.

In her work, Greenstein reflected on the challenges of analysing the
complex, multi-layered data that she had gathered. She also provided
a detailed commentary about the process of transforming the video
into a strip cartoon (including advice about useful free software).

Greenstein monitored her own language and actions in terms of
the adult–child hierarchies, noting examples of her being authori-
tarian or inaccessible.

On two occasions during the research, Greenstein raised with the
student participants the question of sharing the work with others.
One audience suggested was the other pupils in the SNU. The participants rejected this suggestion for fear that the 'exposure of their
ideas to the school community might "get us into trouble"' (2014,
78). The link between the data collection for 'the school I would like'
and their own education was also rejected because of a 'feeling they
have nothing to gain because "we won't be going to that school
anyway"' (2014, 78). The students did consent to the data being
used in publications. Greenstein went on to discuss the notions
of reciprocity and gains: 'This gain is not necessarily limited to the
implementation of research findings but is often connected to the
empowering aspects of participating in the research itself, which,
being non-judgemental and confidential may provide a safe place for
conversing with adults and encouraging self-reflection' (2014, 78).

Reflections on the research
Greenstein's research used play as a way to both engage the pupils
and open up possibilities. In the concluding remarks, she sounded
a note of caution that the method of data collection is no sinecure:
'[A]ny method is not in itself emancipatory or even participatory.

Researchers should always carefully and reflexively engage with the particular situation they face in their research and allow for co-construction of meaning alongside the participants' (2014, 79).

Activity 1
Lundy (2007) used the terms 'space', 'voice', influence' and 'audience'. Reread the account of Greenstein's research and think about these terms. In your view, was a 'space' created? (Hint: think beyond physical space.)

Activity 2
How does Greenstein's approach compare with a more traditional research approach, such as asking for a written response?

Activity 3
Lundy suggested that participation is an iterative process (see Figure 3.1). Greenstein's methodology involved a series of activities. How do you think this iterative process influenced the quality of the data produced and the relationship between the researcher and the children? (Hint: imagine the research with only a single data collection activity and one meeting between the research and the children. Now answer the questions.)

Activity 4
The participants had given consent to be involved in the research and it was reported that this was reaffirmed during the process with no participant being required to be involved in an activity. However, they withheld consent to the data being shared in particular ways. In so doing, they chose to restrict the influence and audience. In your view, what are the implications of this and can you suggest anything that might have altered their decision?

Can Article 12 of the UNCRC be understood in isolation?

The CRAE report cited above stated that '[u]nderstanding the inter-connected nature of the Articles of the UNCRC, both in themselves and within a wider human rights framework, and how those provisions can be used together to promote, protect and ensure children's best interests

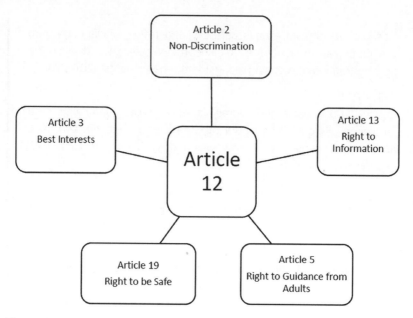

Figure 3.2 Links between Article 12 and other Articles in UNCRC. *Source: Based on Lundy, 2007, 932*

is especially important for local authorities who care for some of the most vulnerable children in our society (2009, 8).

Similarly, Lundy argued that Article 12 can only be understood fully when 'it is considered in the light of other relevant UNCRC provisions' (2007, 933). She portrayed the relevant Articles alongside Article 12 in a graphic.

Lundy posits that a full understanding of Article 12 needs to take into account five other Articles, namely Articles 2, 3, 5, 13 and 19. These are explained below using the summary of the UNCRC produced by UNICEF (http://www.unicef.org/crc/files/Rights_overview.pdf). However, this approach has a limitation, since any condensed version simplifies the original.

- *Article 2: Non-Discrimination.* The Convention applies to all children, whatever their race, religion or abilities; whatever they think or say, whatever type of family they come from. It doesn't matter where children live, what language they speak, what their parents do, whether they are boys or girls, what their culture is, whether they have a disability or whether they are rich or poor. No child should be treated unfairly on any basis.

- *Article 3: Best Interests.* The best interests of children must be the primary concern in making decisions that may affect them. All adults should do what is best for children. When adults make decisions, they should think about how their decisions will affect children. This particularly applies to budget, policy and law makers.

- *Article 5: Right to Guidance from Adults.* Governments should respect the rights and responsibilities of families to direct and guide their children so that, as they grow, they learn to use their rights properly. Helping children to understand their rights does not mean pushing them to make choices with consequences that they are too young to handle. Article 5 encourages parents to deal with rights issues 'in a manner consistent with the evolving capacities of the child'. The Convention does not take responsibility for children away from their parents and give more authority to governments. It does place on governments the responsibility to protect and assist families in fulfilling their essential role as nurturers of children.

- *Article 13: Right to Information.* Children have the right to get and share information, as long as the information is not damaging to them or others. In exercising the right to freedom of expression, children have the responsibility to also respect the rights, freedoms and reputations of others. The freedom of expression includes the right to share information in any way they choose, including by talking, drawing or writing.

- *Article 19: Right to be Safe.* Children have the right to be protected from being hurt and mistreated, physically or mentally. Governments should ensure that children are properly cared for and protect them from violence, abuse and neglect by their parents, or anyone else who looks after them.

As you read the examples in the subsequent chapters of this book, you should reflect on: Article 12 of the UNCRC; the concepts of space, voice, influence and audience; and the iterative process between the right to express a view and the right to have views given due weight. You should also keep in mind the other Articles that Lundy has identified as relevant and, for each piece of research, consider whether you think they are relevant.

'The right to have views given due weight' underpins Part III of this book. It considers how stakeholder perspectives can inform and enhance inclusive education, and considers Article 2, which relates to non-discrimination. Throughout, inclusive education is used as the context in which to consider the UNCRC. This is consistent with the approach of Lundy, whose comments provide a useful summary to this section: 'A practical consequence of the indivisibility, interdependence and interconnectedness of all human rights is that the meaning of individual provisions of the UNCRC can only be read and interpreted in conjunction with the other rights protected by the Convention' (2007, 932).

What are the links between Article 12 and inclusive education?

Inclusive education can be regarded as being, in part, about (school) reform. In relation to education reform, Levin suggested five pragmatic arguments for student participation as being linked to one or more of the following principles:

1 Effective implementation of change requires participation by and buy-in from all those involved, students no less than teachers;
2 Students have unique knowledge and perspectives that can make reform efforts more successful and improve their implementation;
3 Students' views can help to mobilize staff and parent opinion in favour of meaningful reform;
4 Constructivist learning, which is increasingly important to high standards reform, requires a more active student role in schooling;
5 Students are the producers of school outcomes, so their involvement is fundamental to all improvement.

(2000, 156–7)

None of these is inconsistent with inclusive education. However, the link between the two sets of values is much stronger than simply avoiding inconsistencies. Internationally, the interconnections have been recognized (for example, by the European Agency for Development in Special Needs Education):

> Participation is an essential condition of inclusion, which is best understood in the context of a complex series of interactions between individuals, groups and the environment in which children and young people learn, live and grow. Schools are a crucial part of this environment. Inclusion is a dynamic field that is changing in light of new priorities and policy imperatives, alongside new understandings and insights into schooling and pedagogy.
>
> (European Agency for Development in Special Needs Education, 2011, 8)

This comment acknowledges child development when it talks about 'learn, live and grow'. Thus participation needs to be understood in terms of both the Human Rights dimension but also in terms of child development; both are relevant. Based on case studies undertaken in Nicaragua, Shier and colleagues sought to combine these two perspectives. The next example of research draws attention to some of Shier's publications on participation.

Example of research: (Re)conceptualizing participation

This example illustrates the evolution in the conceptualization of participation by reference to the work of a single author. Shier moved from the UK to work in Nicaragua.

- In 2001, he published an article entitled 'Pathways to participation: openings, opportunities and obligations' which introduced the notions of 'openings, opportunities and obligations' (Shier, 2001). This captures the move away from participation being a possibility to a full enactment of Article 12. It usefully distinguishes between those practices that meet the expectations of that Article and those that don't.
- Drawing on evidence from Nicaragua and the UK, Shier wrote an article 'Children as Public Actors: Navigating the Tensions' (Shier, 2010) which unpacked some of the complexities and tensions involved. He identified fifteen tensions and argued that the tensions fell into three groups:
    - tensions between participation as control and participation as empowerment (e.g. government agendas versus children's' agendas; consultation versus shared decision making);
    - tensions specific to children as a social group (e.g. mimicking adult structures versus inventing new ones; child protection versus child empowerment);
    - process versus product (e.g. getting a quick result versus including everyone).
- In 2014, he and colleagues published another model linked to their analysis of four case studies of children and young people's successful political advocacy in Nicaragua, e.g. 'Children and young people from La Dalia in the heart of the northern coffee-growing zone told us about their role in

helping to draw up a new Municipal Education Development Plan 2007–8. The former Mayor of La Dalia confirmed that young people's involvement in shaping the local plan, and the Ministry of Education corroborated this' (Shier et al., 2014, 5).

- The authors accepted that human rights are 'universal and the same for all' (2014, 3) whereas humans are 'unique and individual' (2014, 3). They used 'the concept of yin-yang to signify the coherence of the two complementary ideas ... The complementarity of the two approaches brings wholeness and integrity to the work.' (2014, 3).

Human rights: Universal, the → same for all

← Children and young people: Unique and diverse

Figure 3.3 Extract from the visualization of the conceptual framework for the study. *Source; Based on Shier et al., 2014, 3*

They added eight key concepts that assisted with the analysis of the case studies;

- Children and young people participate in different social settings;
- Different levels of participation and empowerment;
- Spaces for children's participation;
- Children and young people's citizenship;
- Who participates? Inclusion and exclusion;
- Participation and democracy;
- Empowerment versus disguised social control;
- Children and young people influencing public policy.

Reflections on the research

Shier has a sustained engagement with participation both as a practitioner and as a researcher. Whilst the theme of his work has remained consistent, the focus of his publications has changed.

Creating visual representations or models is fraught with hazards. In this visualization, the 'yin and yang' appear to be balanced and equal. This would be an oversimplification. The key message is about complementarity. Despite that cautionary note, it is worth considering whether the model, which was developed in the context of political participation, can be applied in other contexts.

Activity 1

The yin-yang motif represents the sociological perspective of participation with the psychological underpinnings of child development. In the context of inclusive education, can you identify ways in which this might be useful? Are there ways in which it might be problematic or limiting?

Activity 2

As you read the subsequent examples of research within this book, can you determine the discipline or disciplines (e.g. sociology, psychology, law) within which they are situated?

Interview with Harry Shier about his research

Harry Shier, Centre for Children's Rights, Queen's University Belfast, UK; CESESMA, Nicaragua

Sue Pearson: How do you think your ideas about children's participation have developed over the years? What were the key influences?

Harry Shier: I think of myself as a person who seeks to embody and enact ideas of learning, growth and change in my life, but as I reflected on this question, what struck me was how many of my early ideas about children's participation have persisted and taken root. These would include for example: (1) Participation is a human right, and therefore, although there are many reasons why children's participation is beneficial to society, none of these reasons is needed to justify it. The fact that it is every child's right is sufficient justification in itself. (2) We should strive to learn about and work on children and adolescents' agendas, rather than always inviting them to work on our preset agendas (whether in research or policy-making). (3) Following from this, we should look for ways to nurture and support children and adolescents' proactive participation (what we call *protaginismo infantil* in Latin America), i.e. actions based on their initiatives and where they make the key decisions (I would also note that this is constantly stifled by the way we adults always have to maintain control over resources, particularly controlling and constraining children and adolescents' mobilization). (4) I believe the lasting legacy of Roger Hart's work is his naming of the various forms of false participation that abound in this field, which he called 'manipulation', 'decoration' and 'tokenism' (Hart, 1992). We need to pay more attention to these as persistent problems, learning to recognize them and weed them out wherever we can. (5) We need to stop restricting children and adolescents' opportunities to speak out as advocates for themselves and others on the grounds of an excessive, overbearing protectionism, which it seems to me often has more to do with covering our own backs than genuinely protecting children.

So, having mentioned some of my ideas that haven't changed at all, I will now answer your question. There are many ways my thinking has changed over the years and continues to change, but I can think of four that I have thought through enough to share.

(1) I now have a much clearer grasp on the idea of 'empowerment'. When I reread 'Pathways to participation' (Shier, 2001), the one thing I wish I could change is where I said that for children to be empowered adults have to 'give away' some of their power; that is, I used to think of power relations as a 'zero-sum game': If you have more it means I must have less. I no longer see empowerment in this way. In more recent writing (Shier et al., 2014; Shier, 2015), I am clear that adults cannot 'empower children'. Our role is rather to seek to facilitate the processes through which children and adolescents can gradually become empowered, and this involves a fusion of conditions, capacities and self-perception (Shier, 2015, 214). Key influences here would be my *compañeras* and *compañeros* at CESESMA in Nicaragua, and through them, indirectly, the work of Paulo Freire.

(2) Children themselves change as they grow and develop. I think at one point I was taken in by a tendency in the 'new sociology of childhood' literature to deny the very idea of child development. This can still be seen in the number of articles that start with a footnote saying 'Child' means anyone under 18. I believe we must take more account of 'evolving capacities' and the way children and adolescents change as their capacities develop (Lansdown, 2005). And, particularly in our writing, we must stop using the term 'child' as a catch-all that includes babies, toddlers, pre-schoolers, primary schoolers, working children, young adolescents and near adults up to the eve of their eighteenth birthday, as if they all belong to a single, neatly characterizable social actor group that we can label 'children' (and as an aside, I think using 'children and young people' as a work-around is just as bad, as 'young person' has no standard meaning, so unless you define it, you shouldn't use it in any kind of serious discussion). I have started

to use 'children and adolescents' in my own work and, though not unproblematic, I do think it takes us a step forwards. The fact that we recognize and respect children and adolescents as citizens and rights-holders *now* does not mean we have to ignore the way they continue to learn and grow as they develop. Again the key influence here would be my work with CESESMA in Nicaragua, where, as in most of Latin America, child (*niño* or *niña*) is 0–12 and adolescent (*adolescente*) is 13–17: clear, consistent legal definitions that everyone knows and understands.

(3) Some years ago I wrote a paper entitled 'Children as public actors: navigating the tensions' (Shier 2010), the whole idea of which was to identify a number of polarities, or oppositions in thinking about child participation, and look at how experienced adults working in this field had learnt to navigate around and between these (examples were: 'The child as consumer vs. the child as activist'; 'Invited spaces vs. popular spaces'; 'Child protection vs. child empowerment' – there are fifteen in total). Recently I've taken a different approach, and what I then saw as oppositions or polarities causing tension, I now think of as complementarities, requiring integration and balancing. This way of thinking inspired the use of the yin-yang symbol to show how we can integrate ideas about diversity and individuality with the universality or 'same-for-everyone' nature of human rights (Shier et al, 2014, 3). I don't think I could write 'Navigating the Tensions' the same way now.

My key influence here is the Tao Te Ching of Lao Tzu. I've studied this a lot over the years, and even created my own revisioning of it, *The Tao of Development* (Shier, 2007), which you can download from my website http://www.harryshier.net/docs/Harry_Shier-Tao_of_development.pdf.

(4) One example of such a complementarity I've been working on recently is the one that links *getting everyone involved* with *working with those who want to be involved*. I think it is no exaggeration to say that making democracy work – at any level – depends on how we integrate both approaches and get them into balance. I checked some statistics and it seems that 65 per cent of the UK electorate turned out to vote in the 2010 general election (66 per cent in 2015) but only 1.2 per cent belong to a political party. Does democracy require that everyone become a party member, or alternatively that only those who show commitment by joining a party get to vote? Of course not. It requires that everyone has a say; that everyone's vote counts equally, whoever they are, wherever they come from and whether or not they choose to be politically active; and that those who choose to be politically active are able to get on and do it without repression or discrimination. Both the active engagement of the few and the universal representation of

the many are essential aspects of democratic governance, and the trick is to integrate them. Of course children and adolescents don't (yet) have a vote in general elections, but I think the same thinking can usefully be applied to child participation projects in general. On the one hand, it is essential that everyone's views are heard and included and that no individual or group is left out. On the other hand, it makes sense to invite those children and adolescents who are committed and enthusiastic about getting actively involved to take leading roles in the project, whether as researchers, reporters, data analysts, advocates or spokespeople. If you follow this approach, I think the ethical question is: Are you capable of identifying and dismantling the barriers that privilege some children and adolescents and discriminate against others in terms of who gets involved? An example of this occurred in my most recent research in Nicaragua. We had a team of seventeen young researchers (aged 9–15) and, although we were fully aware that there were a number of disabled children living in our catchment area, none of them were included in our final team. So I must ask myself: Did they have the same opportunity as everyone else to come forward and get involved in the project? They may not have wanted to, but that's not the issue. The issue is, Did they have an equal chance? For example: Were the selection criteria entirely relevant and necessary? Did we identify those children, or groups of children, who might have wanted to join the team but faced obstacles to putting themselves forward? And those who might have needed additional support to play a full and equal role in the team once selected? And what about those who would have loved to participate but never heard about the project because no-one made the effort to reach them? In this particular project, with the benefit of hindsight, I don't think we got it right; but these are now questions to be asked at the start of every future participation process.

A key influence here is Malala Yousafzai (Yousafzai and Lamb, 2013). While we cannot expect all children and adolescents to do what Malala did – and continues to do – that's not the point. We must learn to support, respect and honour those who do. Malala is just one, but she now has the support she needs, and she is a voice that speaks for millions who might not otherwise be heard.

Sue Pearson: Some children were very involved in this research whilst others weren't. Did this create any issues for the children or for you as the researcher?

Harry Shier: This is covered in the previous answer, but to sum up: Every child and adolescent has an incontestable right to be heard, but they are not under an obligation to be actively engaged in research or advocacy work if they are not interested. The ethical challenge for adults facilitating such work is to ensure that no one is excluded through either direct or indirect discrimination, and this requires consistent positive efforts on our part.

Sue Pearson: When you are developing a research project, at what point do you start to think about how it can make an impact?

Harry Shier: Before I start developing a research project, I've already thought about the potential impact. For me, research is a tool that can be used to help children and adolescents defend their rights and so improve their lives; research is at the service of advocacy. I don't deny that knowledge has value in itself, and I know there are researchers who dedicate their lives to seeking it on that basis, but that's not my interest. And this applies equally to supporting child researchers. The question I ask them at the start of a project is not 'What do you want to research?', but, 'What are the problems you face in your family, school or community, that new knowledge from research might help you tackle?' (See Shier 2012, 4–6, for an example of this approach in action.) So the research question itself is derived from considerations of potential impact. I wouldn't be doing research otherwise.

From the perspective of teachers, what are the assets and barriers to participation in (inclusive) education?

Shier's yin-yang model was developed in relation to political participation, and our focus now returns to education. A concern for both political and educational participation is the identification of barriers to and enablers of participation. This section draws on the perspectives of teachers, since they are influential in the children's experiences of and learning within participation, and also learning with the children about inclusive education.

Participation has been associated with reducing barriers and increasing cohesion within groups, communities and wider society. Thus far the opportunities and benefits of participation in relation to (inclusive) education have been discussed. However, there are (potential) barriers to participation. It is worth noting that the views of some teachers are not universally held by others in the profession. Research undertaken in Scotland in 2009 illustrated this point.

Example of research: Assets and barriers to developing pupil participation

The research was commissioned by Learning and Teach Scotland (LTS). One of the aims was 'To identify possible barriers to the development of pupil participation in schools and to make suggestions about how these can be overcome' (Cross et al., 2009, 5).

Data was gathered between December 2007 and March 2008, using three main methods. An online questionnaire was distributed to 2,631 primary and secondary schools registered with the Heads Together database, an online community for headteachers facilitated by LTS. The survey achieved a response rate of 24 per cent (n = 622). In addition to the survey, ten primary schools and five secondary schools across twelve local authorities submitted documentary materials for analysis. Four local authorities also submitted documents evidencing participation strategies for consideration. Finally, in consultation with LTS, four school case studies (two primary and two secondary) were conducted to consider how activities, practices and values come together to shape the overall participatory ethos of a school and the important role respect plays in developing effective practice.

This account of that research draws on the survey data. The respondents were asked about a number of factors, identified from the literature and from consultation with teachers and pupils, which might be regarded as assets or barriers (Cross et al., 2009, 27). A five-point scale was used with 1 representing an asset and 5 a barrier. The findings related to barriers and assets appear in the table below.

Primary school respondents were more likely than secondary respondents to regard the following as assets:

- The immediate environment and structure of the school building;
- National curricular changes;
- Student attitudes;
- Staff attitudes;
- Parent attitudes.

Table 3.1 Assets and barriers to developing pupil participation

Factor	Asset		Unsure		Barrier	Total number of respondents
	1	2	3	4	5	
The immediate environment and structure of the school building	27.7%	33.0%	20.3%	14.5%	4.5%	488
Local authority policy and practice	22.8%	51.8%	20.1%	4.6%	0.8%	483
National curricular changes	33.7%	50.6%	12.6%	2.5%	0.6%	486
Time available to implement pupil participation	6.8%	26.8%	16.8%	39.5%	10.0%	488
Student attitudes	52.1%	36.2%	7.0%	3.7%	1.0%	486
Staff attitudes	41.3%	44.2%	10.4%	3.5%	0.6%	489
Parent attitudes	33.7%	45.6%	16.0%	3.7%	1.0%	489
Community relations	33.8%	46.7%	16.4%	2.9%	0.2%	488

Source: Based on Cross et al., 2009, 27

There was also an open-ended question about what other factors might pose barriers. The 168 comments were categorized as follows:

- Time constraints – 37 per cent;
- Money or resources – 29 per cent;
- Pupils with low ability, special educational needs (SEN), behaviour problems, or the young age of pupils – 12 per cent;
- Curricular restrictions – 11 per cent;
- The distance children have to travel to school, or school bussing – 11 per cent;
- Pupil apathy, pupil lack of confidence or ethos – 10 per cent;
- Demands made by assessment or accountability – 6.5 per cent;
- Disaffected families or parental apathy – 5 per cent.

Reflections on the research

The authors cautioned that the report was only a snapshot, and that there was scope for longer-term research and evaluation. The Further reading section below includes an example of materials to support monitoring and evaluation.

Activity 1

Time available was seen as the chief barrier and the strongest constraint. What might be the possible reasons for this? How do you think this view could be mitigated? Remember that resources and staffing are finite.

Activity 2

The discussion of Article 12 of the UNCRC highlighted that other Articles have to be taken into account. These included Article 2 about non-discrimination. In the response to an open question about other factors that might be barriers, 12 per cent of the respondents referred to particular groups of pupils. What are the implications for developing inclusive participation?

The bias in the data was towards identifying assets rather than barriers, and yet progress towards all pupils being participants and feeling that their role in meaningful ways has been slow. This is consistent with research undertaken in Wales (Lyle, 2014). Lyle posits that the UNCRC is based on a view of children as active agents rather than non-adults in need of care and protection. She argues that 'educational psychology has a powerful influence on educationalists, which limits their expectations of children (2014, 221). She particularly associated this with young children, although it is worth considering whether it might be extrapolated to some other groups. Her views are far from uncontroversial and further evidence is needed to explore this. If an international perspective is taken, the tensions may be rather different. In cultures where the emphasis is on the collective (whether that is a family, clan or community) this can be in tension with child participation and/or a sense of protection towards those with different resources. The *National Child Participation Guide for Uganda* acknowledges the potential tensions:

> Participation of children as stated in the UNCRC is often seen as foreign, superficial and alien to the African and Ugandan culture. Whenever discussions on issues concerning children arise, it elicits political, cultural, social and emotional concerns. It is often challenged as elitist and interpreted as an intrusion into the jurisdiction of the family head and a threat to parental authority.
>
> (Ministry of Gender, Labour and Social Development and UNICEF, 2008, 14)

But the Guide also challenges that perspective:

> Child participation has been practiced in the African context for decades. However, the form of participation in traditional African society is beginning to disappear because of modern day living that has led to the loss of these practices. The misunderstanding child participation causes today emerges from old contexts. Many African traditions practice child participation without realizing that they are doing so – making it possible for children to access useful information and contribute to decisions.
>
> (2008, 14)

The materials from Uganda highlight the need to consider the form of participation and to do so in a manner that is widely applicable. That is our next focus.

What forms can participation take and what are the implications for how adults act?

Save the Children works globally in the area of child participation and monitoring progress. In their publication, *The Child Participation Global Indicator,* they provide a framework for the possible forms of participation (Save the Children, n.d., 3). The broad categories are shown in the table below.

Table 3.2 Types of children's participation

Consultative	Participation involves adults seeking the views of children to increase their knowledge and understanding of children's lives and the issues affecting them. It recognizes children's beliefs as well as their expertise but is adult-led and managed.
Collaborative	Involves children partnering with adults in some capacity, through which adults and children work in partnership to make decisions and implement projects.
Child-led	Children are empowered to lead their own projects or initiatives either individually or as part of their own organizations, clubs or parliaments. Adults may act as facilitators or offer advice and support to children.
Non-participation	Formal participation, just to tick the box, but without any real meaning or content. Can be decorative or manipulated

Source: Based on Save the Children, n.d., Session 12

Clearly this table sets out different roles for children and adults. However, we need to think about not just the roles of the adults but also how they act and the ethical dimensions. The latter can be summarized as recognizing the potential sensitivity of the issues associated with inclusion, considering the impact of the research on the children and taking steps to avoid harm. Ethical issues can be linked to elements of the UNCRC. For instance, Lundy refers to understanding Article 12 in the light of Article 3, which covers the best interests of the child. The International Save the Children Alliance drew up the *Practice Standards in Children's Participation* (Save the Children, 2005). Save the Children has a long history, both locally and globally, of encouraging participation, of providing training on it and of monitoring and evaluating it. The authors drew up the standards document in consultation with 'Save the Children staff, partner organizations and children in various countries and community settings' (Save the Children, 2005, 17). There are seven standards, and in the full document these are explained in detail, with criteria to determine whether they have been met. The standards are as follows:

- Standard 1: An ethical approach: transparency, honesty and accountability.
- Standard 2: Children's participation is relevant and voluntary.
- Standard 3: A child-friendly, enabling environment.
- Standard 4: Equality of opportunity.
- Standard 5: Staff are effective and confident.
- Standard 6: Participation promotes the safety and protection of children.
- Standard 7: Ensuring follow-up and evaluation.

Given that participation of children is a global activity, the standards have been written to establish principles. However, '[t]here must always be a clear understanding of the implications relating to local social, economic, cultural and traditional practices, as well as to the age and maturity of the child' (2005, 4).

These standards are intended to secure an ethical approach to participation. The forms of participation outlined above drew attention to non-participation, which involves other ethical decisions, the first of which might be: What are the circumstances in which non-participation is acceptable?

Are there indicators for participation in inclusive education?

Much of this chapter has been concerned with participation within education without the use of the lens of inclusive education. That is despite the strong links between inclusion and participation that were identified at the outset. Our attention now returns to those links. The European Agency for Development in Special Needs Education (EADSNE) (2009) was concerned to develop a set of indicators for inclusive education in Europe. Work was subsequently undertaken in a second project to specifically consider participation (EADSNE, 2011). The examples of research provided so far have explored some of the challenges in aligning policy and practice, and considered participation at various levels within and beyond the education system. This is consistent with the approach taken in this report: 'The proposed framework … [i]s not only about policies for supporting inclusive education and increasing participation, but also about how policy is turned into provision and in turn, how existing provision informs policy' (2011, 10). The framework that they developed was seen as relevant to multiple stake-holders including policy-makers, parents and voluntary groups. It clearly established how the term 'participation' would be understood by and cites the work of McConachie et al. who wrote, 'The key concepts of participation are – what does the child want to do, how do most children behave, and what activities have high social, developmental and educational priorities' (2006, 1163). This definition was developed in relation to disability and is 'stronger' than the definitions at the start of this chapter since those did not include the comparison with others or the priority of the activities – although it would be appropriate to probe whose priorities. For instance, there may be differ-ences between the priorities of children, parents and teachers.

EADSNE (2011) structured the indicators around three groupings:

- Indicators on participation (27);
- Indicators on participatory policies and practices (31);
- Indicators on participatory relationships (34).

Additionally they wrote about ways in which to develop further comparable indicators.

Research activity

Review the examples of research that you have encountered so far in this book and try to categorize them using the EADSNE framework. (Hint: some examples will fit more than one category.)

The work of EADSNE was research-informed and it suggested that the framework might help to identify areas where future research is needed. This book is also research-informed but gives particular attention to the views of children and their active involvement in research related to inclusive education.

Chapter activities

The following activities have been designed to help reflect on some of the key concerns over the chapter as a whole.

Activity 1

In the chapter, attention is drawn to Article 12 of the UNCRC but it is asserted that this is best understood in the light of other Articles. Access either the original UNCRC (http://www.unicef.org.uk/Documents/Publication-pdfs/UNCRC_PRESS200910web.pdf) or the child-friendly version (http://www.unicef.org/rightsite/files/uncrcchilldfriendlylanguage.pdf).

1 What links can you suggest between Article 12 and the other Articles?
2 What point do you think the chapter is making about the interconnectedness of the Articles?
3 How might the implementation of Article 12 be affected if the other Articles were disregarded?

Activity 2

The UNCRC Article 12 refers to 'all matters affecting the child'. Reread the chapter and identify all the different links that are made to participation/participatory, e.g. political participation, participatory relationships.

Activity 3

The chapter uses the terms 'inclusion/inclusive education' and 'participation':

1 Look through the chapter and note as many examples as you can of the use of the terms.
2 Drawing on some of these uses of the terms, do you think that inclusion can happen without participation?
3 Further, can inclusion be researched without taking into account the views of children? (Hint: this may depend on the nature of the questions that are being asked.)

Summary

This chapter has considered participation both in general terms and in relation to the UNCRC. It has linked Article 12 to education in general and to inclusive education in particular. Progress towards realizing Article 12 has been notably patchy and slow. Therefore, some of the barriers and enablers (viewed from various standpoints) have been identified. Consideration has been given to how the conceptualization of participation is evolving. Following categorization of participation into three broad forms, attention has been paid to the expectations placed on adults. The whole chapter has been linked to a view of children having agency and rights. The overarching message can be summarized by a quotation from Ban Ki-Moon, the seventh Secretary General of the UN, in his official address on International Youth Day in 2012. He stated that:

> Young men and women are not passive beneficiaries, but equal and effective partners. Their aspirations extend far beyond jobs; youth also want a seat at the table – a real voice in shaping the policies that shape their lives. We need to listen to and engage with young people. We need to establish more and stronger mechanisms for youth participation. The time has come to integrate youth voices more meaningfully into decision-making processes at all levels.
>
> (UN, 2012)

The next chapter responds to that challenge by considering the 'mechanism' of research and the participation of children.

Further reading

The European Agency for Special Needs and Inclusive Education strategic objectives are:

- to promote quality in the field of special needs and inclusive education by maintaining a long-term framework for extended European collaboration;
- to facilitate effective exchange of knowledge and experience among, as well as within, member countries;
- to identify key factors that hinder or support progress and provide countries with information and guidance;
- to analyse and review policy developments in countries in order

to support the development of sustainable and effective inclusive education systems.

(https://www.european-agency.org/about-us/what-we-do)

It has produced a range of linked documents, progressing from a broad focus on the principle of inclusive education to more specific focuses, including on participation. All of these are available online (http://www. european-agency.org).

European Agency for Development in Special Needs Education (2003). *Key Principles for Special Needs Education: Recommendations for Policy Makers.* Middelfart, Denmark: European Agency for Development in Special Needs Education.

European Agency for Development in Special Needs Education (2009). *Key Principles for Promoting Quality in Inclusive Education: Recommendations for Policy Makers.* Odense, Denmark: European Agency for Development in Special Needs Education.

European Agency for Development in Special Needs Education (2011). *Participation in Inclusive Education: A Framework for Developing Indicators.* Odense, Denmark: European Agency for Development in Special Needs Education.

Flutter, J. and J. Rudduck (2004). *Consulting Pupils: What's in It for Schools?* London: RoutledgeFalmer.
This seminal book considers pupils' participation within schools including the implications and potential benefits.

O'Boyle, A. (2013). 'Valuing the Talk of Young People: Are We Nearly There Yet?' *London Review of Education* 11: 127–39.
This article considers why what children say about themselves and education do not seem to be valued in public discourses.

Participation Works Partnership Network for England (n.d.). *Partnership Works.* Available online: http://www.participationworks.org.uk (accessed 20 February 2016).
The Participation Works Network for England (PWNE) is a free network which exists to provide opportunities for adults (for whom participation is part of their daily work) to network, share new ideas and learn more about the participation landscape. It is a partnership made up of the following six agencies: the British Youth Council, Children's Rights Alliance for England, KIDS, National Council for Voluntary Youth Services, National Youth Agency and Save the Children UK.

Save the Children (http://www.savethechildren.org.uk)

This organization has created a set of resources for monitoring and evaluating children's participation in programmes, communities and wider society. These are available at http://www.savethechildren.org.uk/resources/online-library/toolkit-monitoring-and-evaluating-childrens-participation (accessed 20 February 2016).

In 2005, Save the Children developed *Practice Standards in Children's Participation*. Available online: http://www.savethechildren.org.uk/sites/default/files/docs/practice_standards_participation_1.pdf (accessed 20 February 2016).

These standards are applicable in a range of contexts.

Research details

Beyond Article 12

The Children's Rights Alliance for England produced a report in 2009 which analysed the extent to which promoting children's rights is a priority for local authorities in general and children's services in particular. It also identifies emerging themes, and considers where local authorities could do more to implement the UNCRC.

Children's Right Alliance for England (2009). *Beyond Article 12: The Local Implementation of the UN Convention on the Rights of the Child*. Available online: http://www.crae.org.uk/publications-resources/beyond-article-12-the-local-implementation-of-the-un-convention-on-the-rights-of-the-child (accessed 2 June 2015).

'Today's learning objective is to have a party'

This research used playful methods to help explore not just the existing world but also an imagined world. Through the approaches adopted, it illustrates creative approaches to educational research.

Greenstein, A. (2014). 'Today's Learning Objective is to have a Party: Playing Research with Students in a Secondary School Special Needs Unit'. *Journal of Research in Special Educational Needs* 14 (2): 71–81.

(Re)conceptualizing participation

This example of research draws on three articles by Shier which trace his evolving ideas.

Shier, H. (2001). 'Pathways to Participation: Openings, Opportunities and Obligations'. *Children & Society* 15 (2): 107–17.

Shier, H. (2010). 'Children as public actors: navigating the tensions'. *Children & Society* 24 (1): 24–37.

Shier, H., M. H. Méndez, M. Centeno, I. Arróliga and M. González (2014). 'How Children and Young People Influence Policy-makers: Lessons from Nicaragua'. *Children & Society* 28 (1): 1–14.

Assets and barriers to developing pupil participation

This research was commissioned by Learning and Teaching Scotland (LTS) to evaluate the nature of pupil participation in primary and secondary schools across Scotland.

Cross, A. B., S. Hall, M. Hulme, J. Lewin and S. McKinney (2009). *Pupil Participation in Scottish Schools: Final Report.* Available online: http://eprints.gla.ac.uk/49601/1/id49601.pdf (accessed 13 March 2016)

4

Inclusive Research

Chapter outline

Introduction and key questions

The first chapter of the book included a section on participation by children in general, which was then developed in Chapter 3. Consistent with our changed understandings of childhood and alterations in our engagement with issues such as ethnicity, gender and disability, there have been shifts in research. The case has been made that children are experts in their lives and that there are policy imperatives for involving children in research. This position has been influenced by the UNCRC. In their book, Walmsley and Johnson employed the term 'inclusive research' and described this as 'research that involves people who may otherwise have been seen as subjects of research as instigators of ideas, research designers, interviewers, data analysts, authors, disseminators and users' (2003, 10). They acknowledged that the principles of qualitative, participatory and feminist research have informed inclusive research. This chapter draws on more recent research and discussions of inclusive education to illustrate the potential and limitations of inclusive research.

In traditional research, the researcher exerts more power than the researched. For instance, the researcher may design a questionnaire (without input from children), children respond to this and the data are exclusively used by the researcher. This is a position which is not consistent with the previous discussion of participation both as a right of children and a characteristic of inclusive education. The research examples in this book will draw your attention to approaches where the power balances are more equal. There is a particular focus on those who, in traditional research, are prone to being overlooked or silenced. The approach adopted will help you to challenge the suggestions in the first chapter as to why some children may be overlooked (Wickenden and Kembhavi-Tam, 2014).

The prime focus of this chapter is not on the findings of the research; those appear in the chapters in Part III of the book. Rather, the emphasis is on who was involved in the research and the nature of their relationship to the enquiry. However, reading this chapter should help you contextualize the research examples cited in the book.

In this chapter we explore the roles of children and adults in research associated with inclusive education. The following questions will be addressed:

- What is meant by the term 'inclusive research'?
- Why is it important to consider the roles of children in research related to inclusive education?
- What roles can children play?
- What issues do those undertaking inclusive research need to consider?

What is meant by the term 'inclusive research'?

In the context of learning difficulties, Walmsley and Johnson (2003) suggested some principles that should apply to inclusive research. They wrote:

- that the research must address issues that really matter to people with learning disabilities and which ultimately lead to improved lives for them
- that it must access and represent their views and experiences

- that people with learning disabilities need to be treated with respect by the research community.

(2003,16)

These principles challenged the orthodoxy of research setting the agenda, prescribing the roles of others and frequently using the data in ways that exclude those who provided it (e.g. academic journal articles about marginalized groups).

The term 'inclusive research' is viewed as a useful umbrella term covering a wide range of approaches that may have been rooted in participatory, emancipatory or feminist research. Although Walmsley and Johnson focused on learning difficulties, the principles of inclusive research have been applied more widely. Nind provides examples related to health or interagency, looking at the experiences of older people, carers and health and social care professionals in relation to the risk of older people falling (2014a, 43).

Whilst research of this type has advantages, it should not be seen as a panacea. There are good reasons for using other forms of research and the question has to be what approach or approaches are fit for purpose. For instance, in Chapter 2, we compared access to education in different countries based on statistical information that is data that does not require the involvement of children for its collection. The mediation of financial and policy factors by schools and individual teachers could not be researched in an 'inclusive' manner.

Nind has provided a useful commentary about her own position as a researcher:

> I am someone who does research *on, with* and *for* people with learning disabilities (and also other learners, educationalists and researchers). I have a strong interest in researching inclusively, but I am not exclusively allied to it. (I deliberately use this phrase *doing research inclusively* with the active verb, preferring it to the apparently more fixed *inclusive research,* as it implies a greater flexibility.)

(2014a, 83–4)

But even if a piece of research has been conducted inclusively, is that sufficient to claim it is 'good' research? Nind and Vinha (2012) suggested that judgements should be about the quality of the research as well as whether it is inclusive. Their publication highlighted the lack of debate about what constitutes quality in inclusive research.

Example of research: Quality in inclusive research

Nind and Vinha conducted a piece of research the objectives of which were to:

- Take stock of what we know about people with learning disabilities taking part in research about them;
- Produce guidance to help when people with learning disabilities are working together with others and on their own doing research;
- Develop materials and case studies based on new practices;
- Produce criteria for judging quality in inclusive research.

(2012, 18)

They conducted a series of focus groups involving policy-makers and funders, and participant-researchers (i.e. those who were participants and researchers or co-researchers with people with learning disabilities). They selected this approach so that it would provide a space in which those taking part in the study could talk, share and generate knowledge between them.

An outcome of research was an understanding of quality in research *and* inclusivity. Nind and Vinha suggested that research meets those two criteria when:

1 The research answers questions we could not otherwise answer, but that are important;
2 The research reaches participants, communities and knowledge in ways that we could not otherwise access;
3 The research involves using and reflecting on the insider, cultural knowledge of people with learning disabilities;
4 The research is authentic (recognized by the people involved);
5 The research makes an impact on the lives of people with learning disabilities

(2012, 43–4)

Reflections on the research

The researchers adjusted their approach in the light of feedback and availability of participants. They redrafted their materials in line with Easy Read, which specializes in making information accessible for people with learning disabilities (www.easy-read-online.co.uk). For example, the report included explanations of research-related terminology which appear close to where the term is used. There is a bullet point that says 'Our method was talking together in **focus groups**' (2012, 3; emphasis in original). Alongside a box surrounds an explanation in blue print which reads '**Focus groups** are small groups who talk about ideas on a research topic' (2012, 3; emphasis in original).

Activity 1
At the end of Chapter 1 you were invited to think about whether some sources were more convincing than others, and, if so, why. To what extent do the suggestions from this research about inclusivity and quality help you to make those judgements?

Activity 2
This piece of research focused on people with learning disabilities. Could it be applied to children with learning difficulties? Could it be applied to other groups who are vulnerable to marginalization?

Why is it important to consider the roles of children in research related to inclusive education?

There has been considerable research undertaken about inclusive education, although complexities, ambiguities and confusions exist. As Nind commented:

Conceptually this area of education research is messy. Part of the project has been seeking to define inclusive education and relationships between inclusion, exclusion, integration, diversity and so on. Despite policy rhetoric that has done more to confuse than clarify, and the existence of multiple movements rather than single movements, we have made some headway. Like progression towards inclusive education itself, however this headway is faltering. Practitioners can cite research that says inclusive education is a success/ failure/ risky venture without solid evidence/exciting adventure offering great promise. Despite such ambiguity, inclusive education is not going away as a talking point or mental reference point; the research has had an effect on the collective mindset and, for those wanting them, there are credible and worthwhile pointers to be found in the research.

(2011, 18)

One possible response to Nind's comments would be to say that the field is extremely complex and to shy away from including the views of children. There are several reasons why this is not appropriate. Under the UNCRC (see Chapter 2), children have a right to have their views heard in matters that have an impact on their lives – and education clearly has an impact on their lives. We also note changing views of childhood (see Chapter 1), from a position where children were seen as in need of protection and care to one where they are seen as socially competent actors with agency. There is evidence that listening to the views of children can inform and enhance teaching and learning both for the individual and more generally. This is illustrated at various points in this book but is particularly clear in Chapters 5, 6 and 7. Taking into account children's perceptions is associated with work to improve the effectiveness of schools. Additionally, the process of being consulted is an educational process itself; a preparation for citizenship. Furthermore, research into inclusive education should be consistent with its principles.

Whilst there has been progress towards involving children in research, this has been inconsistent across learner groups, with some groups more or less likely to be represented. Thus children with limited communication abilities are under-represented; perhaps because of a perception that they don't have views to express, or concerns that accessing those views would be costly and time-consuming or that gaining ethical consent from the children would be problematic. In other cases, there may be definitional issues. Smith (2005) researched underachievement and claimed her study was distinctive since it considered underachievement across the whole ability range; she argued that it is possible to have underachieving high-achievers as well as underachieving low-achievers. Some groups and individuals (e.g. looked-after children) may have become distrustful of the probing questions of adults and may view a researcher as 'just another nosey adult'. Additionally, research funding may be more available where there is a narrow focus on a defined group rather than an emphasis on the more fluid, broad concept of inclusive education. This could result in some groups being particularly frequently researched. Thus there is more research on the group of pupils with dyslexia than on those who experience a reading difficulty.

Challenges and opportunities are associated with ensuring that no group of children is 'muted' as a consequence of any child-related or context-related factors. However, the traditional boundaries between different groupings (e.g. children and adults, those with and without disabilities) have been and are being rethought. The activities of self-advocacy groups such as

People First, which is run by and for people with learning disabilities, have challenged views of their insightfulness, competence and willingness to be involved and opened up new possibilities. That international organization works to support people with learning difficulties to have more choice and control. The website, People First of Canada, makes an explicit link between the work of the movement and progress towards inclusion (http://www.peoplefirstofcanada.ca/about-us/history). It isn't acceptable to say that any child is too young, too difficult to communicate with or too difficult to recruit to a research project, or that any child would not have views to express. All children should have access to education, although Chapter 1 has provided evidence that this is not the case despite strong advocacy. In 1967, Segal published a book entitled *No Child is Ineducable*. This was a passionate call to value the potential of every child, and influenced educational thinking. In relation to research, Freire was vehement: 'The silenced are not just incidental to the curiosity of the researcher but are the masters of inquiry into the underlying cause of the events in their world. In this context, research becomes a means of moving them beyond silence into a quest to proclaim to the world' (Freire, 1982, 34).

If children who feel marginalized and excluded from education are also under-represented (or unrepresented) in educational research, this can be a further source of disadvantage. They are being excluded from a learning experience which includes gaining insights into the research process. Children have valuable perspectives to offer, and, as experts in their own lives, may hold views that differ from those of their parents or teachers or policy-makers – a situation which the adults may find challenging. Children may have concerns that have been unrecognized by the adults around them but which are genuine and pressing for them. A student whom I taught illustrated this. At secondary school she was not involved in any of the meetings about her educational provision which took place. The adults involved did not address the issue of her access to the sixth form common room, which she (as a wheelchair user) could not use. It simply didn't occur to them. For her, that lack of access was a major – if not *the* major – frustration. Academically, she was buoyant – but she also valued social engagement.

The evidence is that children who in the past may have been overlooked by researchers can contribute both to the data and to the research process. We need to ensure that all children can be and are involved in research associated with their education. All children benefit from being educated about research. Children's interest in research as a process is illustrated in the following example.

Example of research: Follow-up meeting for participants

A postgraduate student and her supervisor reported on a follow-up activity with a group of primary school children who had been involved in a participatory research project related to 'children's experience and perceptions of adaption and intercultural encounters' (Pinter and Zandian, 2015, 238). The participants attended a state primary school which is near an international university and therefore educates children from many countries.

The researchers used participatory approaches linked to the question: 'What would be most helpful to you if you had to live in a new country?' They approached this through a Diamond Nine Ranking Activity. The children were given 'a large diamond shaped cardboard and ten statements on small cards. They were asked to discuss and organize the ten ideas by ranking them according to their perceived importance' (2015, 238). Initially the task was completed with the children in pairs and then in groups of four, which enabled reflection on the similarities and differences in the children's opinions. The children also developed 'suggestions for newcomers' which took the form of five things the children thought that others 'should or should not do in order to fit in more easily in a new educational environment' (2015, 238). Both of these activities provided ample opportunities for discussion. This data informed the assignment and that could have been the end of the research project.

The authors wanted to share the research findings with the children and requested another meeting with them several months after the activities. The data gathered through the participatory activities had been used by one of the researchers to complete an MA dissertation. At this meeting, the children were shown the MA dissertation, an eleven-page mini-version of the dissertation and a poster. Three questions were prepared in order to guide the discussion:

- How did you like the research tools? What changes would you recommend to the tools?
- Looking at the findings, who do you think should read/know about this MA dissertation?
- How do you think you benefitted from participating in this research?

The children made unexpected and unsolicited comments that reflected interest extending beyond these questions. These related to how the children saw themselves and the roles they played. The authors grouped these spontaneous comments around the themes of:

- pseudonyms and transcribed talk;
  'The PG researcher …. is just about to ask the next set of questions, when one of the children, Tina, looking at the dissertation left open on the table, suddenly asks the question "Who is Sally?"' (2015, 241). (Sally was one of the pseudonyms and this question prompted a discussion of their use in the dissertation.)
- voice and perceived role in research;
  'Tina commented, "[I]t is amazing how, how the things we said lots of other researchers have found out as well. So like … lots of people's opinions are the same so, if they do do something about helping the problem like the newcomers it will probably be okay"' (2015, 243).
- changes in understanding.
  In the follow-up session, Tina comments, '[E]mm like I didn't think it would turn out like how it was. Like I didn't actually fully understand like what you were doing for your research but now I do, because you shared what your results came up with and like … just like whatever you did, I didn't expect it' (2015, 245).

In the follow-up activity, the children diverted attention away from the pre-prepared questions to the matters that interested them. They had 'real' questions about the research process as well as the findings. The article concludes: 'The more we understand about how child participants see research and their place in it, the more effectively we can design our research methods in subsequent studies' (2015, 247).

Reflections on the research
This is a rare account of a follow-up to a participatory research activity, and illustrates the children's interest in the research process as well as the findings. The title 'I thought it would be tiny little one phrase that we said, in a huge big pile of papers' reflects the children's confusion about their role and involvement. During the follow-up activity, they were able to clarify issues about research and researchers.

Activity 1

In the follow-up session, these researchers took notice of the unsolicited comments of the children, i.e. those that diverted attention from the planned questions. Kellett supported this view, noting that it is important 'to listen to children and not just hear what they have to say' (Kellett, 2010, 197).

1 How do you understand the difference between hearing and listening?
2 If we accept that researchers need to listen rather than just hear, what would be the implications for researchers?
3 How would it shape what the researchers do?

Activity 2

As noted above, the data gathered through the participatory activities was used by one of the researchers to complete an MA dissertation and 'in a conventional sense, this was the end of the research process' (Pinter and Zandian, 2015, 239). The follow-up activity provided a space for learning by both the children and the researchers. In your view, what are the potential benefits and challenges of including follow-up activities in research plans? Try to identify different kinds of activities that the follow-up work might involve. [Hint: perhaps start by thinking about a particular topic and a particular group of participants.)

What roles can children play?

The title of this section assumes that there are multiple possible roles for children that extend beyond being data providers. Many of these involve shifts in the power balances between the researched and the researcher, as highlighted in Chapter 1. Shaw et al. (2011) portrayed the continuum of power-relationships.

Even where the role of children is restricted to being sources of data, they have some limited power. In what ways might children who are interviewees in adult-led research exert power?

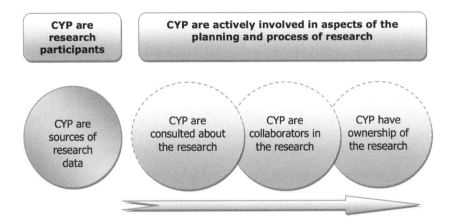

CYP have increasing control of the research process

Figure 4.1 Model of children's involvement in research. *Source: Based on Shaw et al., 2011* (These authors used the term 'Children and young people' and the abbreviation CYP.)

Example of research: Children as interviewees exerting power

McLeod undertook research to explore the communication between social workers and looked-after children in order to gain an understanding of why it is difficult to establish an effective dialogue with disaffected young people. In 2001, she had investigated how well social workers listened to looked-after children: 'The central finding … was something of a conundrum: while the social workers believed they were listening, and could describe detailed efforts they had made to elicit children's views, the young people in the main, did not feel they had been heard' (2007, 280). The interviewees were asked:

- whether they felt social workers listened to them;
- whether their social workers explained things to them and asked them for their views;
- what part they had played in care-planning and/or service development;
- whether they had any grievances and what they felt they could do about them.

This article 'tried to evaluate not just the information it [the data] provided about the young people's views, but also the process of interaction' (2007, 281).

The researcher, who is a senior lecturer in Social Work, identified that the young people used tactics in a bid to take control of the agenda. She categorized their tactics into eight types, each of which she saw as bids to take hold of the agenda.

Avoidance: two interviewees declined to be involved in the research, whilst another agreed but never turned up for appointments.

Active resistance: one interviewee 'ran riot, throwing toys around the room and all [the researcher's] efforts to engage him failed'. The researcher's commentary on this is that 'many looked-after children have no desire to have social workers inflicted upon them, but they have no choice. They resist the only ways they know.'

Aggression: one interviewee was openly hostile.

Passive resistance: an interviewee who claimed to be happy to talk to the researcher only responded in monosyllables.

Fantasy: several of the interviewees provided unreliable information which the researcher suspected (and later confirmed) was inaccurate.

Denial: one interviewee chose to be economical with the truth which may have been a way of maintaining some control over the communication.

Exaggeration: one interviewee overstated the case as a way of making a point.

Changing the subject: in an interview which touched on how little the interviewee had seen of his mother prior to her death, he took control by changing the topic.

In reflecting on the interviews, the researcher said there was a possible link between their 'less successful' aspects and her lack of skill. However she suggested an alternative view that the communication was only ineffective if viewed from her perspective. The strategies of the children might have enabled them to achieve their aims. McLeod (2007, 284) cites the work of Rich who viewed any interview as an interaction: 'two people talking to and affecting each other. It is merely a convenience to describe one of them as the interviewer' (1968, 3). McLeod argues that 'if we want to truly hear young people's voices we have to find out what is on their agenda' (2007, 284).

Reflections on the research

This research was undertaken by a social worker; a member of a group of people with whom the children would have had past experiences. Children's concerns about the consequences of saying more might have been a factor in how they responded to the interview schedule.

Activity 1

Can you think of any instances in which someone you interviewed used any of the strategies described above, or where you, as an interviewee, used them? (This may include metaphorical use – not necessarily literally throwing toys around.)

Activity 2

How might the identified strategies (e.g. change of topic, denial, etc.) have been avoided? (Hint: you may want to think about what the researcher could say or how the conversation could have been supported, e.g. with images or artefacts.)

Children, especially those who have been marginalized, may feel unable to express themselves by conventional means but may display their power in a variety of ways, as illustrated above. How can they enact their agency? Lewis drew our attention to 'Silence in the context of "child voice"' (Lewis, 2010). She entitled one section of her article 'Recognising, noting, responding to, interpreting and reporting silence' (2010, 18). She argued that 'the interpretation of silence should become an integral part of the analysis and over time could contribute to the development of methodologies of silence alongside methodologies of voice' (2010, 20). Although there is an emphasis on accessing 'children's voice' in current publications (including this book), it should not be done uncritically.

We have noted that the traditional power balances between the researcher(s) and researched are no longer seen as fixed; other relationships are in play. It is argued that children can be active participants in all aspects of research. Words often associated with researching inclusively include flexible, responsive and creative. These are evident in the next example, which is from Spain.

Example of research: Using biographical narrative methodology to explore social exclusion in Spain

This study explored what barriers and support the young people (18–25) had experienced in school, personally and in work. Rojas et al. contested that the research experience and skills of the participants need to be taken into account, and stressed 'the importance of researchers being capable of imagining other ways to approach and to tackle a reality not necessarily foreseen by them initially' (2013, 158). Their sample (n = 48) included some 'belonging to minority ethnic and cultural groups, some disabled and some economically underprivileged groups' (2013, 156). The researchers needed to modify their approaches in the light of differences in the respondents' varied experiences and circumstances. The challenges that they reported were:

- preferential use of non-verbal forms of expressing in the communicative exchanges – they found that they could not understand the young peoples' discourse 'without considering the non-verbal communication mechanisms they habitually use';
- arbitrary and quite unsystematic organization of dates or life events – whilst all the respondents could recall situations or people, for some the timeframe seemed unimportant and references to time were sometimes very broad (e.g. 'when I was young');
- preference for the use of closed questions;
- use of particular reference schemes in interpreting, understanding and valuing important moments in life;
- opting for values and beliefs different from those of the dominant culture.

They reported how these observations led them to modify the data collection process by substituting one activity for another or modifying the technique. They emphasized that none of the changes that they made was associated with any one particular group.

Activity 1
The researchers noted the interviewees' preference for closed questions. Why do you think this might be their preference? What are the implications?

Activity 2

There are references to marginalized groups, vulnerability and dominant culture. Reflect on Chapter 2 which discussed inclusive education including the comments on exclusion. In that context, what are your views about a term such as 'dominant culture'?

Shaw et al., in their publication entitled 'Guidelines for Research with Children and Young People' (2011), provided a useful matrix of the models of involvement. The authors noted that the National Children's Bureau who published this document doesn't advocate (NCB) noted that it doesn't 'advocate a model of involvement that gives CYP *total* control over the research process, as we believe that this could potentially undermine the quality of the research and/or result in unethical or illegal practices' (2011, 8; emphasis in original).

Whilst an analysis such as appears in Table 4.1 is useful, it is only one way in which to make the connections between the research processes and the involvement of children. It appears clear and logical, but that may mask some of the complexities. To help you think about the ways in which the research processes have been categorized and the forms of involvement, some research examples are included in this chapter. You should also return to this table as you read other research examples.

The first example reports on research undertaken in Mongolia and Zambia (Morgan and Sengedorj, 2015). UNICEF provides some statistics about Mongolia at: http://www.unicef.org/infobycountry/mongolia_ statistics.html, and for Zambia at: http://www.unicef.org/infobycountry/ zambia_statistics.html. The common theme in this research across the two countries is what topics children would want to research.

Table 4.1 Features of different models of involvement

Models of involvement Aspects of CYP's role	CYP are sources of research data	CYP are consulted about the research	CYP are collaborators in the research	CYP have ownership of the research
Decision-making	Adults in control of all the decisions (although individual CYP can decide whether or not to take part)	Adults take CYP's views into account when making decisions	Decision-making shared, or negotiated, between adults and CYP	Adults provide advice and guidance to CYP and support them to make informed decisions
Developing research idea or proposal, designing and planning research	No involvement (unless participating in pilot study)	CYP may be consulted during the development stage	CYP and adults may develop and plan the research together	CYP initiated research idea and have major influence on design and methodology
Duration of involvement with the research	At data collection points only	CYP's involvement likely to be sporadic (at key decision-making points)	CYP potentially involved at any or all stages of research	CYP likely to be involved throughout, from conception to dissemination
Research participants providing data	Yes	No	No	No
Involvement in collection and analysis of the data	No	Unlikely, though may be consulted on tools or interpretation of findings	May be actively involved in some aspects(e.g. designing tools, data gathering, interpretation)	CYP potentially involved in all aspects of the research process (if they wish)
Reporting/ disseminating	No involvement. However, findings of research should be fed back to the participants if possible	May be asked to comment on draft report or dissemination plans	CYP may have role in report-writing (e.g. for CYP audience) and contribute to dissemination activities	CYP may take a lead in some reporting and dissemination activities

Source: Based on Shaw et al., 2011

Example of research: if you were the researcher, what would you research?

The title above forms part of the title of an article by Morgan and Sengedorj (2015) which posed this and other questions to children in Mongolia and Zambia. The children (n = 72) were aged between seven and fourteen years and came from varied backgrounds.

Table 4.2 Participants involved in the research

Mongolia (Ulaanbaatar)		Zambia (Lusaka, Kiwe and Livingstone)	
Background	n	Background	n
Children who lived on the streets	6	Children who lived on the streets	14
Children who lived in a centre for former 'street children'	8	Children from mainstream schools	21
Summer camp in the countryside for children who lived in the centre for former 'street children'	15		
Children from an after-school club	8		

In Mongolia, the researchers used discussion groups (n = 3) with twenty-two of the children, and observations and informal discussions at the summer camp. In Zambia, there were small group discussions and one-to-one interviews.

The following questions with associated probes were used to facilitate discussions:

1 What do you understand by the term research?
2 If you were a researcher, what would you research about education and schools?
3 How would you research these questions?
4 What do we need to think about to keep children safe and comfortable when they are answering the questions?
5 Who should carry out the research? Children, children/adults or adults?

The children's responses to the first question tended to focus on 'scientific research' and how researchers 'who wear a white coat' try to find out the answer to a question or 'a problem'' (2015, 208). Their responses to the second question were grounded in their experiences, e.g. not having enough money for school equipment, how lessons were boring and not fun, and not being able to attend school because they were poor. Morgan and Sengedorj suggested that:

- the children's responses may reflect their own preoccupations with what was important to them in the here and now;
- children bring their own experiences, values and beliefs to the research process;
- the power balances may have meant that the children felt they needed to give any answer to the adult who was asking even if they weren't sure what the question was about;
- the children may have used previous experience with 'foreigners' to guide their responses.

Nonetheless, the children provided ideas for research which they thought should be conducted. In terms of appropriate methods, some of the children mentioned groups whilst others preferred one-to-one interviews. Children commented on the relationship with the interviewer and on the need for knowing the researcher and trusting them.

In terms of interviews the children suggested that they could be made 'fun'. Children were asked about the use of photographs and other visual methods. These children had limited opportunities to take photographs and 'had previous experiences of their picture being taken, by journalists or tourists, without their consent' (2015, 211). They could see how photographs might help the researcher but some of the children thought they might be a source of distress. Most children were comfortable with tape-recording interviews although some 'did not want their voice on the tape'. The researchers commented on how similar the children's views were to those of adults. They questioned whether children need 'special methods' to research their lives. Drawing on the work of Leeson (2013), they posit that using particular methods with children is a way of indicating that children are different. The principle of being sensitive to the participants applies equally to adults and children. Children should not be treated as a homogenous group.

The discussions also broached the topic of ethics. In terms of who should conduct the research, there was a range of different viewpoints, with many children feeling it would be best 'if the children did the research or of it was a combination of adult and child-led. The researchers cited a boy aged thirteen from a mainstream school in Mongolia, who said: "Children can understand children"' (Morgan and Sengedorj, 2015, 213). This illustrates some of the ambivalence in their views; sometimes they emphasized the similarities between children and adults, and at other times referred to the differences.

Reflections on the research

The researchers were careful to explain to the children that suggesting ideas for research was not a promise that the research would take place. However, there was evidence that children have ideas about what matters to them that could be researched.

Activity 1

This research suggests that whilst some research methods (such as photography) are meant to be empowering, they may disempower some children. What could researchers do to increase the proportion of children who are empowered? What are the implications?

Activity 2

The statement cited above (that 'Children can understand children') could be interpreted as meaning that only those belonging to a particular grouping can understand that group. What are the advantages and disadvantages of this position for those conducting research?

The children in this research were data providers but they clearly had ideas about what they would like to research and how they might do so. Perhaps the challenge to adults is that we should ask more often what is important to children and what ideas for research they have.

The statement that 'Children can understand children' can also be linked to the analysis and interpretation aspects of research. The example below comes from research which involved People First, the advocacy group mentioned earlier.

Example of research: Inclusive data analysis

Kramer et al. undertook a research project within which the numerical data was presented to adults with learning difficulties in three different formats. They argued that 'gathering, analyzing and interpreting data can be empowering to people with intellectual disabilities by potentially raising their awareness of their situation and facilitating a desire to change that situation if they find it unsatisfactory' (2011, 264).

The adults with learning difficulties were members of People First, a self-advocacy group. The overall aim of the project was to 'increase group capacity for advocacy, starting with the specific goal of running a People First meeting. A data collection tool was designed to document and help group members reflect on the extent to which they controlled the meeting. This included items such as:

- setting the agenda;
- preparing for the meeting;
- running the meeting;
- organizing the materials;
- participating in the meeting;
- making decisions.

Each of these had subsections which were cued by pictures. Control was rated for each item that was on the 'Who did what' checklist. The categories were 'advisers', 'People First members and advisers together' and 'People First members'. For each checklist item, the number of ratings created the frequency data.

The university researchers presented the numerical data in three formats:

- bar graphs;
- pie charts;
- line graphs.

These were presented to the People First officers, who expressed a preference for bar graphs. The university researchers then produced one slide for every checklist item. Each slide included the checklist item, the picture associated with the item and the bar graph. These were presented to the members, who conducted some small focus groups, each of which included a university researcher or group adviser. The composition of the groups was negotiated with the members. Each group analysed the data on a selection of slides chosen because they were particularly relevant to the goal of running the meetings. The university researcher checked their understanding. The next step was to interpret the data with questions such as:

- Why do you think this happened?
- What does it mean for People First?
- How does it make you feel?
- Are you OK with this?
- What worked well and what didn't?

The People First qualitative comments were documented in handwritten notes, recorded and transcribed.

All members of People First (either with or without support) were able to analyse the data and specifically to identify the 'tallest' bar in the graph. Involvement in the interpretation was patchy with some members not responding, some talking only about feelings and other members put 'forth detailed responses that described the reasons for the change in control and the implications for the future' (2011, 267–8).

In discussing this part of the project, the researchers stressed the importance of chunking the data (using bar charts for each item). There was no comparative element to the research so each question could be dealt with separately. They also commented on the importance of the social networks and support within the focus groups, the importance of debating within the group as a form of peer review and the value of the members being familiar with the 'Who did what' checklist. There were concerns about the suitability of the process for those who do not use verbal communication.

Activity 1

In reporting on this project, the researchers suggest that '[o]ne limitation to this study concerns the generalizability of the process and findings; the findings may be reflective only of this particular self-advocacy group and their experiences. In addition, the findings may not generalize to other self-advocates with fewer or more functional skills' (2011, 272).

1 What are your views about the importance of research being generalizable?

2 If it is accepted that these methods aren't generalizable, how would you start to plan for individuals with different resources to be co-analysts? (Hint: the emphasis in the quotation was on strengths.)

Activity 2

The article comments, 'Though beyond the original scope of the study, the university researchers are aware that this study stopped short of incorporating an inclusive authorship strategy' (2011, 272).

1 What do you understand by the term 'inclusive authorship strategy'?
2 What opportunities and challenges would such a strategy provide?

What issues do those undertaking inclusive research need to consider?

This section highlights some issues that researchers need to consider. It should be read in conjunction with the examples of research in all the chapters since they illustrate how others have conducted research.

An overarching principle is that all research should be conducted ethically. The ethical guidelines produced by the British Educational Research Association are widely used (BERA, 2011). In Chapter 3, reference was made to the *Practice Standards in Children's Participation* (Save the Children, 2005) which are used internationally. In combination these provide sound guidance.

The chapter has begun to question whether there are methods of data collection that are particular to children. This is a topic that re-emerges in Chapter 8. The next sections illustrate some of the decisions that researchers and co-researchers need to make.

In designing the sample consideration needs to be given to who the participants are representing. This is not a question unique to inclusive research but it nonetheless is an important one. Many of the pieces of research, though not all, involve participants who are perceived to have something in common whether that is a developmental disorder (e.g. dyslexia, autism) or a contextual factor (e.g. attending a particular type of provision). In selecting participants in this way, there is a privileging of that single factor. The criteria used to select the participants in a piece of research may be dissonant with the child's self-identity, a point made by Wickenden (2011).

Example of research: Talk to me as a teenager

Wickenden researched the making of friendships by disabled young people who have little or no speech. This article was part of a wider study which 'used ethnographic and narrative approaches to explore aspects of identity and lifeworld of a group of disabled teenagers who have physical impairments and use alternative and augmentative communication (AAC)' (2011, 1). In reporting back to the participants five themes with user-friendly names were used. In relation to 'Selfhood – How the Teenagers see Themselves' (2011, 12) Wickenden reported that they 'see themselves as having a number of diverse aspects to their identities (such as chatty, good at maths, supporting Chelsea, being a laugh, and being helpful amongst others). They did not see their disabled status as the most important part of them and did not like this identity to be foregrounded by others' (2011, 12). They emphasized the 'normalities' of their lives.

Wickenden commented on how the children saw themselves but also how they perceive they are seen by others.

> There is a clear contrast between the way the participants perceive that they are seen by those who know them well and by less familiar people or strangers. This was confirmed by the data from other people talking about them. Familiar people such as family members, close friends and long-term professional helpers indeed view them in ways that are similar to the way the participants see themselves.
>
> (2011, 13)

These participants saw themselves as having multiple identities and might not be comfortable if the researcher focused on just one identity. They suggest that people who know them see them in ways that are similar to their self perceptions but those who don't know them may not.

Activity 1

Wickenden's research involved 'children who have little or no speech and who use a number of other ways to talk' (2011, 1). She wrote,

'They are probably excluded [from research] because of perceived methodological difficulties in ascertaining the views of those with severe communication impairments and perhaps because it is often assumed that they would have nothing interesting to say about themselves or their lives' (2011, 1). What ethical issues do you think are raised by these judgements?

Activity 2

A quotation from Natalie aged fifteen, 'Talk *to me like a teenage girl*' (Wickenden 2011, 24) provided the inspiration for this title for this article. This crystallized the dilemma for research if multiple identities exist.

1 Do you think that individuals have multiple identities? (Hint: think about how you see yourself in different contexts and/or relationships.)
2 If multiple identities exist is this relevant in the context of research? If so, how could they be taken into account?

In Chapter 2, we considered whether inclusive education is concerned with individuals, some children or all children. (You may wish to return to Chapter 2 and the debate about who the concept of inclusion refers to.) This consideration is also evident in research designs with examples illustrating different approaches. Some researchers have used a broad, generic category such as 'young people who have been marginalised', arguing that 'some of the distinctions based upon predetermined categories are artificial and add little to the discourse of inclusion' (Rose and Shevlin, 2004, 155). Others critique the concept of marginalization. For instance, Messiou suggests there are four ways of conceptualizing marginalization namely:

1 The child is experiencing some kind of marginalization, and it is recognized by everyone, including him/herself.
2 The child feels that he/she is marginalized, but most others do not recognize this.
3 The child is found in what appear to be marginalized situations but does not feel it or view it as marginalization.
4 The child is experiencing marginalization but does not admit it.

(2006, 46)

A resolution of these complexities is to include all those in a group or setting; some of the research examples adopt this approach.

Where research has narrowed the focus to a group or groups, it raises a further set of interesting questions.

- Are there groups where a great deal of research is undertaken and others that are under-researched?
- If so, why and what are the consequences?

Certainly it is the view of some researchers that there is under-representation of some groups. When Save the Children (2003) researched children who miss out on education, they adopted the notion of the 'interrupted learner' which refers to those who miss out on a substantial period of education and where no replacement provision is made. Within this umbrella term, there are many groups and for some there is a corpus of research (e.g. looked-after children, teenage mothers). They therefore narrowed their research to four cohort groups where there was very limited research:

- Young people with chronic illness
- Young people labelled as having emotional and behavioral difficulties (EBD)
- Refugees and asylum-seeking young people
- Young people affected by domestic violence.

(2003, 12)

A further set of questions relates to whether research undertaken with one group could inform research with other groups or indeed whether research undertaken by individuals from one discipline can inform others with different backgrounds. The premise of this book is that this can and should happen. The selected examples of research cover a wide range of issues from researching with young children to young adults, and diverse topics including gender, race and disability. This is intentional and consistent with the 'broad' definition of inclusion. The examples are also multiple disciplinary. The very first editorial of the *International Journal of Inclusive Education* explicitly promoted this approach. Slee stated that his interest in establishing the journal 'derives from lessons drawn from feminist and anti-racist educators while trying to make sense of policy-making in the area of what is reflectively called "special educational needs" ... It seemed to me that those engaged in this area of work needed to enter into an extended conversation with feminists and anti-racist educators and researchers to learn more about cultural politics' (Slee 1997, i–ii). As a researcher he was arguing the case for learning across research topics and across researchers from different disciplines. There is a rich and diverse range of material to draw upon and there needs to be a structure to make it more navigable. However, the decisions made about where particular research examples appear is a matter of judgement. Be aware that material referenced in one chapter may have relevance for another aspect of inclusion.

Many of the examples of the research included in this book involve one-off activities that capture a snapshot of a situation. A minority of the examples involve a sustained piece of research which, for example, tracks the individual or the context over time. Both approaches have strengths and challenges. One-off events that capture views at a single point in time may be vulnerable to the data reflecting a particular contextual factor. So, if the participant has had a bad experience that day that might be reflected in the data, or a really productive day might also bias the data. Those comments would be true of any research but two arguments have been made for a more sustained relationship between the research and co-researchers/participants. In relation to Article 12, Lundy (2007) argued that participation is an iterative process. When individuals experience 'being heard', they are more likely to express their views. A second reason for a more sustained relationship was raised in this chapter. Wickenden (2011) reported that the level of familiarity between the child and other person influenced the alignment between the child's self perception and how they perceived they were viewed.

On the theme of contextual factors, it is worth reiterating that education and schooling are not synonyms. Indeed one of the later research examples (Singal and Swann, 2011) explicitly contrasts learning within and beyond school. This chapter has included research involving children with no or limited access to school (Morgan and Sengedorj, 2015). It has also recognized that the identities of children are only partly associated with their experiences as pupils.

In summary, this section has highlighted the need to consider ethical issues, methods of data collection, the research design including sampling, the potential for learning across disciplines and topics, the duration of the research and a view that education occurs within and beyond schools.

Chapter Activities

The following activities have been designed to help reflect on some of the key concerns over the chapter as a whole.

Activity 1

The chapter comments that 'Children have valuable perspectives to offer, and, as experts in their own lives, may hold views that differ from those of their parents or teachers or policy-makers – a situation which the adults may find challenging. Children may have concerns that have been unrecognized by the adults but which are genuine and pressing for them'.

1 Identify examples within the chapter where research has revealed children's views that differ from adults or children's perspectives that challenge adult perceptions and opinions.
2 What is your understanding of why such views and perspectives may not have been accessed in the past, or why they might easily not be accessed within the current education system?
3 How might you make use of these views and perspectives in developing: (i) your own understanding of inclusive education; and/or (ii) your own understanding of what constitutes good practice in research into inclusive education?

Activity 2

The chapter uses the terms 'participation' and 'participant'.

1 Look through the chapter and note as many examples as you can of the use of the terms. What do you think are the main points that are being made about the nature of participation and the role of participant?
2 The chapter argues that our ideas about 'participation' and the child as 'participant' in enquiry have been changed by new understandings concerning children, research and inclusion. What do you think are the strengths and limitations of these different understandings?

Summary

This chapter has:

- explored what is meant by the term 'inclusive research';
- justified why the views of children, all children, are important;
- considered the different relationships between adults and children in research;
- highlighted some of the issues that those undertaking inclusive research need to consider.

Further reading

Nind, M. (2014). *What is Inclusive Research?* London: Bloomsbury.

The term 'inclusive research' was used in relation to disability research. It is an umbrella term that draws on other approaches to research including participatory research, feminist research and emancipatory research. A common feature across these is a shift in the power balances between the researcher and those who in traditional research might be referred to as 'the researched'. Nind's book defines all the terminology and uses a number of case studies to illustrate the issues.

There is an associated podcast at: http://www.ncrm.ac.uk/resources/podcasts/view.php/what-is-inclusive-research (accessed 7 April 2016).

Nind, M. and H. Vinha (2012). 'Doing Research Inclusively, Doing Research Well?' Available online: https://www.southampton.ac.uk/assets/imported/transforms/content-block/UsefulDownloads_Download/97706C004C4F4E68A8B54DB90EE0977D/full_report_doing_research.pdf (accessed 7 April 2016).

Those of you considering undertaking some inclusive research will find this publication valuable. The authors were involved in an Economic and Social Research Council (ESRC) study of inclusive research with a particular focus on learning difficulties. One of the outcomes was guidance for other researchers which is written in a very accessible manner.

Smit, S. (2012). 'Pupils as Co-researchers'. Available online: https://www.youtube.com/watch?v=L8p8fLBx54I (accessed 6 April 2016).

In this video (15 minutes) students and teacher examine an extra-curricular learning environment together. In September 2009 the professoriate

'Behaviour and Research in Educational Praxis' of the University of Utrecht, led by Petra Ponte, started a study on student participation at various Dutch primary schools. '[L]etting pupils analyse and examine their own education in association with their teacher, [led] them to get more voice in its design'.

Stevenson, M. (2014). 'Participatory Data Analysis Alongside Co-researchers who have Down Syndrome'. *Journal of Applied Research in Intellectual Disabilities* 27 (1): 23–33.

This is another example of research involving co-researchers with Down syndrome.

Research details

Quality in inclusive research

Nind and Vinha were funded by the ESRC and addressed the issue of 'Doing Research Inclusively, Doing Research Well?'. Given the values of the researchers and the need to make the findings accessible there is a website linked to this project and both a traditional research report and an accessible version. These materials appear as part of their website http://www. doingresearchinclusively.org.

Nind, M. and H. Vinha (2012). 'Doing Research Inclusively, Doing Research Well?' Available online: https://www.southampton.ac.uk/assets/imported/transforms/content-block/UsefulDownloads_Download/97706C004C4F4E68A8B54DB90EE0977D/full_report_doing_research.pdf (accessed 7 April 2016).

Follow-up meeting for participants

Part of the requirements of a MA programme involved a dissertation. For this data was collected from some children. The data collection could have been the final contact between the researcher and the children. This article reports on what happened when the researcher continued the relationship by returning to discuss her research.

Pinter, A. and S. Zandian (2015). '"I thought it would be tiny little one phrase that we said, in a huge big pile of papers": Children's Reflections on their Involvement in Participatory Research'. *Qualitative Research* 15 (2), 235–50.

Children as interviewees exerting power

Research involves power with the potential for the participants being positioned as less powerful. This article reports on the nuanced ways in which some children can exert power.

McLeod, A. (2007). 'Whose Agenda? Issues of Power and Relationship when Listening to Looked-after Young People'. *Child & Family Social Work* 12 (3): 278–86.

Using biographical narrative methodology to explore social exclusion in Spain

These Spanish researchers provide insights into the need for flexibility in inclusive research to enable the voices of all to be heard.

Rojas, S., T. Susinos and A. Calvo (2013). '"Giving Voice" in Research Processes: An Inclusive Methodology for Researching into Social Exclusion in Spain'. *International Journal of Inclusive Education* 17 (2): 156–73.

If you were the researcher, what would you research?

This research was undertaken with children who had no or fragmented education. Despite that they had views and ideas about topics for research and possible approaches.

Morgan, J. and T. Sengedorj (2015). '"If you were the researcher what would you research?": Understanding Children's Perspectives on Educational Research in Mongolia and Zambia'. *International Journal of Research & Method in Education* 38 (2): 200–18.

Inclusive data analysis

This is one of a small number of reports of research which involves co-analysis. It suggests that it is both possible and advantageous to the research and to those involved. Whilst it involved adults, this principle is more widely applicable.

Kramer, J. M., J. C. Kramer, E. García-Iriarte and J. Hammel (2011). 'Following through to the End: The Use of Inclusive Strategies to Analyse and Interpret Data in Participatory Action Research with Individuals with Intellectual Disabilities'. *Journal of Applied Research in Intellectual Disabilities* 24 (3): 263–73.

Talk to me as a teenager

This article is linked to a wider study which used ethnographic and narrative approaches to explore aspects of identity and the lifeworlds of a group of disabled teenagers who have physical impairments and use AAC (Augmentative and Alternative Communication).

Wickenden, M. (2011). '"Talk to me as a teenager": Experiences of Friendship for Disabled Teenagers who have Little or No Speech'. *Childhoods Today* 5 (1): 1–35.

Part III

Implications for Children's Lives: Using Children's Perspectives to Inform Inclusive Education

5

Children's Access to Places and Spaces

Introduction and key questions

Concerns with the 'place' of education for particular groups of children have been a recurrent theme in the debates about inclusive education. One meaning of this term relates to whether children have access to schooling; whether they have a place. We have already noted that access to primary education is not universal. A second meaning of 'place' is about the nature of the placement. For example, there were (and are) strongly held views about whether or not the development of inclusive education implies the closing of all special school provision for children with special educational needs. Further examples include the debates about bussing minority groups to predominantly white schools to combat segregation or the relative merits of single-sex versus co-educational classes and schools.

Recently, more nuanced approaches have emerged. As Hemingway and Armstrong framed it, 'notions such as "space" and "place" are used as metaphors for understandings and practices related to belonging and not belonging, inclusion and exclusion' (2012, 480).

This chapter introduces you to some of these issues by considering the following questions:

- In the context of inclusive education, is it easy to make international comparisons?
- Do the places where children are educated influence how they see themselves and how they are seen?
- How do children view the various environments within a school?
- Are the social spaces within schools inclusive?
- Are there examples of adults creating spaces for participation?
- Does learning within schools differ from learning in other settings?

In the context of inclusive education, is it easy to make international comparisons?

The answer to this has to be 'No – but there is much to be gained by thinking about the factors involved'. In relation to education in general, there is regular reporting in the press of international comparisons of education. For instance, the Organisation for Economic Co-operation and Development (OECD) publishes league tables of education standards across the world. It reports on the thirty-four countries of the OECD and partner countries. The reports are substantial; the one published in 2014 provides data on the structure, finances and performance of education systems, and contains more than 150 charts, 300 tables and over 100,000 figures (http://www.oecd.org/education/eag.htm).

There is also a triennial international survey which aims to evaluate education systems worldwide by testing the skills and knowledge of fifteen-year-old students (http://www.oecd.org/pisa/home). Additionally, there is a four-year cycle of international comparisons of trends in maths and science achievement in 4th and 8th grade. This is commonly referred to as TIMSS (Trends in International Mathematics and Science Study). For the past fifteen years there has also been the Progress in International Reading Literacy Study. The data from both these surveys is available at http://timssandpirls.bc.edu. Whilst these don't specifically address inclusive education, they do illustrate that international comparisons are made. It is also apparent that these are used and that they are reported in the press. They raise concerns both about the progress of educational development and about the need to enhance the capacity for (economic) development (although it is important not to deny the challenges involved in interpreting the data given factors such as histories, culture and resources). For example, there are country-level variations in the aims of education. Whilst some may view producing an elite group who can lead (economic) development as desirable, others prioritize social cohesion.

More recently, attention has turned to the potential of international comparisons related to inclusive education. D'Alessio and Watkins, in the editorial to a special issue of *Research in Comparative and International Education* devoted to inclusive education, considered the key issues involved. They argued that the challenges linked to international comparisons of education are amplified when the focus is inclusive education. In the editorial, they stated that:

> two 'problem' areas are discussed: (i) the incomparability of terminology – words such as inclusion may or may not have the same meaning when translated into other languages and also other contexts; and (ii) the inherent methodological difficulties within the 'target' population of research in inclusive education – pupils with special educational needs are not identified, assessed or offered provision in the same ways within countries. This means that comparisons of approaches within countries are problematic – and comparison of these countries at an international level becomes extremely difficult.
>
> (2009, 233)

Their observations were made in the context of provision for children with special educational needs, but similar levels of complexity are evident elsewhere. The World Bank tracks gender equality in education. There is some optimism about progress towards gender equality in access to education, but the World Bank cautions that:

[r]emarkable progress has been made toward achieving gender equality in education. Over the past three decades the ratio of girls to boys enrolled in school has risen at all levels. ... Still, major gaps remain between boys and girls. In Africa and South Asia for example, boys remain 1.55 times more likely to complete secondary education than girls. Many countries will not meet the education Millennium Development Goals (MDGs) by 2015. Almost 30 percent of low- and middle-income countries are off-track or seriously off-track to meet the education MDG of universal primary education. Additionally, more than 20 percent of low- and middle-income countries are off-track or seriously off-track to meet the MDG of empowering women and girls by achieving gender parity in education.

(World Bank, 2015)

That quotation serves as a reminder of the complexities of the issues and also their dynamic nature. This chapter explores placement with reference to inclusive education. Any analysis needs to be based on data, but there are complications – for instance, in relation to children with special educational needs. Howgego et al. stated that:

No statistics are available on special school attendance in developing countries, but in the European context 2.3% of learners are educated in segregated settings, either in separate classes in mainstream schools, or in a special school (WHO, 2011: 210). The number of special schools has increased in India, in line with the development of inclusive education (Singal, 2008), but they tend to be urban-based, and so this does not necessarily involve separation from families and communities, as would be the case with attendance of a residential special school.

(2014, 12)

Some have argued that for systems/countries to develop their capacities for responding to diversity there may need to be an interim stage in which there is the provision of special schools. This contrasts with the ethos of the Salamanca Statement which promotes the practice of children with special educational needs attending their neighbourhood schools with their peers. For example, Urwick and Elliott (in the context of Lesotho, a low-income country) argued that there may be a transitional phase that involves some special school provision. They stated, 'A phase of development in which there is considerable use of specialised facilities and selected schools is seen as necessary if more children with disabilities are to have meaningful opportunities for learning' (2010, 137). This is a helpful reminder that inclusive education is not solely about placement but also about participation and progress.

Urwick and Elliot (2010) highlight a tension between children attending their local schools and having access to teachers with appropriate expertise. The existence and potential role of special schools and specialist provisions in the context of inclusion is contentious.

Activity 1

Why do you think that Urwick and Elliot saw special schools as necessary? (Hint: think about access to specialist staff and resources.)

Activity 2

Urwick and Elliott saw the necessity of special schools as a phase in the development of provision. In your view, what are the advantages and disadvantages of developing a system of special schools?

This adult-centric discussion has been provided to illustrate some of the complexities involved and some of the gaps in the available data. It also sets the scene for some child-based data. Within this chapter, the term 'presence' will be associated with two dimensions. At the most basic level, presence can be thought of in terms of whether a child has a place in a school. However, whilst being on the roll of a school is necessary, it is insufficient. Therefore, the chapter will also consider children's presence in terms of their engagement with the (educational) activities within their schools.

Evidence about children missing out on any form of formal education or having very limited access was discussed earlier. An interesting question is how individuals and their significant others understand the benefits of having at least some access to schooling. The following example of research was based in Madhya Pradesh, India, where recently there have been improvements in access to education for those with disabilities.

Example of research: Achieved and desired outcomes

This research example is one part of a larger research study, the Disability Education and Poverty Project (DEPP) which itself is part of a broader activity, the Research Consortium on Educational Outcomes and Poverty. The DEPP project operates in Ghana, Kenya, Pakistan and India. The research reports on some of the qualitative data from India specifically that linked to the questions 'how do young people with disabilities characterise their lives; and, in particular what are their perceptions of how their schooling experiences have impacted on their lives?' (Singal et al., 2011, 1206)

Theoretically, the researchers drew on the work of Bourdieu, who introduced ideas about forms of capital other than financial. Singal et al. refer to economic, social and cultural capital. They argue that variations in these may impact on the access to education and that the outcomes of education may be understood in these terms.

The participants were aged 15–30 years and had hearing (HI), visual (VI) or physical (mobility) impairments (PI). These aspects were selected since there is a tradition of provision in these areas. The researchers also considered whether the participants lived in rural or urban areas, their locations, their genders and the age at which each experienced the onset of their impairments. The data was collected through interviews, each of which involved two interviewers; one interviewer asked most of the questions and one took notes. In total, thirty young people were interviewed.

Table 5.1 Distribution of sample population by impairment, residence, schooling level and gender: Dewas District, Madhya Pradesh, India

	School 0–5		Schooling 6–9		Schooling 10+		
Impairment	**Male**	**Female**	**Male**	**Female**	**Male**	**Female**	**Total**
HI: Urban	1	2	1	2	0	0	6
HI: Rural	2	0	2	0	0	0	4
PI: Urban	1	2	0	1	1	0	5
PI: Rural	1	0	2	2	0	0	5
VI: Urban	0	1	0	0	2	2	5
VI: Rural	2	0	0	0	2	1	5
Totals	7	5	5	5	5	3	30

Source: Based on Singal et al., 2011, 1208.

Interviews were also conducted with 'significant others, namely parents or, in two cases where parents were not available, a sibling and the spouse' (Singal et al., 2011, 1208). Based on the interview data, the researchers asserted that the views of the outcomes of education of the young people and their significant others differed. The significant others focused on a 'better quality of life and reduced dependency on others' (2011, 1210). In contrast, the young people 'were convinced that education would make a big difference to their lives, not just in terms of the knowledge they would have gained, but also on how they saw themselves and were seen by others' (2011, 1215). The authors succinctly summarized these different perspectives: 'Whereas the "significant others" (primarily, parents) regard schooling as a failure if it does not lead to jobs, the young people themselves focus on education's enabling role' (2011, 1205).

Activity 1

The discussion so far has portrayed education and access to education as 'good things', but without giving attention to the desirable outcomes.

1 What outcomes do you want from education?
2 Do your 'significant others' share these ambitions?
3 To what extent do your aspirations link to the idea of an inclusive society?

Activity 2

A link exists between education and employment. Singal et al. assert that 'Economic independence is greatly valued by all people, but is of particular relevance to people with disabilities to assert their individuality and reaffirm their rightful place in mainstream society' (2011, 1216).

1 Do you agree that economic independence is valued by all people?
2 Why do you think the authors felt they needed to draw particular attention to the ambitions of people with disabilities? (Hint: think about the changes in how disability is viewed.)

Do the places where children are educated influence how they see themselves and how they are seen?

The example above considered from different perspectives the potential benefits of having a place in education. However there have been debates about the type of school attended; for example, a mainstream school or a special school. Cigman (2007) argued that there are two positions on inclusive education:

1 the 'radical' position, which involves the dismantling of all special schools and all children attending mainstream schools;
2 the 'moderate' position, which involves the retention of some special schools for some children who 'need' particular types of assistance and support.

An element of progress towards inclusive education has been a number of initiatives involving links between mainstream schools and special schools. In some instances the focus has been primarily social (i.e. engaging in social activities together) whilst in others it has been more about learning together. There are usually preparatory activities prior to the formation of more formal links. A concern is to understand the associations between place of education and identity.

Some research (e.g. Griffiths, 2007) considers both mainstream and special school pupils' perceptions of each other and of the schools they attend. The concern of Griffiths was not to evaluate issues of placement but rather to look at the barriers linked to how the two groups viewed each other. Does the nature of the school that children attend impact on how they are seen?

Example of research: 'They're gonna think we're the dumb lot because we go to the special school'

This study was an initial phase, a baseline, to 'clarify some of the potential obstacles, in preparation for the subsequent collaborative action phase' (Griffiths, 2007, 78) in a link between a mainstream primary school and a special school in the UK.

Initially, thirteen pupils in Year 8 of a mainstream school (aged 12–13) and thirteen pupils in Key Stage 3 (aged 11–14) in a special school were identified. Of the twenty-six pupils, eventually sixteen split equally across the settings were involved. The authors explained that 'Five mainstream pupils were unable to participate fully in the study, two owing to illegible notes, one for a recurrent no-response and two for the expression of very negative attitudes to participation that my mainstream colleagues felt would have substantial implications for the continuation of the study at the stage where inclusive activities would begin' (2007, 80). Given that five mainstream pupils did not take part the number of special school pupils was also reduced.

The participants were shown some slides with images of the other school, an overview of the research and an introduction to the teacher from the other school. The children were then interviewed by their own teacher using the following prompts:

- What do you think pupils at X School will be like?
- What do you think X pupils will think of you?
- What do you think X school will be like?
- What do you think X pupils will think about your school?

(The letter X has been used to replace the names of the schools involved.)

The data indicated that many of the special school pupils had 'very negative perceptions of themselves as learners. Moreover what was especially alarming was that a number of pupils attributed their low status to the fact they attended a special school' (2007, 81).

Two quotations from a special school pupil (Special School Pupil 1) provided by Griffiths were:

They're gonna think we're the dumb lot because we go to the special school.

(2007, 81)

> *If we don't act like spackers, then they'll think we're normal.*
> (2007, 82)

In relation to the second comment, her analysis was that:

> The acute awareness of difference and exclusion reflected in this comment signifies a pupil to whom special school attendance is a major social disadvantage and one that is indicative of an inherent and visible disability that will cause members of the mainstream to intimidate and exclude him. There is also the suggestion that, although the pupil views his 'differences' as permanent, it is possible for them to be hidden or disguised of the sake of social acceptance.
> (2007, 82)

She stressed that the findings are not generalizable and that the pupils may have been confused about the terms 'special' and 'mainstream'. The opening to her discussion synthesized a concern she had that 'The convergence of a group of special school pupils with low self-esteem and a group of mainstream pupils who inherently perceive themselves as the superior of the two groups could prove to be a "time bomb" in terms of inclusive practice' (2007, 84).

She also identified an ethical dilemma that may occur in other research, particularly when teachers research their own practice. The two researchers wanted to 'produce an unbiased and organic representation of the thoughts and preconceptions held by the pupils with whom we work ... to leave an unconstructive comment or a negative attitude unquestioned is contrary to our perceived purpose as teachers' (2007, 86).

Reflections on the research

Griffiths suggested that the key distinction between the two groups of pupils is their educational placement. However she later acknowledged that personal insecurities, previous experiences or rumours may have shaped their views. For instance, one special school pupil said, 'I think they'll say I'm ugly because I've got goofy teeth' (2007, 82), whilst another special school pupil said, 'I think they will be nasty, because the other school were' (2007, 82).

Activity 1

Griffiths identified the tension between faithfully collecting the views of the pupils and the desire to address unhelpful perceptions.

1 Why do you think this tension might exist?
2 If you were the researcher, what would you do during and after the data collection to manage the tensions?

Activity 2
The article described the attitudes as a 'time-bomb'.

1 Why do you think this term might have been used?
2 Do you regard such emotive language as justified?
3 How would you defuse the situation?

How do children view the various environments within a school?

The emphasis in the research examples above has been on access and location. The discussion has referred to schools as institutions. In reality, each school involves multiple micro-environments – whether those are office spaces, classrooms, corridors, playgrounds or toilets. In terms of inclusion, children may have different experiences in and views of these as places. This more detailed understanding of school as a place is evident in the children's comments in research undertaken by Ryan in Belfast.

Example of research: 'Inclusion is more than a place'

The research was undertaken in Belfast. The primary objective 'was based on the principle that the voice and opinions of children and young people were central' (Ryan, 2009, 78). The second objective was to 'explore the differences between the perceptions of children and young people with special educational needs and/or disability towards inclusion and other pupils' (2009, 78).

Schools were invited to a meeting outlining the research project. Of the fifteen that attended, seven agreed to take part. The schools reported their findings in 2006 and there was an analysis of these to produce conclusions and recommendations. These were structured around several themes.

- *Reasonable adjustments.* This is a term referring to changes a school could be expected to make for an individual or groups of children. The first observation was that there are 'no stock answers' (2009, 82) and that the individual child needs to be involved. The second was that there were 'financial considerations' (2009, 82) to be made, but if an adjustment made for a child was perceived as excluding, then the money was not well spent. Again, children's views need to be taken into account.
- *Toilets.* These were mentioned by a number of children across the schools with the main issue being 'the smell'.
- *Sensory stimulation.* 'A number of pupils reported that they felt excluded from the dining hall or canteen due to the level of noise' (2009, 83). In addition, the schools had visually enriched environments within their classes and the school generally. However, 'for some pupils with special educational needs, this visually stimulating environment is just the last thing they need' (2009, 83).
- *Office space.* There were differing views about the role of the head teacher's office, which associated it either with rewards or sanctions. Similarly, the function of the staff room was reported as both 'a space away from the pupils', or, as one pupil said, 'a place to hide' (2009, 83).

Activity 1

These pupils raised issues of smell, noise and visual stimulation. To what extent do you think these issues widened the factors associated with developing an inclusive school?

Activity 2

Ryan commented that 'The overwhelming lessons learnt is that "reasonable adjustments" may not fully be considered reasonable where the pupil at the centre of the need for adjustments had not had an input into the decision-making process' (2009, 83).

1 Can you make links between this statement and the discussion about participation in Chapter 2?
2 What are the implications of this position for the understanding of inclusive education and how to develop it?

Interview with David Ryan about professional research, reflection and engaging children and young people

David Ryan. Adviser for Special Educational Needs and Inclusion, Children and Young People's Services, Education Authority for Northern Ireland, Belfast Region, and Associate Lecturer, Stranmillis University College, Belfast.

Sue Pearson: What links do you see between your roles and professional enquiry?

David Ryan: Throughout my professional career, which has been spent for over twenty-five years in the field of SEN and inclusion, (as a teacher, advisory teacher, statement officer and Adviser) I have always been curious. I would often ask myself why things were the way they were, applying what I called 'Why five?' In other words, ask a question and then ask another question – up to about five times to seek to get a little bit closer to the truth.

Often I found that a lot of what was portrayed as professional practice was not based on any sound educational or research footing. I would receive answers to my questions such as:

'We have always done it that way.'
'Why?'
'Miss Jones set it up that way twenty years ago.'
'Why?'
'I don't know why!'

This curiosity led me to question a number of what were thought of as 'established truths' and found that in actual fact what may have been good practice in the past, may no longer have been so.

Sue Pearson: Is there an overarching concern that has influenced your approach?

David Ryan: The greatest failing in the field was the very idea that when it came to pupls with SEN or disability that the experts knew best. It was only when I became a parent of a child with SEND (special educational needs and disability) that I began to question this as well. Why didn't 'the experts' ask the children, and why didn't we ask the parents? This was difficult, as at that time I had no professional footing in research, and I very much had to find my own way.

The first research I undertook was with pupils in schools to find out where they felt included and excluded in schools. The first major learning point was to find ways to use a similar (non-professional) language with pupils. I had to use the language they were familiar with and not the unfamiliar language of research. This led to the publication on visual narrative.

There was some local media interest in this research. The BBC Northern Ireland's Reporter, Maggie Taggart, attended the launch, as it was found that, at that time, it was quite unusual to provide children with a voice through research, and as adults we had much to learn. I didn't know that children with ASD (autism spectrum disorder) may have tactile sensitivities which can make the outside skin of mobile classrooms problematic for them.

Soon after that I did start doctoral research, and was able to take on board the idea of theoretical framework for research. I found the work of the French sociologist Pierre Bourdieu had much to commend it when it came to challenging the language assumption, as it was Bourdieu who spoke of the difference between the unfamiliar language of instruction used by teachers in schools and the familiar language used by children at home.

The next research involved pupils with SEBD (social, emotional and behavioural difficulties) at a PRU in Belfast, to see how complementary therapies impacted on their behaviour. This was a case where the language used became a real challenge, where some of the pupils joked with me that they had to translate what I was saying in professional language, before they could understand it. The idea of emancipatory research was prevalent through this research, as I saw the importance of ensuring that the most vulnerable and often disenfranchised children would have a voice. It was encouraging that the findings of the research were reported at ISEC 2010, an international conference, in Belfast and the young people were able to take part in the delivery of the paper.

My next major challenge was to take on board the relationship between SEN, educational disadvantage and the idea that the vast majority of these children came from inner-city areas with high levels of multiple deprivation.

Belfast is well known for its murals – community artwork painted on the gable ends of terraced houses. In one of the areas where this research took place, one of the murals has the slogan 'Nothing for us or about us, without us'. This speaks volumes, and in this research I asked teachers to identify the pupils they considered to be underachieving, and then interviewed the parents in their homes, the pupils and the teachers in order to get to the heart of what factors were influential in the process.

Sue Pearson: What do you think you have learnt by combining research and practice?

David Ryan: I think that there are two learning points from my personal reflection on practice. The first is that research is necessary to inform, inspire and improve the practice of myself and others. I have to be a professional who uses research, as opposed to an academic researcher who is a research professional. Whilst both approaches are necessary, I feel that it is the professional practitioners who are in the field who are able to contribute the most to knowledge. For this reason, all teachers should be critically reflecting on their practice, reading about other 'outstanding', 'best' and 'good' practice, including what happens in other jurisdictions to improve their own practice. In addition, when something works well in their own classroom, they should write about it, shout about it and share it. How else will others find out it, if a professional research approach is not adopted?

The second learning point is the absolute importance of ensuring that pupils, regardless of whether they have SEBD or not, are given not just a voice in their education, but that their views will become the basis of planning which is personalized for their needs. The same is true of all children, including the gifted and talented. The increased use of tablet technology in schools is going a long way to making this a reality. Imagine a situation where a new head teacher is appointed, and he or she wishes to implement appraisal for the teaching staff, based on them meeting targets. The head teacher decides not to trouble the teachers with their targets as they are too busy. At the end of the school year, the head teacher then calls in the teaching staff to see if they have successfully achieved their targets. 'How could I have met my targets if I didn't know what they were?' Surely the same could be said to be true of what professionals do when it comes to target setting for pupils with SEND – have we taken the time to agree the targets in collaboration with the child, or do we as 'the professional' or 'the expert' simply set them irrespective of the view of the child?

Others have conducted similar research to that of Ryan (2009) that confirms and extends these findings. For example, the research of Adderley et al. (2015) identified 'shouting' by teachers as an issue (noise). It had different impacts on pupils and their views of the approachability of staff. The children were also able to suggest ways to improve the situation:

Aaron: *I think our teacher could be a lot happier, because if [they are] really mad then it gets us sad, well not sad, but our work is a lot worse than it could be if [they were] happy. Our work would be better.*

(2015, 114)

A fuller discussion of social, emotional factors appears later in Chapter 7.

Returning to the place of education, another recurrent theme is seating. It surfaced in the research by Adderley et al., who found that children frequently raised the issue of 'where and with whom they sat' (2015, 116). It also appeared in research undertaken in Tanzania and Zambia (Miles and Kaplan, 2005). The researcher exposed the teacher in each setting to images from the other one. The images from Zambia portrayed different ways to arrange a classroom even when resources are limited. These provoked a discussion about whether those with sensory impairments should sit together and whether children should take it in turns to sit on the floor. The latter could 'open up discussions around whether uncomfortable seating is a cause of inequality in the classroom or a reason for dropping out of the class' (Miles and Kaplan, 2005, 82).

These summaries of the research have placed images in the foreground of discussion. To help you develop a more rounded view of visual data collection, you should read the article by Woolner et al. (2007), who wished to actively involve stakeholders (including children) in school design. The researchers used a range of visual methods of data collection, and reported on their experiences and also on the richness of the data produced.

Are the social spaces within schools inclusive?

Thus far consideration has been given to the location and the environment of the school building. However, the social spaces (e.g. corridors, playgrounds) are also significant to children. They can be either places for socializing or sites of exclusion and loneliness. Despite this, there appears to be a dearth of relevant research. Woolley (2013) argues that that there is some literature available from the USA which identifies societal and structural barriers in outdoor play spaces, and that more research is required. Pearce and Bailey (2011) made a similar point and highlighted that non-curricular play is a mandatory element of the school day in each of the UK's home countries. It constitutes approximately seven hours of children's time per week, equating to about a quarter of their school day. These researchers conducted a study to gather evidence about children's perceptions of playgrounds.

Example of research: Football pitches and Barbie dolls

The research by Pearce and Bailey took place in a primary school in south-west London. 'Every child in the schools (n=137) participated in curriculum-related activities although thirteen had not given consent to take part in the associated research … and their data was omitted' (2011, 1364). They used a sequence of activities, moving from a presentation to a tour of the site to a drawing task, which was followed by a short conversation and finally some focus group conversation. The data was analysed using four themes (each with sub-themes). The themes were social play, physically active play, risk and gender. The report here is restricted to gender. It states: 'There was an overwhelming sense in the conversations with the children at this school that gender segregation and stereotyping was simply taken for granted. It was interesting, for example, that the only non-stereotypically male activity described positively by a boy was from a Year 1 pupil who had recently entered England and his comments were reicieved with astonishment by his peers' (2011, 1372).

The children made a number of suggestions about how to improve the provision, and a number of these were implemented. Pearce and Bailey report these examples:

- The introduction of segregated areas, with one for the children to play football in and another for them to play other games in. This was intended to reduce the dominance of football and increase play areas for those not wanting to play football.
- The introduction of a garden area, and the purchase of more equipment (such as hula-hoops) to encourage girls to be more physically active.
- Training older children to be 'buddies' to younger children and encourage friend-making between those children so that they feel less lonely in the playground.

(adapted from Pearce and Bailey, 2011, 1375–6)

Activity 1

Look back to Chapter 3, which considered participation. Lundy emphasized an iterative process between the right to be heard and the right to have views given due weight. Based on the summary of this research, can you see that process?

Activity 2
These pupils appeared to take gender stereotypes for granted.

1 Do you find that acceptable?
2 If not, what do you think should be done?

Are there examples of adults creating spaces for participation?

In the international literature, another theme that emerges is that of 'spaces'. For example, Cobbett et al. (2013) wrote 'Creating "Participatory Spaces": Involving Children in Planning Sex Education Lessons in Kenya, Ghana and Swaziland'. Nind et al. (2012) wrote 'Creating Spaces to Belong: Listening to the Voice of Girls with Behavioural, Emotional and Social Difficulties through Digital Visual and Narrative Methods'. Epstein and Lipschultz (2012) wrote 'Getting Personal? Student Talk about Racism', which reported on an after-school programme to discuss racism. Only one of these examples is illustrated here (Cobbett et al., 2013) and it relates to planning sex education lessons – an essential but sensitive topic.

Example of research: Creating 'participatory spaces'

Cobbett et al. (2013) identified four core positions which informed the conceptual background to the research:

- based on Bernstein's work, they wanted to bring the lived experiences of the children into the school;
- they were influenced by the work of Rudduck and Flutter (2000) whose work drew attention to the importance and value of pupils' perspectives;
- they were led by previous research by one of the researchers, which had shown the potential of dialogue in working though socio-cultural tensions;
- they were influenced by the work of Kesby on participatory spaces (2005, 2007), which stresses that influences within

and beyond the participatory space need to be taken into account.

The curriculum development groups (CDGs) operated in three primary schools in Kenya, three in Ghana and two in Swaziland. Each involved four children (two boys and two girls) and had the broad aims: 'to bring pupils' voices and views into the planning of HIV, AIDS and sex education lessons; to facilitate dialogue between pupils, teachers and community stakeholder about what should be taught and how' (2013, S81).

The researchers described a cyclical change within the group so that as adults became more open, the pupils did also. A similar evolution was noted in listening. They quoted one girl, who said, 'I've learnt that when it comes to this discussion of HIV, there is no one who is older, smaller or "I'm afraid of this one" [mentality]; like I'm afraid to talk because that parent is older than me. We just talk freely like you are in the same age level' (Senzelewe, female pupil, Interview term two, School B, Swaziland) (2013, S80).

Reflections on the research
The researchers noted that the changes in the schools based on this participatory activity varied. For some it reaffirmed an 'abstinence only' approach, whilst others moved to an emphasis on a delay to sexual activity and better information about safe sex.

Activity 1
The literature about participatory spaces sometimes questions the value of facilitation and guidance, whereas these researchers thought that 'the governance employed by the researcher did seem to enable equal participation within the facilitated space' (2013, S79). The circumstances within which participatory groups operate vary as do the contributions of individuals.

1 How would you interpret and evaluate 'equal participation'?
2 Under what circumstances do you think having external individuals to provide governance and facilitation would be valuable?

Activity 2
This research was around the sensitive topics of sex and sexuality. In your view, what other topics would benefit from pupils' contributing to planning the curriculum? (Hint: there has been reference to how diversity is represented and how that might result in stereotyping and judgements.)

Does learning within schools differ from learning in other settings?

Throughout this chapter, the focus has been on formal education – even where that extends to play within formal settings. However, learning is not restricted to the school environment. It is an ongoing process in all the environments the child enters and in all the interactions that happen. It isn't restricted to childhood, but is a lifelong activity. In some instances, children who are seen as 'in need of inclusion' in the context of schooling are viewed very differently in other settings. This raises questions about the similarities and differences of learning within and beyond the school, and what can be gained by a deeper understanding of this issue.

Schooling is a formal subset of education; a formal part of a much wider concept. If we accept that distinction, then it is interesting to question how children see learning in different contexts and what can be gained from their insights. This was an issue addressed by Singal and Swann (2011), who researched children's perceptions of themselves inside and outside school.

Example of research: Learning inside and outside school

This research involved eleven children from a school in a London borough. The school had used the Pupil Attitudes to Self and School (PASS) survey. On each item the children are classified as of great concern' (red), 'of some concern' (amber) or 'of no concern' (green). The first stage in selecting the sample involved identifying pupils in Years 5 and 6, who had three or more amber and/or red codes.

Within this sample we then focused on areas of the survey that were of particular significance to our project, namely:

- perceived learning capability;
- self-regard;
- preparedness for learning; and
- learner confidence.'

(Singal and Swann, 2011, 471)

Table 5.2 provides details of the participants. In England, at the time of the research, pupils with SEN were divided into three categories.

Those with more complex needs had Statements of Educational Needs. Pupils within a second category were supported by teachers within their school, with some external support. This was known as School Action Plus (SAP). For other pupils, the class teacher made the provision for the child with support from the Special Educational Needs Co-ordinator (SENCO). This was referred to as School Action (SA).

Table 5.2 Participants in the research

Year	Sex	Ethnicity	SEN	EAL	Academic performance
5	F	White British	SAP	–	Lower than average
	M	Japanese	SA	Yes	Lower than average
	F	White British	SA	–	Lower than average
	F	Somali	SAP	Yes	Lower than average
	F	Nigerian	-	–	Above average
	M	Indian	-	Yes	Above average
6	M	White British	-	–	Average
	M	Pakistani	SAP	–	Lower than average
	M	White British	SAP	Yes	Lower than average
	M	White British	SA	–	Average
	M	White British	SA	–	Average

Source; Based on Singal and Swann, 2011, 472

The research involved a series of activities:

- an initial semi-focused interview to develop an understanding of how the children saw themselves as learners at home and school;
- a drop-in fortnightly lunch club so the children could talk informally with the researcher;
- the provision of disposable cameras for the children to record images;
- photo-elicitation interviews in which the children discussed the albums of photographs. (Photo-elicitation is a research method which uses images to elicit comments.) The children were asked to take images with the following themes:

- Things that are important to me;
- Things that I find hard to learn;
- Pictures of me learning;
- Things that make me happy.

The findings were grouped under three headings:

- Constructions of the children as learners;
- Children's experiences of learning inside and outside school;
- Differences in learning processes inside and outside school.

The summary only refers to the last of these. The authors stated that 'Children had a lot less to say about how they learnt inside the school. The key category was listening' (2011, 478). The children also spoke of the absence of the teachers' attention and the value of drawing on the knowledge of their peers. They had more to say about learning outside school; as the authors stated, 'children have nuanced (and sometimes very lengthy) descriptions' (2011, 478). In this context, the children emphasized observation and the 'perceived competence of the person being observed' (2011, 479). How they perceived themselves as learners in the two settings also differed.

Table 5.3 Children's view of learning within and outside school

Children's views on differences in learning processes	
Within school	**Outside school**
'the focus was predominantly on listening to the teacher' (p. 478)	'observation seemed to be more prominent in their outside school experiences' (p. 479)
'was marked by the absence of teacher attention' (p. 478)	'they felt confident enough to 'find their own way' (p. 480)
'dependence on the teacher' (p. 480)	'confident to try things, face challenges and explore the world' (p. 480)

The authors commented that 'it is mystifying that children who are so confident in their learning outside school should feel so inadequate inside school' (2011, 480). In the conclusion, the researchers argued that we need to bring together the two worlds that the children inhabit to the benefit of schooling.

Activity 1

Thinking back over your own past learning experiences (and your current ones), can you detect differences in how you view and talk about learning that takes place in various settings?

Activity 2

In the context of inclusive education, what are the implications of this research? (These ideas will be developed in subsequent chapters.)

Chapter activities

The following activities are designed to help reflect back on some of the key concerns over the chapter as a whole.

Activity 1

Consider the following summary of two positions featured within this chapter:

> Some have argued that for systems/countries to develop their capacities for responding to diversity there may need to be an interim stage in which there is the provision of special schools. This contrasts with the ethos of the Salamanca Statement which promotes the practice of children with special educational needs attending their neighbourhood schools with their peers.

1 Look back through the chapter and summarize the critical response to both of these perspectives.
2 Review these responses and consider what they tell us about: (i) attitudes towards children; (ii) attitudes towards difference; (iii) attitudes towards education.

Activity 2

The chapter contains many accounts of children's perspectives on their experiences and of their ideas about their education. Identify three different quotations or points made by the children. For each point:

1 Try and understand the context of the quotation and points and what factors have combined to stimulate, or create, the child's perspective.

2 Say what factors might affect whether and how the child's perspective might lead to positive change within their education.

3 Say how the quotation or point might affect your understanding of what constitutes a good education and how you approach children being involved in schooling.

Summary

The chapter has:

- alerted you to the benefits and challenges of drawing on an international literature;
- examined the potential influence of where children are educated;
- explored how children view environments within schools;
- illustrated the creation of spaces for participation;
- compared learning within and beyond schools.

Further reading

Hemingway, J. and F. Armstrong (2014). *Space, Place and Inclusive Learning.* London: Routledge.

At the Institute of Education, University of London, a symposium was convened on the topic, 'Space, Place and Inclusive Learning'. Papers from this formed a double issue of the *International Journal of Inclusive Education*, 16 (5–6) and were later published as a book There was an international strand to the papers that included ones based in the UK, Australia and Italy.

UNESCO (2012). 'World Atlas of Gender Equality in Education'. Available online: http://www.uis.unesco.org/Education/Documents/unesco-world-atlas-gender-education-2012.pdf (accessed 6 April 2016).

Education for All was launched in 2000, when the countries of the world agreed to 'eliminate gender disparities in primary and secondary education by 2005, and achieve gender equality in education by 2015, with a focus on ensuring girls' full and equal access to and achievement in basic education of good quality'. This document, published in 2012, is an atlas of the situation at that time. It graphically demonstrates the variations and complexities.

Woolner, P., E. Hall, K. Wall and D. Dennison (2007). 'Getting Together to Improve the School Environment: User Consultation, Participatory Design and Student Voice'. *Improving Schools* 10 (3): 233–48.

In the context of a major building project in an English school, the authors considered a range of participatory approaches to eliciting the views of children.

Research details

Achieved and desired outcomes

This qualitative research was undertaken in India and gathered data from thirty young people with disabilities and their significant others. It also collected some contextual information.

Singal, N., R. Jeffery, A. Jain and N. Sood (2011). 'The Enabling Role of Education in the Lives of Young People with Disabilities in India: Achieved and Desired Outcomes'. *International Journal of Inclusive Education* 15 (10): 1205–18.

'They're gonna think we're the dumb lot because we go to the special school'

This was teacher-conducted research that considered pupil perceptions in preparation for a subsequent collaboration between a mainstream primary school and a special school.

Griffiths, E. (2007). '"They're gonna think we're the dumb lot because we go to the special school": A Teacher Research Study of how Mainstream and Special School Pupils View Each Other'. *Research in Education* (78): 78–87.

'Inclusion is more than a place'

The children involved in the study, including some with SEN, were equipped with cameras and encouraged to develop visual narratives about how the school could be changed to make it more inclusive.

Ryan, D. (2009). '"Inclusion is more than a place": Exploring Pupil Views and Voice in Belfast Schools through Visual Narrative'. *British Journal of Special Education* 36 (2): 77–84.

Football pitches and Barbie dolls

Using child-orientated approaches, this research reported on children's views of playgrounds and playtimes.

Pearce, G. and R. P. Bailey (2011). 'Football Pitches and Barbie Dolls: Young Children's Perceptions of their School Playground'. *Early Child Development and Care* 181 (10): 1361–79.

Creating 'participatory spaces'

Sexuality education is complex and can be associated with taboos and tensions. This research is about consulting pupils in a 'new' space so that new understandings can be developed.

Cobbett, M., C. McLaughlin and S. Kiragu (2013). 'Creating "Participatory Spaces": Involving Children in Planning Sex Education Lessons in Kenya, Ghana and Swaziland'. *Sex Education* 13: S70–83.

Learning inside and outside school

This research involved children who were identified as underachieving within their schools. The sample involved eleven children in the final two years of primary education. Interview data and image-based data was collected.

Singal, N. and M. Swann (2011). 'Children's Perceptions of Themselves as Learner Inside and Outside School'. *Research Papers in Education:* 26 (4): 469–84.

6

Developing an Inclusive Curriculum Informed by Children's Perspectives

Introduction and key questions

In Part III, the focus has been on access to education and the nature of the placements within it. Our attention now turns to the nature and quality of the education provided. It may seem puzzling to consider pupils' perspectives on the curriculum, since it may feel as if this is a given, or that it is the province of adults either within the school or in formal bodies beyond the school. In reality, the situation is more complex in at least two ways. First, there is a long-standing recognition that the curriculum is not static. A notable example of this can be found in the *Report of the Consultative Committee on Differentiation of the Curriculum for Boys and Girls Respectively in Secondary Schools* (which is also a reminder that the issue of gender equality in education has a long history). What was written then regarding the dynamic nature of the curriculum remains true today:

> 'The problems of the curriculum, by their very nature, do not admit to any final solution: each generation has to think them over again for itself'
> (Board of Education Consultative Committee and Hadow, 1923, ii).

This quotation raises the question of who in the generation should do the thinking. In the context of inclusive education, Paulo Freire's views on this are pertinent: 'Attempting to liberate the oppressed without their reflective participation in the act of liberation is to treat them as objects which must be saved from a burning building' (1982, 65).

Children have views about the curriculum which can and should be accessed. This chapter will illuminate these ideas by first considering how the term 'curriculum' can be defined and then by responding to the following questions:

- In relation to inclusive education, what do international documents say about the curriculum?
- How can the term 'child-centred curriculum' be understood?
- Can children's knowledge inform the school curriculum?
- Can children produce educational resources relevant to inclusive education?
- What do children want from education?
- Are there shared views about transitions?

The examples of research included are to a greater or lesser extent context dependent, and so are not necessarily relevant to every circumstance. They are provided to stimulate thinking about questions that are being asked by others, how these people are researching the topics and (as far as possible) how the data can be used.

Defining 'the curriculum'

There are multiple possible ways of defining 'the curriculum'. These range from itemizing the time allocated to every subject, to saying that it is the totality of the learners' experiences via models that map various dimensions such as skills, subjects, teaching and learning approaches or capacities. This variation will be illustrated by some examples.

The World Bank has worked with a number of countries on projects related to the curriculum. In 2014, the World Bank and the Ministry of Education and Training in Vietnam worked together to produce a report, *Proposed Guidance Framework for Development of Curriculum and Teaching Materials to Avoid Prejudice on Vulnerable Children Groups* (World Bank, 2014). Part of that document describes Vietnam's general education and states that:

> The curriculum is built for all students nationwide. The current curriculum, especially for primary education, is built with study time trend of two sessions / day. Under the current curriculum, all students are required to study and complete the following subjects:
> - The elementary education curriculum has ten compulsory subjects: Vietnamese, Mathematics, Natural and Social Science, History and Geography, Music, Art, Gym, Craft, Techniques.
> - Lower secondary education program consists of thirteen compulsory subjects: Language, Mathematics, Physics, Chemistry, Biology, History, Geography, Foreign Language, Education and citizenship, Music, Art, Gym, and Technology.
> - Upper secondary education curriculum consists of twelve compulsory subjects: Language, Mathematics, Physics, Chemistry, Biology, History, Geography, Foreign Language, Civic education, Fitness, Technology, and Computer Science.
>
> (2014, 12)

The approach taken in Scotland for the *Curriculum for Excellence* sets out aims linked to coherence, flexibility and enrichment. It states that 'it is the totality of experiences which are planned for children and young people through their education – a canvas upon which their learning experiences are formed' (Education Scotland, 2004, 230).

The approach of the Scottish Government, as articulated on the website (Education Scotland), is to identify four capacities that the curriculum is designed to develop. Each child should be enabled 'to be a successful learner, a

confident individual, a responsible citizen and an effective contributor' (http://
www.educationscotland.gov.uk/learningandteaching/thecurriculum/
whatiscurriculumforexcellence/thepurposeofthecurriculum/index.asp).

In the documentation specific reference is made to inclusion. For
example, the literacy and English section states that 'The experiences and
outcomes have been written in an inclusive way which will allow teachers
to interpret them for the needs of individual children and young people
who use Braille, sign language and other forms of communication. This is
exemplified in the words '"engaging with others" and "interacting" within
the listening and talking outcomes' (Scottish Executive, 2004, 125).

The example from Scotland has a helpful degree of flexibility that can
accommodate most aspects of inclusion. This chapter will illustrate that
children have roles other than as recipients of a curriculum.

Activity

If you were asked to describe the curriculum of a school you have
attended, how would you respond?

You now have three different ways in which to describe
'curriculum', one of your own, and those of the World Bank and
Scotland. There are differences. Consider the reasons why the
descriptions vary. (Hint: think about factors such as audience,
purpose, level of detail.)

UNESCO (n.d.) acknowledges that there are different perspectives on
curriculum, which are often differentiated by including a modifier before
the word 'curriculum'. Examples are:

- *intended curriculum*: what societies envisage as important in teaching
  and learning;
- *written and/or official curriculum*;
- *implemented curriculum*: what actually happens in the classroom
  (based on the intended curriculum);
- *achieved or learned curriculum*: what the children actually learn;
- *hidden curriculum*: the unintended development of personal values
  and beliefs of learners.

These can be useful distinctions. For instance, where pupils' perspectives are taken into account, these can shed light on discrepancies between the intended curriculum and the achieved curriculum. Researchers are sometimes precise in the definitions of curriculum that they are using but you will see in other instances this is not the case. The variation in the meanings ascribed to terms such as 'curriculum', 'inclusion', 'poverty', and 'dyslexia' is a recurrent and problematic aspect of the literature. The changes in definitions may be inevitable as thinking and values evolve. Confining a literature review to a consistent definition can be problematic as you will see in Chapter 8. Some of the responsibility has to be with the reader who should probe and critically reflect on the terminology, the intended meaning and any connotations. (Connotations refer to meanings or feelings that are involved beyond the literal meaning. Thus a red rose is literally a red flower but it may also be a symbol of love.)

The discussion within this chapter about inclusive education needs to be set within the wider context of international debates about developing a curriculum for the twenty-first century. Naturally these discussions are ongoing and complex given they need to take into account changes to and differences in variables such as the starting positions of the countries, their priorities, available resources, capacity for change and political and cultural factors. A way forward is to consider underlying principles that are interpreted in the light of local circumstances. You may come across the mantra 'Think global, act local'. This seems apposite in relation to curriculum just as it has been used in relation to inclusion (Mittler, 2008).

Even if the focus is on thinking globally, there may not be consensus and some publications are a reflection of the priorities of the authors. For example, the World Conference on Art Education produced a report entitled *Road Map for Arts Education; Building Creative Capacities for the 21st Century* (Wagner, 2006) This provides regional reports (Asia and the Pacific, Latin America and the Caribbean, Europe and North America, Africa and Arab States), national reports and an international report including some recommendations which are targeted at different groups (e.g. UNESCO, and governments and political leaders). Some might view this report as representing the perspectives of a lobby group but it is referenced to an overarching vision for education in the twenty-first century, indeed one that makes reference to inclusion. This links back to the idea that each generation must refresh the curriculum.

In relation to inclusive education, what do international documents say about the curriculum?

When countries are devising or endorsing curriculum frameworks, they are cognizant of international trends and policies. Additionally, international comparisons of selected outcomes of education are undertaken and are often reported in the press with emotive headlines, e.g. 'Falling behind'. The comparisons have the allure of simplicity but there are questions to be asked about what is being measured, how it is being measured, the values underpinning the measures and the relevance to inclusive education. From the example above it is clear that education can be linked to creativity, an aspect which is not easily measured and is accorded different values in particular countries or social groups. Further, the starting points of education systems vary so that crude statements about the position in the international rankings tend to mask the complexities by telling a partial story. For example, the chapter on placement referred to TIMSS and Progress in International Reading Literacy Study (PIRLS) as international assessment of pupils. Governments take note of these alongside other international comparisons to ensure that their countries are not 'falling behind'. The results usually attract press coverage and a debate about teachers, the curriculum, resources, etc. Thus there is a comparative/competitive discourse across countries and within countries. But there are also shared initiatives. Amongst these is a report *Learning: The Treasure Within* (Delors, 1996). This document is viewed as a reference point and a vision for education which is applicable across national boundaries. The report sought to envisage an education that would be fit for the twenty-first century: it updated and refined the notion of lifelong learning 'so as to reconcile three forces: competition, which provides incentives; co-operation, which gives strength; and solidarity, which unites' (1996, 16).

It also placed emphasis on the four pillars that form the foundations of education:

- learning to know;
- learning to do;
- learning to live together, learning to live with others;
- learning to be.

In relation to the third of these, the report argued it would be achieved 'by developing an understanding of others and their history, traditions and spiritual values and, on this basis, creating a new spirit which, guided by recognition of our growing interdependence and a common analysis of the risks and challenges of the future, would induce people to implement common projects or to manage the inevitable conflicts in an intelligent and peaceful way' (1996, 20).

We have identified two major UNESCO initiatives, *Education for All* and the Delors Report. The relationship between these has been reviewed in *Revisiting Learning: The Treasure Within. Assessing the Influence of the 1996 Delors Report* (UNESCO, 2013). The question posed in the review was 'How does the Delors vision relate to EfA?' (2013, 7–8). It noted both some common ground but also a lack of consensus. It made the point that 'developed' countries now view EfA as 'more relevant to low income countries' (2013, 8). This is not a view upheld in this book. Taking the phrase 'Education for All' literally sits uncomfortably with the identified marginalization and exclusion within 'developed countries'. Examples of these aspects were provided in Chapter 2.

The occasional paper (UNESCO, 2013) also commented on the narrowing of the debate associated with the Millennium Development Goals (MDG), which focused on universal primary education and gender equality. This is not the perspective adopted in this book, which considers all phases of education except higher education and other factors relevant to education such as race, ethnicity and SEN.

In the same era, there were international debates about the education of particular groups of pupils. For instance, in June 1994, representatives of ninety-two countries and twenty-five international organizations came together at the World Conference on Special Needs Education in Salamanca, Spain. A product of this conference was the Salamanca Statement (UNESCO, 1994), which is regarded as highly influential in relation to inclusive education. It states that:

- every child has a fundamental right to education, and must be given the opportunity to achieve and maintain an acceptable level of learning;
- every child has unique characteristics, interests, abilities and learning needs;
- education systems should be designed and education programmes implemented to take into account the wide diversity of these characteristics and needs;
- those with special educational needs must have access to regular schools which should accommodate them within a child-centred pedagogy capable of meeting these needs.

(1994, viii)

In the quotation, the themes of diversity, design and child-centredness are apparent. More recently, the UNESCO report *The Central Role of Education in the Millennium Goals* makes reference to the curriculum:

schools may be open but parts of the curricula may be offensive to certain population groups.

(2010, 9)

schools have introduced Disaster Risk Reduction strategies into the curriculum and children have been involved in developing preparedness and evacuation plans.

(2010, 15)

Fighting child mortality and improving girls' empowerment may be assisted by curricula on cleanliness, basic sanitation, and measures to minimize contagious diseases.

(2010, 17)

These comments respectively allude to the curriculum as a risk to inclusion by being offensive to some, a subject in which pupils can be co-designers, and as something which has long-term implications including mortality and empowerment.

We have already shown that the term 'curriculum' can be described in terms of distinct subjects with an arrangement for each phase of education (e.g. the example related to Vietnam). In relation to this, UNESCO cautions that discontinuities in the curriculum impede inclusion: 'For example, across many regions, the way curriculum frameworks are structured has been shown to be a huge barrier to participation and learning within school communities. Indeed, a strong hierarchical separation between primary and secondary education, between lower and upper secondary education … create interruptions and discontinuities in learning' (2010, 21).

Example of research: progression rates

The World Bank provides data about progression rates from primary to secondary school in developing countries. This is structured by gender and available in different formats (table, graph, map and metadata). You can refine them to focus on the country, the region or the income. The graph for girls can be found at http://data.worldbank.org/indicator/SE.SEC.PROG.FE.ZS/countries?display=graph and that for boys at http://data.worldbank.org/indicator/SE.SEC.PROG.MA.ZS/countries?display=graph.

   You can change to a map using the white button at the top of the graph.

Activity 1
Look at this data (and the associated maps) and consider whether there is evidence that progression should *not* be viewed as automatic and unproblematic.

Activity 2
Change to the table view and select a country where the progression rate interests you. Why does it interest you? Now click on the name of the country and information about a wide range of indicators will appear. Are any of these relevant to inclusive education? (Hint: think back to the vignettes produced by the World Bank and cited in Chapter 2.)

These examples are all from international documents but similar concerns appear at national, school and classroom level. Therefore at national, local and school settings it would be possible to provide many more examples that form parallels to (or extend) these examples. However, the point has been made that the term 'curriculum' can be (and is) interpreted in various ways and that there are ongoing concerns about how to develop curricula that are in harmony with inclusive education. This chapter selectively addresses some of the issues outlined above. The next section considers the 'child-centred curriculum', a term used in the Salamanca Statement (UNESCO, 1994).

How can the term 'child-centred curriculum' be understood?

The term 'child-centred', which appears in the Salamanca Statement, is open to interpretation. Does it mean that only topics of interest to the child are taught? Does it imply an individualized curriculum? Is it a curriculum based on the 'best interests of the child'? Is it an alternative to the national curriculum? There is some degree of consensus between authors, but what is needed is a shared framework to facilitate shared understandings.

In this context the work of Bernstein is helpful, since it provides a widely recognized, internationally applied way of talking about and analysing the curriculum. He used the terms 'classification' and 'framing'. Classification is 'the means by which power relations are transformed into specialized discourses, and framing is the means where by the principles of control are transformed into specialized discursive practices (pedagogic relations) which attempt to relay a given distribution of power' (Bernstein, 2000, xvii, brackets in original).

Where curriculum subjects are seen as independent 'silos', the classification is viewed as strong, whilst in project-based work it may be weaker. Bernstein actually used the term 'insulation' to refer to the spaces between categories. That insulation may be necessary to maintain subject specialisms but you will have seen the comments above that strong classification can create barriers to inclusive education. The phases of education are also examples of boundaries. A later section of this chapter will consider transitions across phase boundaries. Bernstein distinguished between strong framing, in which teachers have control, and weak framing, which is generally associated with child-centred learning.

The relevance of Bernstein's ideas to inclusive education may not be immediately apparent. However, he provided an example which may be helpful.

Where classification and frames were relatively strong, one would expect that if a pupil presented some work to the teacher which the teacher thought was unexpectedly good, he/she might say 'That's a good piece of work. Did you do it yourself?' Whereas if the classification and especially the framing was relatively weak, in the same situation, the teacher might say, 'That's really exciting. Did you do it by yourself?' If the pupils said that he did, the teacher might then add 'You might have got even more out of it if you had talked it over with some of the group.'

(Bernstein, 1975, 9)

Activity 1

Which of the two scenarios above (i.e. strong framing and classification or relatively weak classification and framing) is most consistent with:

1 pupil participation?
2 inclusive education?

Activity 2

Reread the materials related to the Vietnam curriculum. Do you think that:

1 the classification is strong or relatively weak?
2 the framing is strong of relatively weak?

The strength of classification and framing can vary and Bernstein used the term 'relatively weak'. It is helpful to think of each in terms of a continuum. For example, weak to strong framing could be represented as F^{--}, F^-, F^+, F^{++}. There is a similar scale for classification. (The details of the representation of continuum in pieces of research may vary but the principle is that there is a continuum.) Analysing teaching in this way can help to unpack the degree of child-centredness. For instance, are the boundaries between subjects strong or weak, and what are the relationships between teachers and children? Child-centred learning is likely to have weak classification and weak framing.

The next example of research used the work of Bernstein as one of the analytical lenses for tracking pedagogic and curriculum change. A reason for selecting this example is that it involved student researchers as part of the process of curriculum development.

Example of research: The role of student researchers in the process of curriculum development

Leat and Reid assert that 'Education in the UK is regarded as traditionally offering a curriculum with both strong classification (separate subjects) and strong framing (little choice of what is studied, passive roles for students and transmission teaching)' (2012, 194).

The context for this case study was 'a mixed high school, serving an ex-mining locality with a recent history of job losses and high unemployment. Most of the students were of white British origin. The proportion of students with learning difficulties and/or disabilities was above average and attainment in public examinations below the national average' (2012, 194). To address this situation, the school sought to develop 'an assessment/progression framework for enquiry skills, [and] in which the onus was on student self-assessment' (2012, 194).

The project initially involved seven teachers (two each from English, Maths and Science, and one from Art), an academic supervisor and support from a deputy head teacher. Subsequently, a number of student researchers (SRs) were recruited and trained. Their responsibilities included:

- developing the dimensions of the framework for peer and self-assessment of learning of enquiry skills;
- adapting the information communications technology (ICT) shell in which evidence related to the framework could be stored, structured accessed and presented;
- providing support and feedback to teachers on their efforts to enact enquiry-based teaching;
- acting as research participants for a computer science PhD student.

Over time, the number of SRs varied and usually they worked in groups of 2–4, with a member of staff who taught them.

The article presented data from different sources, but for the purposes of this book only that related to SRs is reported. Data was collected from the pupils through two rounds of interviews. In the first, pupil view templates (PVT) were used. In these there are images of a teacher and a learner. For each there is both a speech bubble and a thought bubble. These were left blank for the SRs to complete. The layout permitted the student to distinguish between what the people are saying and what they are thinking. The examples below illustrate this.

The first pair of extracts from the PVT data relate to a 'non-project' teacher:

(Speech bubble – student view of teacher talking to the class) Listen! I'm trying to tell you what to do! If you don't listen, you won't know what to do next. How do you expect to learn anything if you don't listen to what I am saying? Any time you waste will be taken away from your break time.

(Thought bubble – student view of what teacher is thinking) Why don't they ever listen? They just interrupt and then nobody knows what to do. I wish there was a way to get their attention. I want them to learn – how am I meant to be a good teacher if they don't listen to what I am saying?

(2012, 200)

The second pair of extracts from the PVT data relate to a project (enquiry) teacher:

(Speech bubble – teacher talking to the class) In enquiry you ask a question and then you are going to investigate this and find out the answer. Try to use the habits of mind* and metacognitive skills.

(Thought bubble – student perception of teacher thoughts) I am really pleased that the students are paying attention to what I am saying. They are responding with interest and awe. I am really happy that I know more about how students learn.

(2012, 200)

*'Habits of Mind' is a set of sixteen problem-solving, life-related skills (Costa and Kallick, 2000).

Leat and Reid outlined four key roles SRs had in the school's curriculum development process, namely:

- 'practical work in the development of an assessment framework by making it comprehensible and accessible for other students';
- playing a part in 'shifting the organisational and power structures in the school';
- contributing to 'changes in the project teachers' practices of

thinking, planning, teaching and assessing';
- having a 'material effect on elements of the curriculum

(2012, 202)

Leat and Reid used Bernstein's terms to analyse and describe the outcomes of the project. They reported that the framing became weaker with a greater sense of collaboration between the teacher and the pupils. With reference to classification, they stated that the Habits of Mind framework, which is applicable across subject areas, 'dented the classification system, eroding subject boundaries' (2012, 201). It also helped to develop 'a more elaborate and explicit understanding of the attributes of learning' (2012, 201).

Leat and Reid critiqued Bernstein's work, stating that the 'generally abstract language does not quite do justice to the feeling generated in some of the SRs, who found the experience transformative':

- *'Yeah – it has made me think about what I can do and want to do when I leave, it has given me more confidence.*
- *I didn't know learning was like this ... it's really good because I know what I can do more – to get better at things'*

(2012, 203)

The teachers' perceptions also altered: 'The teachers began to see the students more clearly as people who need to develop and mature as learners and human beings – a process measured more by confidence and competence in all manner of settings' (2012, 202).

Reflections on the research
There was coherence to this project; the strands were about enquiry and self-assessment, and those involved included the children. There were positive reflections on how at least some of the SRs had benefitted from this experience. It may be helpful to you to think about the distinction between knowing about something and experiencing it.

Activity 1
The data collection included the PVT, which sought data on both what the individual was saying and what they were thinking. Do you view this as a useful distinction? Can you identify any situations related to inclusive education when such an approach might be valuable?

Activity 2

What were your reactions to reading the expectation that pupils, albeit SRs, were expected to provide support and feedback to teachers and that they were credited with having contributed 'to changes in the project teachers' practices of thinking, planning, teaching and assessing' (2012, 202)? What does this tell you about the potential role of children within schools?

Activity 3

A theme in Part I of the book is that of a move away from seeing children as dependent, without agency and vulnerable towards recognizing them as having agency and identity. Reread the final quotation about teachers' perceptions on p.156. What links can you make between that and the different perspectives on childhood?

Interview with David Leat, Anna Reid and Ulrike Thomas about their research

Prof David Leat, Dr Anna Reid and Ulrike Thomas, Newcastle University

Sue Pearson: Some accounts of curriculum portray it as adult-dominated and inflexible with many curriculum decisions taken beyond the school. Yet you say 'Control over choice of subject matter and the rules governing relationships between teachers and pupils were shifting' (Leat and Reid, 2012, 201). In the context of inclusive education, do you have any views about the control of the curriculum?

David Leat: It would be my view/prejudice that broadly since the introduction of a National Curriculum in England, there has been decreasing involvement of teachers let alone students in the choice of curriculum content. Initially this was via input regulation (highly detailed attainment targets) – however the degree of content specification via orders has been reduced. This might have freed up curriculum control but input regulation has been replaced by output regulation in the form of targets and associated accountabilities, policed by OfSTED. Schools as organizations, departments and individual teachers have internalized this form of surveillance with the effect of much teaching to the test and institutionalized lesson formats, typified at one time by three-part lessons but over time shifting more towards teaching to objectives and measuring progress on narrow measures. This is despite some OfSTED statements that this is not what is required. Teachers are variously labelled, monitored, showcased and moulded. Much of this pressure is passed to students and those who buy into it (and even those who don't) have aspects of their identity shaped by the experience. So generally teachers and students have little experience of having choice or control over the curriculum or pedagogy. Amongst teachers there is a fair degree of suppressed values and limited agency – but there are some who manage to stand a little outside the pressure. For me it is notable how well most students respond to having some choice and control over curriculum and it is one of the reasons that Art seems to remain a very popular subject with many students (even when they don't elect to take it). So we have increasingly strong framing in many classrooms. The consequence is classrooms may be much less inclusive because students disengage – they may behave OK but they are not intrinsically motivated and don't see any value in education other than for certification.

Such a curriculum approach (objectives led) usually leads to an Initiation-Response-Feedback (IRF) style discourse pattern with a limited role for students in that discourse. I remember talking to Bob Lingard at a conference about his work on socially just inclusive pedagogies in Queensland and asked him what the schools were like which did operationalize the project's four principles (connections, valuing difference, social care and intellectual challenge) and he said it was typified in a school that did Philosophy for Children (P4C). That was no surprise as P4C tries very hard to be inclusive and in good hands gets well away from set curriculum, convergent objectives and IRF.

Anna Reid: I ended up writing my doctoral thesis about this project. The key point of my discussion was concepts of teachers' 'contractual agency' and 'internal agency' in relation to the curriculum. Depending on their varying beliefs about the value and importance of enquiry-based learning (EBL), some teachers did what they thought they could 'get away with' in relation to the regimented context in which they were working. Others didn't get this far and kept their actions to themselves. I found this really frustrating and really went to town on my critique of 'performativity' in schools.

Sue Pearson: You wrote that some SRs found 'the experience transformative' (Leat and Reid, 2012, 203). Can you elaborate on the transformational aspect?

David Leat: I would start by saying two things. First some of the teachers genuinely managed to hand over considerable control to students.

Secondly some and one in particular really opened up his thinking about the project and its consequences to the students. So some students saw new dimensions to their teachers and got a much wider view of what learning can be – for example appreciating that working with other people successfully is a real talent or that finding humour in something is valued or showing some resilience might be recognized. This was a completely new language for them about learning and as a result they reshaped aspects of their identity. What was quite frightening however was the fact that when most got into Year 10 they got very strategic (gaming the system?) and decided that getting good notes from a didactic teacher covering the 'stuff' was the best bet for good results. There were some exceptions however. Both Anna and I are very interested in Dialogic Self Theory and we would see many of the students changing through developing new 'I' positions and generally becoming more multi-voiced.

I would add that some of the classrooms came much closer to being learning communities with greater relational equity. But it is clearly fragile stuff and the policy context is so ferocious that it is difficult to sustain such approaches over long periods of time for most pupils – it only goes on in pockets and corners.

So going back to Bernstein, regulative discourse and instructional discourse and recognition rules and other concepts are very powerful (we are fans generally), but they can miss the affective and felt aspects of more divergent, creative curriculum approaches.

Anna Reid: It is really transformational for some SRs. A cohort of SRs received exactly the same theoretical and practical input from me as their teachers did. This led to one teacher in particular recalling seeing the 'glint' in a SR's eye as they supported their teacher's attempts to implement EBL approaches to learning. I feel the experience of some SRs was transformative because they experienced insights into teaching and learning which they had never encountered before, and they enjoyed relationships with their teachers which were far less hierarchical and more equal because they felt they were in it together.

Ulrike Thomas: Weakened classification and framing encouraged 'more of the pupil/student to be made public, more of his thoughts feelings and values … As a result the socialization could be more intensive and perhaps more penetrating' (Bernstein, 1975, 109). He was also aware that this could lead to the production 'of new defences against the potential intrusiveness of the integrated code and its open learning contexts' (1975, 109). I felt this is what happened to some of the students as they approached their GSCEs – they enjoyed and saw tremendous value in EBL, but ultimately the external narrative about good grades, good job or 'going to uni' was just too powerful!

Sue Pearson: What did you discover about the process of research, and specifically including SRs, from this experience?

David Leat: I suppose it was another step for me away from what one might call mainstream agendas (those more likely to be funded). Although I am not anti-quantitative approaches I am increasingly persuaded of the importance of approaches that expose lived experience and meaning making. It was also another step in learning about partnership, co-production approaches to research. It is not exactly that your participants (although with luck and effort they become partners) co-own the research, rather that there is outcome/product that matters to them that you the researcher are contributing to. There is a degree of reciprocity. I guess it also underlined the importance of ongoing relationships and trust in such settings, which Anna was very good at.

Anna Reid: Research is contextual; agency is ecological. Relationships are key when trying to implement and then report on the impact of implementing an initiative which goes against the dominant culture.

The emphasis in the project discussed above was initially on self-assessment and enquiry learning which were deemed by the adults to be priorities for the school. Both of these are congruent with developing inclusive education. There was some evidence that pupils as researchers can be involved in the development of a more inclusive curriculum with associated benefits for all pupils. Additionally, there are personal benefits to those who are involved in the research. However, the term 'curriculum' also encompasses what is taught to students; in Delors' terms, 'learning to know'. A common view is that decisions about material taught are the province of the adults whether they are teachers or others with roles within education. In the context of pupil participation, it is worth considering whether the knowledge and views of children can/should be drawn upon to inform curriculum planning. The following example of research returns to the distinction between education and school that was made in Chapter 5 on placement. You were invited to consider the distinctions the children make between learning within and beyond the school. The next section explores whether the knowledge gained beyond the school can inform the school curriculum.

Can children's knowledge inform the school curriculum?

In the era of HIV/AIDS it may be the responsibility of adults to determine that there should be education about HIV/AIDS, but young people have knowledge that may have been gained in a range of settings. McLaughlin and Swartz (2011) question whether pupils' knowledge of HIV/AIDS could be used to improve the input of schools and by extension reduce the incidence of HIV/AIDS.

Example of research: Utilizing young people's knowledge of HIV/AIDS

HIV/AIDS is impacting on the lives of children in terms of their access to education, their ability to live full and healthy lives and their enjoyment of childhood. McLaughlin and Swartz stated that of those with HIV/AIDS, 67 per cent live in sub-Saharan Africa.

This research was undertaken in Kenya, South Africa and the United Republic of Tanzania and involved eight schools. McLaughlin and Swartz provided a background to the study in sections on young people at risk, HIV-related education, and teachers and HIV-related education. They stated that their research questions were heavily influenced by the work of Bernstein (1971) on different types of knowledge:

- What are the primary sources and contents of sexual knowledge for young people in sub-Saharan Africa, and how do these forms of knowledge differ in their content and process of acquisition?
- How do these different forms of knowledge interact with AIDS education received in the classroom, and how might young people's sexual knowledge be used to effect change in pedagogy and curriculum?

(2011, 433)

The research involved three steps as set out in Table 6.1 on p. 162.

Table 6.1 Methods used at each of the eight schools

Phase One : rapid ethnography	Rapid ethnography – observation of sex education and other classes over one week
	Building relationships with research participants
Phase Two: perceptions of pupils, teachers and community members	20 X 2 'Sources of sexual knowledge' auto-photography activities and initial interviews with pupils
	4 'current and desired sex education' mini documentaries and 4 focus groups of 4 or 5 students each
	10 final interviews with pupils, specifically about gender, religion and culture
	4 focus groups with 6 teachers
	6 interviews with 6 teachers
	6 interviews with 6 community leaders
Phase Three: agreeing on the implications for education	Consultative dialogue with each school
	Considering data
	Recommending action for the school and beyond
	Producing a toolkit for schools to use

Source: Based on McLauglin and Swartz, 2011, 435

In this account the prime focus is the data from the children and overlaps with data from the other groups. In terms of discourses about sexual knowledge, children clearly drew on 'knowledge from the community, including peers; and the formal discourse of school' (2011, 436). They also drew on experience. The researchers suggested that: 'Informal sources were teaching them about power, gender, poverty, abuse and sexuality' (2011, 437). In contrast, formal (school) discourses were about 'regulation, abstinence, protection or taking care, health and treatment' (2011, 437).

Tentative conclusions can be drawn from this article:

- Young people want to have 'open and honest dialogues with teachers' who they see as a group who can help.
- Teachers have a sound knowledge of young people's sexuality and the need for HIV/AIDS education.
- Some teachers had received training and were confident about delivering sex education.
- Seeing the pupil and stakeholder data provided a constructive climate for discussion.
- A hybrid curriculum that draws on formal and informal knowledge to educate pupils and teacher is a possibility.
- The challenge is to design local curricula that do this.

Reflections on the research

This example illustrates how the curriculum needs to respond to changing conditions (in this case HIV/AIDS), and in that sense is consistent with the quotation at the start of the chapter about each generation rethinking the curriculum. Some would argue that inadequate attention has been given to designing an inclusive curriculum as this example illustrates.

Activity 1

This research makes a case for the involvement of teachers, community leaders and young people in planning education related to HIV/AIDS. What do you think were the key elements of the 'approach' to curriculum development that they used? (Hint: there is information in the article about the activities undertaken and who was involved. You may want to reread the interview with David Ryan in Chapter 5.)

Activity 2

Do you think this (inclusive) approach could be applied to designing other elements of the curriculum?

Can children co-produce educational resources relevant to inclusive education?

In Chapter 2 on inclusive education, we considered data about how characteristics of individuals are associated with 'goodies' and 'baddies'. No doubt you remember the associations with bad teeth. Stereotyping on any basis is detrimental. It tends to set expectations based on a characteristic without regard to the whole person. The important question is how we combat stereotypes, and there are several examples of attempts to do this. For instance, until relatively recently, disabled children were absent from children's fiction. However, there is now children's fiction which contains positive images of disability. You should look at the Letterbox Library (http://www.letterboxlibrary.com) to see how diversity, including but not restricted to disability, is now evident in children's fiction. But could some of the work produced by children provide insights into the discourses of race, class and gender? In Lundy's terms (2007), is there a way for them to express their views? But further, is there a way in which this can be heard by a wide audience?

Example of research: Picturing oppression

This Canadian research (Sensoy, 2011) involved a month-long project in which twenty seventh graders 'created photo essays that would communicate to "the world" what it means to live with race, class or gender oppression' (2011, 323). It was guided by two research questions:

> How do students working with a critical pedagogue conceptualise their own experiences with race, class and gender in ways that either interrupt or reinscribe dominant mainstream curricular narratives?

> To what extent can visual methods serve to open up and expand researchers' understanding of students' conceptions of their lived experiences in the context of a critical pedagogy classroom?

> (2011, 323)

This account reports on the first of those questions.

The context of the school was 'low-rise, low-income housing' (2011, 324) with an ethno-racial mix of mainly White with 'large Asian heritage populations (primarily from India, Pakistan, China, Korea and the Philippines) as well as large immigrant populations from Eastern Europe and former Soviet States' (2011, 324). The adults involved were the teacher of the class who was in her thirties and was described as 'the child of an immigrant family to Canada, a South Asian woman; and a graduate student working on a Masters degree in equity issues in education' (2011, 326). The students (n=20) included eleven boys and nine girls. The researchers noted that '13 were born in a country other than Canada and an additional two who were born in Canada are of Aboriginal ancestry' (2011, 327). The researchers made reference to counter-stories which are 'narrative(s) in which members of marginalized groups – those that have experienced oppression along a primary identity – empower and repair group and individual identities by responding to those stories generated about them in mainstream accounts' (2011, 324).

The class teacher and the researcher shared with the students a 'visual' puzzle in the form of the famous photograph of the 'unknown rebel' in Tiananmen Square. The students' task was to think about the questions of first, what the photograph was about, and second, what pictures means.

One student reported back that he had a personal connection to the picture; his father had been in 'Tiananmen Square on the day that the photograph was taken, and was able to identify "the June 4th Incident"' (2011, 329). The student and his father had discussed this incident, and the student shared his memory of this with the class. This provided a positive context for the pupils to 'combine their school-based work with their own real-life experiences and knowledge' (2011, 329). The focus was on race, class and sexism. The pupils were given detailed instructions about what to think about, what to do, what was and wasn't acceptable in terms of taking images and what would happen with the images. They were given a disposable camera and had Friday to Monday to take images.

In the research findings, the researchers addressed a set of themes:

- *Thinking literally, thinking metaphorically (2011, 332)*. For instance, some students, perhaps influenced by school books, portrayed race as a matter of colour, whilst Latif, a student of Albanian Muslim heritage, developed a metaphorical account using images and poetry: https://www.youtube.com/watch?v=gwTPgtb2xGl
- *I want them to 'feel' what it is like (2011, 335)*. Kofti used one photo to challenge individuals to look beyond the colour of someone's skin: https://www.youtube.com/watch?v=kHaZvcZafzQ, whilst Kiet challenged

gender stereotypes: https://www.youtube.com/watch?v=5xY6uQ48rBc

- *Unsettled expertise (2011, 336).* In this activity, some of the expected perceptions of 'high' and 'low' achievers were challenged. Some of the former found it harder than the latter.

The materials that the students produced were part of an educational experience for the participants; they illustrated complex understandings of race, gender and sex that challenged the more simplistic treatment of these ideas in school-based materials; and they provided a resource with global reach.

Reflections on the research

This was an activity undertaken in one classroom, and yet there are hundreds of views of the YouTube materials – the work has reached a much wider 'audience'.

Activity 1

Sensoy comments that 'What is compelling about the counter stories they produced is not so much the insights they offer about students' ideas on race, class or gender, but the capacity (or limitations) of students integrating their lived experience and knowledge with school-based knowledge' (2011, 340). In the context of inclusive education, what do you see as the significance of this statement? (Hint: You might want to think about factors including the profile of the staff, the representation of diversity in school resources, community involvement, the physical barriers between the school and the community the pupils come from.)

Activity 2

In the light of this example, can you think about other ways in which visual approaches could be utilized, either as part of an inclusive curriculum or to promote inclusive education?

What do children want from education?

The children's materials reported by Sensoy (2011) included one piece entitled. 'Do I have to be the same to fit in?' That question leads us into thinking about the futures that children anticipate after education. What dreams or aspirations do they have? What, if any, links are there with the 'Four Pillars of Learning' in *Learning: the treasure within* (Delors, 1996)? What are the links between the futures that children think about and the views of teachers? Obviously, it is impossible to generalize answers to any of these questions, but the next research example will alert you to some of the issues.

We have noted that education can be viewed as promoting personal growth, but is also linked to economic growth. There is a sense that some children in particular circumstances (and their families or communities) lack aspiration. These low aspirations can be linked to low achievement, creating a self-fulfilling prophecy; an 'aspiration trap'. However, this approach locates the 'blame' as being with the children (and their families or communities). You may notice this type of discourse in some political statements or press coverage. In schools, you may hear comments that 'it is the parents that you really want to see who never come to parents' evening'. It may be accurate to note that they are absent but it is too easy to see this as intentional and interpret it as a lack of interest in education. However, their absence may be a product of other factors such as having to juggle multiple responsibilities or having painful memories of their own schooling which make entering educational premises problematic.

Flechtner argues that 'aspiration traps are particularly harmful to people at the bottom of the socio-economic ladder' (2014, 2). The next example of research was undertaken in Australia in a low socio-economic area, and will alert you to some of the complexities beyond the superficial stereotyping.

Example of research: 'I want to get a piece of paper that says I can do stuff'

McInerney and Smyth argue that the concept of low aspirations is evident in Australian educational policy. They note that 'Young people from low SES (socioeconomic status) are presumed to lack ambition, drive and energy. Much of the responsibility for school failure, diminished employment prospects and financial hardship they experience is seen to reside in a combination of cultural, family and individual deficiencies' (2014, 241).

Between April 2011 and March 2012, they conducted the research in an area that has 'an employment rate of 7.3% … and close to 30%

(well above the state average) of those aged between 15 and 19 years of age are not engaged in work, further education or training' (2014, 242). Their data gathering involved observations, document analysis and interviews (n=60).

They provided three 'narrative portraits', a term referring to highly condensed versions of the narratives which preserve the key points. All the interviewees experienced 'a degree of social and economic deprivation' (2014, 244).

To analyse their data, they drew on 'funds of knowledge' theory which has previously been used to contest views about low SES students. Moll et al. used this term to 'to refer to the historically accumulated and culturally developed bodies of knowledge and skills essential for household or individual functioning and well-being' (1992, 133). McInerney and Smyth expanded the explanatory powers of this theory in three ways:

- they accepted that children's funds of knowledge may be independent of that of adults (e.g. in the arena of computing);
- they sought to acknowledge more fully 'the significance of social class, gender and power differentials operating within and between households and neighbourhoods' (2014, 246);
- they acknowledged the 'opportunity structures' that existed.

Their analysis of the data was grouped around the themes of:

- individuals and households;
- institutions and communities;
- public policy.

In their conclusion, they commented that:

> What they [the participants] have to say about their lives, their interests and their aspirations challenges a good deal of the deficit thinking about young people and their parents/ carers in low SES communities. Liam, Emilia, Tony and the other young participants have faith in their schooling and believe that success in the senior years will lead to worthwhile and engaging pathways in higher education, training and employment.
>
> (2014, 250)

and:

> We have highlighted a lack of opportunity structures to

support low SES students' participation in higher education, training and employment and have suggested that the key to improving the life chances for these students depends on developing public policies that address the fundamental causes of economic inequality.

(2014, 250)

Reflections on the research

This piece of qualitative research is strongly written, but there are some methodological issues that you may want to consider. The narrative portraits required a condensing of the complete interviews, and that process would have been challenging for the researchers. In addition, the researchers suggested that the three narratives are 'broadly reflective of the group as a whole', which is a matter of judgement. Neither of these comments is intended to undermine this research or cast doubt on the researchers. They are to remind you of the challenges of dealing with a wealth of qualitative material – in this case, sixty interviews.

You might find it useful to consider the proposition that a test of good research is whether someone else, given access to the raw data, would produce a similar set of findings and arrive at a comparable set of conclusions.

Activity 1

The quotations above refer to both 'deficit theories' and 'public policies'. In Chapter 2, we noted that there has been a shift in thinking about disability from the medical model where any difficulties were viewed as deficits in the child to recognizing the interaction between the child, the context and the adults. The former is inconsistent with inclusive education but the latter is better aligned. Drawing on those examples and the material in this research example:

1 Consider the links between how an issue is theorized and policy development and implementation.
2 Might outmoded theories impede the enactment of policy? (You may find it useful to reread Chapter 3 on Participation.)

Activity 2

The heading for this example of research was a verbatim quotation from a comment by a participant, which was used within the title of the research article. The researchers suggest it is consistent with a utilitarian view of education.

1 In the context of inclusive education, how do you view accreditation ('getting a piece of paper')?

2 What are the challenges and benefits for teachers and pupils?

Are there shared views about transitions?

The example of research that we have just considered was, in part, concerned with the opportunities that education can provide and what some of the barriers and affordances might be. Mittler suggested that transition was a topic that should be rethought. In the context of the UK and transition from school, he wrote, 'Young people and parents continue to complain that the services and support which they received during childhood simply disappear once they leave school' (2008, 6).

Earlier in this chapter, Bernstein's ideas about classification were introduced. It was argued that in the context of inclusion, strong classifications are potentially problematic. The quotation from Mittler could be interpreted as a strong classification.

This section is concerned with 'boundaries' with education, e.g. the transition from primary school to secondary. Before addressing that topic, a couple of important observations should be made. First, a critique of Millennium Development Goals is that they focus on primary education rather than a more holistic view of education. Goal 2 is about universal primary education. Whilst this has not yet been achieved, there is a concern that the broader views of *Educational for All* should not be lost. In fact, many countries have committed themselves to at least some secondary education (http://data.unicef.org/education/secondary). UNICEF suggests that the barriers are similar to those related to primary education, but are 'intensified'. They classify them as related to:

- costs;
- distance to travel;
- the pressure to start earning.

Even where progression to secondary schooling is the norm, there are reports of variations between groups of pupils, a situation that suggests the need for a more inclusive approach. West et al. (2010) reported on a longitudinal study. The sample comprised 2,000 Scottish pupils who were surveyed at ages 11, 13, 15 and 18/19. The complexities of the issues are evident in the following quotation.

> Personal factors, however, are the most important predictors of both transitions, though not all in the same way. Respondents of lower ability, judged more anxious by class-teachers, who had been victimised, had lower self-esteem, and were less well prepared for secondary school, expressed more school and peer concerns (effect sizes being stronger for peer concerns except in the case of ability). Those who were more aggressive and disengaged from primary school had a poorer school, but better peer transition.
>
> (2010, 34)

The importance of this transition from primary to secondary education is not only evident in the range of reports that have been published but also the extent of research activity. However, it is potentially difficult to make sense of the accumulated body of materials. Which pieces of research are robust? To what extent do the findings corroborate each other? What are the gaps in the research? The next example of research illustrates how researchers undertake analysis of previously published material. In the process, the quality of the research, the links between different pieces and the key themes which emerged were identified.

The work of Topping (2011) was selected because it demonstrates the value of seeking multiple perspectives on a topic. In this instance, distinctions are made between the concerns of teachers and children (and parents).

Example of research: Differences between teachers' and children's perceptions of transition

Using online databases and the terms 'transition* or transfer* AND primary-secondary OR elementary-high' (Topping, 2011, 269), the researcher identified 325 international studies. (Using the truncation transfer and adding an asterisk is a way to ensure that articles using any of the variants of 'transfer', e.g. transferring, are identified.)

There was then a rigorous approach to selecting the data for the review. Of the 325 identified, all the abstracts were read as part of a selection process. This led to 127 papers being read in full. Based on this, eighty-eight were retained. Those papers were reviewed systematically. Differences between the views of teachers and of children emerged. These were used as organizing principles in the review.

The review found that pupils' perspectives were largely associated with socio-emotional aspects. Topping grouped the material around the themes of:

- Peer networks;
- Bullying;
- External networks;
- Self-esteem and mental health;
- Special groups.

The teachers' perspectives principally were associated with attainment and were grouped around:

- Curriculum problems in secondary schools;
- School strategies;
- Special groups.

In relation to special groups, the pupils' perspectives focused on high-poverty pupils, ethnic minority pupils and children with disabilities. The section on teachers' perspectives made reference to children who were younger within their year, children from poorer homes, less able children from larger and less well-educated families, children from ethnic minorities and children with disabilities: 'Pupils (and parents) are pre-occupied with short-term, personal, socio-emotional issues. Teachers are preoccupied with longer-term, institutional-led attainment issues' (2011, 280).

The article includes suggestions for practice and policy in transition divided into those that work and those that partially work.

Activity 1
This research indicates a difference between the findings based on data from teachers and those based on data from children. What do you perceive as the main differences between their views? How might these differences relate to inclusion?

Activity 2
Topping further suggests that whilst teachers are providing some support, it is, in the view of the parents and children, 'the wrong thing' (2011, 279). He then connects this to blame – teachers blaming children, children and parents blaming teachers. How do you think stakeholders could be supported to move from a blame culture to a more positive, inclusive culture? (Hint: you may want to consider consultation, communication and Chapter 3 on Children's Participation).

Chapter activities

Activity 1

This chapter has illustrated that children have roles other than as *recipients* of a curriculum.

1 Create notes on the way the chapter has summarized key features of these different roles.
2 What are your opinions about these roles? What do you see as their potential strengths and limitations?
3 Reflect on your responses – do you think a child in an educational setting you have worked in would see their strengths and limitations in ways that are parallel or different to yours? Why do you think these parallels and differences might exist? How might you use such awareness in working with children?

Activity 2

The chapter has explored 'curriculum' and 'inclusion' in a number of different contexts.

1 Read through the chapter and look at the ways in which different contexts relate to how any 'curriculum' is theorized and developed. Are there parallels and differences? What factors seem to affect how curricula are understood, formed and implemented?
2 Summarize the different ways in which you think 'curriculum' and 'context' relate to each other within the chapter's review.

Summary

This chapter has:

- considered how the term 'curriculum' can be understood and analysed;
- illustrated what international documents related to inclusion say about the curriculum;
- clarified the term 'child-centred curriculum';
- provided evidence that children can create curriculum materials;
- promoted thinking about what children want from education;
- reflected on the impact of discontinuities in education.

Further reading

Fletchner, S. (2014) 'Aspiration Traps: When Poverty Stifles Hope'. Available online: http://www.worldbank.org/content/dam/Worldbank/document/ Poverty%20documents/inequality-in-focus-january2014-final.pdf (accessed 28 February 2016).
The World Bank's *Inequality in Focus* newsletter informs the public policy debate on equity, inequality of opportunity and socio-economic mobility.

Lewis, A. and B. Norwich (2005). *Special Teaching for Special Children? Pedagogies for Inclusion*. Maidenhead: Open University Press.
This edited book provides a theoretical framework for thinking about pedagogies of inclusion. Experts in particular fields make links between that framework and identified groups of children, e.g. autistic spectrum disorder, dyslexia, dyspraxia.

Organisation for Economic Co-operation and Development (2012). 'Equity and Quality in Education Supporting Disadvantaged Students and Schools'. Available online: /z-wcorg/ database Available from http://public.eblib.com/ choice/publicfullrecord.aspx?p=873379 (accessed 18 March 2016).
It is argued that the highest performing education systems are those that combine equity with quality. This document provides data about international comparisons. It will, for example, help you to contextualize the example of research about the aspirations of Australian children.

Sriprakash, A. (2010). 'Child-centred Education and the Promise of Democratic Learning: Pedagogic Messages in Rural Indian Primary Schools'. *International Journal of Educational Development* 30 (3): 297–304.
This article reports on an initiative aimed at developing child-centred education as part of a response to low student retention and achievement in rural government schools in India. It draws upon the work of Bernstein. It illustrates some of the tensions associated with a shift from traditional educational practices to a child-centred approach.

Symonds, J. E. (2008). 'Pupil Researchers Generation X: Educating Pupils as Active Participants – an Investigation into Gathering Sensitive Information from Early Adolescents'. *Research in Education* 80 (1): 63–74.
The article reports on a four-hour session with 11–12-year-olds in which they investigated the effectiveness of a rage of data collection techniques. It also identifies the circumstances within which authentic responses from children are most likely.

Research details

The role of student researchers in the process of curriculum development

This article reports on a case study undertaken in a secondary school in England. It considers the role of student researchers in the development of the curriculum.

Leat, D. and A. Reid (2012). 'Exploring the Role of Student Researchers in the Process of Curriculum Development'. *Curriculum Journal* 23 (2): 189–205.

Utilizing young people's knowledge of HIV/AIDS

Young people gain knowledge from multiple sources and this research considers how a space can be created within which the share knowledge.

McLaughlin, C. and S. Swartz (2011). 'Can we Use Young Peoples Knowledge to Develop Teachers and HIV-related Education?' *Prospects: Quarterly Review of Comparative Education* 41 (3): 429–44.

Picturing oppression

This research took place in an inner-city school in Canada and used images taken by the children to research their lived experiences of class, race and gender.

Sensoy, Ö. (2011). 'Picturing Oppression: Seventh Graders Photo Essays on Racism, Classism, and Sexism'. *International Journal of Qualitative Studies in Education* 24 (3): 323–42.

'I want to get a piece of paper that says I can do stuff'

This Australian research acknowledged that children are experts in their own lives and explores their experiences of their aspirations.

McInerney, P. and J. Smyth (2014). '"I want to get a piece of paper that says I can do stuff": Youth Narratives of Educational Opportunities and Constraints in Low Socio-economic Neighbourhoods'. *Ethnography and Education* 9 (3): 239–52.

Differences between teachers' and children's perceptions of transitions

Topping's literature review identified a number of articles on this topic. Using published material Topping considered the perspectives of different stakeholders; teachers, parents and pupils.

Topping, K. (2011). 'Primary-Secondary Transition: Differences between Teachers' and Children's Perceptions'. *Improving Schools* 14 (3): 268–85.

Children's Sense of Belonging

Introduction and key questions

This chapter considers the social and affective dimensions of inclusion. The approach has been influenced by the work of Hanko, who wrote: 'Studies continue to point out that emotional and social factors affect all learning; show the connections between our feelings, our reasoning and our motivations, and emphasise that direct support strategies geared to meeting the needs of specific children should be developed as whole-school policies in relation to all children and understood by the whole staff' (2003, 125).

Similarly, McIntyre argued that:

If we are serious about using pupil consultation to optimise teaching effectiveness, we need first to deepen our understanding of the social conditions of learning. Then we probably need to develop ways in which the different pupils in particular classrooms can be enabled to engage in dialogue with their teachers about how their particular contrasting social conditions help or hinder their learning.

(2004, 6)

These quotations resonate with the ideas introduced in Chapter 2 about inclusive education in relation to SEN/disability. Inclusion is partly about full access (Chapter 5), curriculum (Chapter 6) but also about a feeling of belonging. That is a broad term which has been taken to refer to social processes.

McIntyre's comment highlights the value of pupils' perspectives on social aspects of education and also the need to access those views in a manner that respects the preferences/resources of the individuals or groups. Both of those aspects are considered in this chapter but the approach adopted extends the concept of education beyond the school. It does this through addressing the following questions:

- What are children's memories of their education?
- Can children provide insights into school culture?
- Do children sometimes use behaviour as a way to exert influence?
- How important to children is a sense of 'belonging'?
- How do 'typically-developing' children view inclusive education?
- What are the possible roles of 'buddying'?

What are children's memories of their education?

Memories of schooling are important both for their impact on the individuals who recollect them, our understanding of the children's experience of schooling and also for their role in providing data for future policy development. Indeed, one of the drivers for the move away from segregated provision for children with disabilities has been the advocacy of those who were educated in that way. The term 'special school survivor' has been used and is indicative of the strength of feeling which exists on the subject. Duffell quotes from the writing of a woman who attended a 'less socially prestigious boarding school'. 'I am a Special Boarding School Survivor. I was at this special school for ten years and absolutely hated it. I am lucky that

I survived – I know of four eighteen years olds who have ended up being detained under the Mental Health Act in a psychiatric hospital from my residential school' (2000, 58).

This is a stark rebuttal of the description of school as 'the best days in your life'. Others who attended special schools have written about their sense of isolation from their peers, how their educational experiences differed from those of their peers and the limitations that they felt were imposed on them by the schools.

Given that inclusive education is both an aim in itself and a way in which to promote a more inclusive society, it seems pertinent to listen to what children have to say as they reflect back on their experiences in provision of education. In Chapter 2, we distinguished between segregated, integrated and inclusive provision. In many countries, these three types of provision are present although the balance varies across and within countries. There is a discussion of the meaning of these terms later in this chapter. However a summary is provided now to set the scene. The expectation in integrated provision is that the children being 'integrated' will adjust to an unaltered school. They can be present if the school can continue without changing. In inclusive education, the schools make changes to recognize the characteristics of the children. The shift towards inclusive education was linked by some to the debate about rights. However, it is appropriate to explore the perceptions of those who have experienced the system. Doing so is challenging because of the variation in education systems between different countries and the evolution of those systems. In light of this, the following examples of research need to be understood within particular geographical contexts, and also with the evolution of inclusive education in mind.

Moriña Díez (2010) thought that hearing the views of children within education is important. She talked to young disabled people about their experiences of education in Spain, a country that espouses inclusion but where the reality may be nearer to integration. Her interest was in the 'barriers and aids' to inclusion.

Example of research: Barriers and aids to inclusion

Moriña Díez argues that 'A close correlation can be found linking social and educational exclusion – the former being more general and the latter more specific' (2010,164). She notes the continuum 'spanning the gap between the lack of access to education and full inclusion' (2010, 164). Integration, in her view, was on that continuum with 'the principle aim of reintegrating an individual or group of individuals who have previously been excluded from the "normal life of school" or in the community at large – the presumption being, of course, that the individual or group in question will have to adapt to the given context without challenging existing societal preconceptions and practices' (2010, 164).

This example of research was part of a larger study of the construction of social exclusion amongst 18–25-year-olds, and involved a subset of nine people with disabilities. Six were between twenty-two and twenty-five years old, and three were between ten and twenty. 'All were people with intellectual, speech and/or hearing, sight or movement-related disabilities' (2010, 166). A personal narrative-based research methodology was adopted. Moriña Díez was eager to stress that 'It is not our objective here to extrapolate the opinions and perceptions expressed by the young people we interviewed. The aim, therefore, was not for their voices to speak for others but rather that … their testimony shed light on the barriers and aids the nine participants encountered along the way' (2010, 166–7). The findings were grouped around five themes, which are explained below using extracts from the research.

'Parallel' school tracks?

> e.g. These children have had to face and adapt to constant
> change: attending an integrated school while simultaneously
> attending support classrooms; changing schools two or
> more time while in the same educational phase; trying to
> harmonise mainstream education with special educational
> needs (SEN) environment.
>
> (2010, 167)

'Normal' educational settings which segregate?

> e.g. One of the most controversial issues appearing over
> and over in the stories these young people told was the
> case of a disabled student who was placed in a mainstream
> 'integrated' educational environment and, as a result, was
> doomed to experience the pain and ostracism of segregation.
>
> (2010, 167)

'Special' educational contexts that bring about disabled students' first experiences in integration? The participants had experience of special environments like the support classroom:

> [T]he the kinds of support the young people in our study have received are contradictory in nature. On the one hand, support environments are spaces for recognition, help and building self-esteem, yet on the other they can be one more cog in the wheel that leads to labelling and marginalisation.
>
> (2010, 169)

A social life limited to 'special contexts'?

> [T[he behaviour patterns and attitudes prevalent among their peers in mainstream environments had done anything but contribute to more widespread acceptance and inclusion in the classroom. On the contrary, the available data indicates that peer behaviour patterns have spurred exclusion in mainstream classrooms.
>
> (2010, 169–70)

A learning paradigm which fails to guarantee equal opportunities for active participation and a sense of belonging for all?

> Reference has been made to problems with social relationships, but the narrative suggested that these extended to academic relationships with peers.

> Further, these students 'spoke of the virtually non-existent contribution to social and academic inclusion on the part of teachers'.
>
> (2010, 171)

This summary seems biased towards the barriers, which is consistent with the author's comment that the participants 'perceived more barriers than boons' (2010, 173). Their views about special schools were relatively positive, and their 'first fledgling friendships and social networks sprouted and grew there, where they felt protected, as equals' (2010, 173). Moriña Díez argues that 'schools should not become accomplices to exclusive educational practice' (2010, 173) and argues for a 'restructuring of the way we think about teaching and learning' (2010, 173).

Activity 1
In the section on 'A social life limited to special context', Moriña

Díez wrote about peer behaviour. She commented that 'this class of "peer-triggered" barriers is by far the most painful in a long line of hurdles which special needs students struggle to overcome, as it regulates opportunities for social interaction in the classroom and school environments to the sidelines and in effect exiles SEN students to the shadows' (2010, 170).

In this quotation Moriña Díez used powerful language (e.g. painful, hurdle, struggle, sidelines, exiles).

1 Reread the quotations from the children and consider the links between how they expressed themselves and Moriña Díez's article.
2 In your view, what contribution does analysing the children's language make to prompting a reconsideration of the experiences of pupils?
3 What do you think the relationship is between the use of language and the promotion of inclusive education? (Hint: refer back to the work of Slee in Chapter 2 who used the notion of 'rebranding'.)

Activity 2

The data was based on narratives collected a considerable time after the young people had left school. In your view, what are the potential issues in terms of the reliability of such data? (Hint: you could consider whether the accounts can be corroborated, how individuals may wish to justify their current position, or whether memories are selective.)

Can children provide insights into school culture?

The research example above has alerted us to the experiences of some children at a particular point in time in a particular educational system, and the focus is restricted to learners with disabilities. However, it does provide a striking commentary on their experiences and the potency of the culture of the schools. In the wider literature about inclusive education, a link has been made to school culture. For example, the *Index for Inclusion: Developing Learning and Participation in Schools* (Booth and Ainscow, 2011), now in its third edition, is a self-review tool for schools which was developed by the Centre for Studies on Inclusive Education (CSIE). There is encouragement for a range of stakeholders (e.g. teachers, parents and pupils) to be involved in the review process.

Versions of the *Index for Inclusion* have been used in multiple international settings – in forty countries in 2011. It is divided into three sections: cultures, policies and practices. It encourages schools to take into account the views of children. More recently Thomas (2013), in an article entitled 'A Review of Thinking and Research about Inclusive Education Policy, with Suggestions for a New Kind of Inclusive Thinking', (re)asserted that there are new models of learning that stress the centrality of community, with an emphasis on meaning, narrative and apprenticeship – in short, the context and culture for learning.

It therefore seems important to consider children's views about the culture of their schools whilst they are (or, in some cases, should be) attending them. Reference has been made to the *Index for Inclusion*, which affords an opportunity for pupils to express views about school culture as part of a wider process of data collection. There is also work on a more focused approach. For instance, Aldridge and Ala'l from Australia report on developing and validating the What's happening in this school? (WHITS) questionnaire. This will 'assess school climate in terms of students' perception of the degree to which they feel welcome and connected, together with a scale to assess student end perceptions of bullying' (2013, 47).

These initiatives have value, but the next example of research serves as a cautionary note about adopting an over-simplistic approach to school culture. Children may experience sub-cultures within schools, sometimes associated with subject boundaries. As a consequence they may behave rather differently in some settings and through their actions demonstrate their appreciation of cultural differences within a single school.

Example of research: Disaffected learners and school musical culture

Rusinek sought to provide evidence that arts education has 'a potential to engage disaffected learners, empowering them and helping them to overcome the danger of educational and social disadvantage and exclusion' (2008, 10). She undertook research in a secondary school in Spain's Valencia region to explore this issue, and addressed three questions:

- What were the characteristics of the music teaching strategies that proved to be effective with disaffected learners?
- How did the teacher's beliefs, musical knowledge and skills shape those teaching strategies, in interaction with the institutional and cultural contexts?
- Why did the group of disaffected learners decide to make efforts to attain musical goals?

Rusinek used a range of data collection methods, including non-participant observations of lessons and concerts, analysis of written material, non-structured interviews and individual and group video stimulated interviews. These were used with a class (n=24) with behavioural and learning problems; they had received '130 written reprimands throughout the year for misbehaving, both individually and collectively' (2008, 11). Despite this, her observations of the students in music led her to state that they 'did not seem to belong to [a] group of rebellious students but to a group of young people wanting to emulate a professional orchestra' (2008, 12).

In analysing the situation, the head of studies and the assistant to the head teacher highlighted factors such as:

- the approach was motivating;
- there was a shared, short-term goal (a concert);
- students had a sense of learner agency;
- there was collaboration and peer-learning;
- there was a sense of responsibility;
- a sense of responsibility was fostered.

Rusinek asserted that the lessons 'worked at the intersection between school and wind band etiquettes, where musical instructions were seasoned with classroom management comments' (2008, 18).

She concluded by stating: 'If learning disaffection may result in social exclusion then there is a lesson to be learnt from this case. The opportunity for inclusion can start in schools, and music educators can do a lot for those young people who are running the risk of a life of failure' (2008, 20).

Reflections on the research
Rusinek regards training for teachers as deficient, and in relation to Spain states that 'the current postgraduate training system was designed in the 1970s for an educational context where young

people complied obediently with adults' instructions' (2008, 10). This is a theme that we will return to in the next chapter.

She (and the children) made links between school-based activities and the 'etiquettes' in musical activities beyond the school.

Activity 1

Consider the following quotation from Rusinek's article:

> The traditional behaviour patterns of students complying obediently with teachers' instructions still survive in the regulations but are not necessarily observed, and this is possible because the interaction between young people and adults has changed faster than our society is able to admit.
>
> (2008, 12)

What links are there between this observation and the earlier discussion about the evolving views of childhood? (Hint: look back at Chapter 3.)

Activity 2

In the above study, the school administrators acknowledge the efficacy of the music teacher's approach but 'admitted their scepticism about the possibility that other teachers would transfer similar approaches to their own teaching practices' (2008, 17). The teachers referred to were using strategies which (on the basis of the number of written reprimands issued) appeared to be unsuccessful in engaging students in teaching and learning. Taking into account this evidence, how could pupil perspectives be used to influence practices more widely? (Hint: reread the example of research 'The role of student researchers in the process of curriculum development' Leat and Reid (2012) in Chapter 6 and the interview with the researchers.)

Do children sometimes use behaviour as a way to exert influence?

Rusinek's article noted that the context 'where young people complied obediently with adults' instructions … does not exist any more' (Rusinek, 2008, 10). This is not unique to Spain. Historical models of the teacher–child relationship are being challenged. The judgements about 'disaffection' made by teachers may be understood as part of that discourse. But children may have experienced or observed disaffection resulting in them also forming views about it. Hartas, in England, acknowledged that there are multiple meanings to participation and set out to 're-examine disaffection through young people's self-identified needs regarding participation, education and training' (2011, 104). This is the focus of the next example of research.

Example of research: Is disaffection another way of having a voice?

Hartas, together with three members of college staff, worked with eighteen students who presented a range of challenges to staff 'due to their perceived limited participation in learning and school life, lack of aspirations and motivations, and their predicted "problematic" transition to training and future employment' (2011, 105). The children were not involved in lessons for three consecutive days whilst they took part in a public forum. During Day 1, they agreed the issues they considered important using prompts such as: 'What makes a good teacher?'; 'Why do you go to school?'; 'If not school, then what?' and 'What do you wish for?'.

The results were grouped around the following themes:

- constraints to participation;
- constraints to learning and pastoral support;
- school-to-training transition.

The discussion opens with a reminder of the aim of the study which was 'two-fold'; 'to offer a public form for a group of young people who were described as being disaffected, … to understand disaffection' (2011, 111). These two themes are reflected in the sub-headings used in the discussion.

A hybridized form of participation, in which comments included:

- challenges to the schools efforts to normalize participation through systems such as student councils;
- assertions that the provisions in schools did not meet the young people's perceived needs;
- assertions that inadequate attention was given to the interaction between participation and systemic barriers;
- contesting 'a form of ephemeral and tokenistic participation and inclusion, which, in their view, the school promoted' (2011, 112).

Deconstructing disaffection, in which comments included:

- the suggestion that 'disaffection may be a response to feelings of dissatisfaction with what the school offers them, of not fitting into the mainstream models of education and training' (2011, 113);
- the suggestion that inclusion needs to be flexible in order for it to be able to recognize difference between people;
- the view that systemic constraints can divert attention, so that disaffection is viewed as related to the individual.

Hartas states that:

The young people's accounts challenged the view that any form of participation can sustain social inclusion, and problematized disaffection as an ascribed identity. The young people contested a form of ephemeral and tokenistic participation and inclusion, which in their view, the school promoted. They felt that this form of participation was irrelevant to their life experiences and did not offer appropriate channels for their voices to be genuinely listened to.

(2011, 112)

Reflections on the research

This research helps to reframe disaffection away from being associated with blaming young people towards understanding the messages that children are seeking to convey. Rather than a narrow focus on children's behaviour, attention also needs to be given to the context including whether that is a contributory factor. Using this lens, you should reread the example of research about music lessons.

Activity 1

Hartas comments that 'young people contested a form of ephemeral and tokenistic participation and inclusion, which in their view, the school promoted' (2011, 112).

1 Return to Chapter 2 on inclusive education. Does that help you to understand the children's critique of their experience of inclusion?
2 Return to Chapter 3 on participation. Does that help you to understand the children's critique their experience of participation?

Activity 2

The students suggest that inclusion should be flexible. In what dimensions could it be flexible? (You may wish to think about what other articles have suggested (e.g. working individually or with peers, education within or beyond school.)

How important to children is a sense of 'belonging'?

The previous section explored children's relationship with schools in terms of disaffection. At the other end of the spectrum, the relationship could be associated with a range of terms, including well-being. For instance, the definition of an educationally inclusive school cited in Chapter 2 made reference to '[the] well-being of every young person' (OfSTED, 2000, 7). That is the focus of this section, which moves from international comparisons of well-being (based on adult views of the term) to children's understandings of the term – including notions of belonging.

Since the publication of the UNCRC, there have been various relevant international reports including *The State of the World's Children 2011: Adolescence – An Age of Opportunity* (UNICEF, 2011) and *Child Poverty in Perspective: An Overview of Child Well-Being in Rich Countries: A Comprehensive Assessment of the Lives and Well-Being of Children and Adolescents in the Economically Advanced Nations* (UNICEF, 2007). UNICEF also reports on the well-being of children. In 2013, UNICEF published a report on child well-being in the twenty-nine most advanced countries (http://www.unicef-irc.org/Report-Card-11). This provides a ranking of countries at the beginning and end of the decade.

The overall ranking of each country is based on the average score for the five dimensions. The UK was ranked sixteenth. To set that in context, the data for the UK, the Netherlands and the USA are set out in Table 7.1, with the columns representing the rankings. The rankings in the table are based on each country's average rank in four dimensions of child well-being

Table 7.1 Ranking of pupils' well-being in developed countries at the start and end of the decade

Country	Early 2000s	Late 2000s	Change in ranking
Netherlands	3	1	+2
Spain	13	18	−5
UK	20	16	+4
USA	20	21	−1

Source: Based on UNICEF, 2013, 44

– material well-being, health, education and behaviours and risks – for which comparable data are available towards the beginning and end of the first decade of the 2000s.

There is also a ranking of children's relationships with peers and parents.

Activity

The data in the rankings is a measure of well-being but a somewhat crude one.

1 Why do you think it might be regarded as 'crude'?
2 If it is crude, why do you think it is gathered and disseminated?
3 What are the risks and opportunities involved in comparing countries?
4 What evidence do you think is missing?

The next example of research complements the UNICEF report in three ways. First, it narrows the focus to education. Second, it gives specific attention to children with disabilities. Finally, it explores children's understanding of the term 'well-being'.

Example of research: To feel belonged

In Australia, a group of researchers have probed 'the meaning of well-being for children and youth with disabilities from their perspectives' (Foley et al., 2012, 375). The study involved twenty participants with a range of disabilities including: cerebral palsy (n=6); autism/Asperger's syndrome (n=7); Down syndrome (n=3); mild to moderate intellectual disability (n=3); and vision impairment (n=1). The data was gathered through two focus groups and an interview with the boy with visual impairment.

Having accessed the relevant academic literature, the researchers sought to 'translate' the ideas into child-friendly language. The research team rejected the term 'happy life' since it is 'emotionally focused and limited in scope' (2012, 378). They adopted the term 'good life' which allowed the participants to interpret it for themselves. They found that 'Six themes of the meaning of wellbeing emerged from the data describing participation. These themes include: the

importance of good friends, family factors, anxiety related to performance at school, coping strategies/resilience, personal growth and
development' (2012, 379).

The researchers suggested that these themes can be further
conceptualized into an overall picture of well-being from the young
person's perspective (2012, 386). They associated that term with
'feelings of being supported, of being included and respected,
of being viewed as valued and capable, and of having feelings of
respect and self-esteem' (2012, 386).

In their conclusion, the researchers made a comparison between
the understandings of well-being in their findings and those evident
in *Indicators of Health and Well-being for Children and Young People
with Disabilities: Mapping the Terrain and Proposing a Human Rights
Approach* (Llewellyn, 2012). They commented that there was an
overlap between the views in that document, which was derived
from UN policies, and the views of the children who participated in
their study. They noted, however, that 'there were a number of ideas
and factors raised by the children which were not reflected within the
wellbeing indicators set developed in the above report' (2012, 388).

These included (but weren't restricted to) the children having
opportunities for showing respect 'in the form of *helping others*'
(2012, 388). Reciprocal relationships is absent from other measures
of well-being. Coping strategies were seen by these respondents
to be important but are also absent from other measures. Foley et
al. grouped these together with feeling valuable and useful, body
image and self-esteem into 'an overarching theme of autonomy'.
The research by Foley et al. also highlighted the roles played by
siblings – a theme absent from adult-centric research.

Reflections on the research
Inclusive research which was considered in Chapter 4 emphasizes
the need to focus on issues that matter to the individuals rather than
ones selected by others. Research into the broad theme of well-
being might have met this criterion, but this research suggests that
we need to guard against assuming that adults and children have
shared definitions of the terms.

Activity 1
These researchers sought to use more accessible terminology in
their research. What do you think are the challenges in doing this?
(Hint: You may find it helpful to look at the resources developed in
Wales about UNCRC which were aimed at children, http://www.

uncrcletsgetitright.co.uk. Think about the strengths and limitations of that approach.)

Activity 2

Arguably a potential value of the use of the adult definition of well-being is that it has been used and is, at least partly, established. What are the challenges and opportunities of changing the definition in the light of children's perspectives?

Interview with Kitty Foley about the 'To feel belonged' research

Kitty Foley, Department of Developmental Disability Neuropsychiatry, University of New South Wales

> *Sue Pearson*: In response to the diverse resources of the participants, you gathered data in different formats (including the groups, one-to-one interviews, writing list, drawings and participants writing and drawing). During the analysis phase did this raise any issues for you, the researchers?
>
> *Kitty Foley*: In approaching this research question, we knew we would be incorporating children with different skills and levels of abilities. Understanding the subjective experience of well-being requires consulting the individuals themselves, no matter their level of ability. It is the researcher's responsibility to adjust methodology in order to provide the best opportunities for participants of all levels to be involved and to express their views.
>
> During the analysis of data, the different forms of data collection were considered while interpreting the data and identifying emergent themes. The source of the data associated with each transcript (e.g. interview or focus group) and observer notes were kept together to allow the researcher to interpret data in context. Drawings from the focus groups were displayed in view of the researcher during analysis, as well as notes about what was drawn. Each piece of data was treated as an expression of a view from the child, whether this be a drawing, a comment in an interview or a statement in a focus group. Due to the differences in preferences in communication style and abilities, one form of expression was not valued more or less than another form of expression. We then analysed the data using thematic analysis. It was important to member

check the findings with the participants, due to the novel approach to data collection and analysis. The process was followed and participants were able to confirm that the findings were in alignment with their opinions and views.

Sue Pearson: If, in the future, you were to repeat this research or something similar is there anything you would do differently?

Kitty Foley: If we were to repeat this research I would aim for a larger sample, to perhaps attempt to identify differences and similarities on the meaning of well-being from the perspectives of children with intellectual and physical disabilities, and perhaps children with disabilities of different ages. Additionally, it would be great to have further explored the credibility of our analysis procedures.

I also would like to try more 'inclusive practice' research strategies by including a reference group of children during the analysis phase. Some other researchers are working with adults with disabilities at every stage of the research project. It would be fantastic to try this with children in a study such as this one.

Translation of research findings into the 'real world' is also a passion of mine. We attempted to do this by mapping the findings on to indicators identified in a report by the Australian Research Alliance for Children and Youth entitled *Child Indicators of Wellbeing and Children with Disabilities: Mapping the Terrains.* We also developed a brief accessible summary of the findings which would be accessible to families and young people with disabilities.

How do 'typically-developing' children view inclusive education?

Some of the previous examples of research have portrayed rather negative accounts of the relationship between children with different resources and their peers, although the last one highlighted reciprocity. Given that inclusion is about all children, it is imperative that attention is also given to the views of all children. A minority have done this whilst some researchers have focused on particular groups (e.g. children with autism), an approach which provides a partial perspective. Another approach is to consider the perspectives of what have been termed 'typically-developing' children. 'Typical development' is a problematic concept since there are differences in the development of all children. Think, for example, about children learning to walk. It is recognized that this happens at different ages but if it is very delayed it may be a source of concern. Therefore, 'typical development' can be understood to refer to children where no concerns have been expressed about their development.

The following example of research (Bates et al., 2014) provides insights into those views, although the focus was restricted to views about the inclusion of pupils with SEN. It is a review of the existing research on this subject. Strict criteria were applied in terms of the methodological quality of the studies included, which reduced the large number of studies that might have been included to a much smaller number. In addition to the substantive findings, that process should help you to critique research related to inclusive education. The four authors, Bates, McCafferty, Quayle and McKenzie, are based in departments linked to psychology; namely clinical psychology, clinical and health psychology and psychology. This illustrates that although inclusive education is often viewed through the disciplinary lens of sociology or education, it is also a focus for other groups. Furthermore it provides another opportunity to consider the language used. The title of the research article is 'Disability and rehabilitation'. You might want to think about the messages conveyed by those terms using the discussion about the medical, the social and the ecological models.

Example of research: 'Typically-developing' students' views and experiences of inclusive education

In their introduction to this article, Bates et al. set out their appraisal of the current situation and its implications: 'In summary, inclusive education is a central, non-optional aspect of the European education system, but is beset with debates that are not easily resolved. Indeed, some argue that it is beyond a consensual definition and that a more fruitful approach is to figure out how to make it work by eliciting the views of key stakeholders' (2014, 1).

This sets a problematic context within which to analyse and synthesize the published material related to the views of 'typically-developing' (TD) students. That was identified through an electronic keyword search, through 'hand-searching journals that had previously published qualitative studies', and through 'a "snowballing" technique, whereby reference lists from key articles were inspected for additional studies' (2014, 2). The authors set clear inclusion criteria:

> (a) Studies are published in English in a peer-reviewed journal, and report primary data.
> (b) Studies examine the views and/or experience of inclusive education, from the perspective of students aged 5–18 years.
> (c) Participants include at least a sub-group of "typically-developing" students (i.e. not having SEN or international equivalents).
> (d) Participants include at least a sub-group of students who are attending "inclusive" school (i.e. where peers with SENs are taught in mainstream classes for a proportion of the syllabus), and/or students must have some degree of contact with SEN peers.
>
> (2014, 2)

Through a process of applying criteria, the original number of articles identified (n=269) was reduced to fourteen, which were then assessed for methodological quality. The authors judged that three were of good quality, seven were of medium quality and four were of poor quality – but all were retained in the study. The findings of the review were presented under three headings, each with sub-headings:

- Attitudes to peers;
  - Befriending peers;
  - Bullying SEN peers;
  - Befriending SEN peers;
  - Poor disability awareness;
  - [The role of] contact in mediating attitudes.
- Views of inclusive education;
  - Students' rationale for inclusive education;
  - Students' experiences of inclusive education.
- Students' ideas for improving inclusive education;
  - Educate students about inclusive education'
  - Teacher training;
  - Increase opportunities for contact.

The concluding paragraph provides a summary of the findings:

> The field of IE [Inclusive Education] is fraught with conflict and debate. Findings from the present review mirror these

tensions: the phrases TD students used to describe IE were alternately filled with confusions, fearfulness, ambivalence and hope. Reading across the 14 studies, students' comments also belied a lack of knowledge about IE or disabilities; and yet, they yearned to fill these gaps, calling for teaching on IE to be written into the curriculum. Clearly, we should pay more attention to what TD students have to say about IE, for their sake and for the sake of their peers.

(2014, 1937)

Activity 1

There was variation in the quality of the research in this area. The judgements were based on the ten questions in one of the checklists which are part of the Critical Skills Appraisal Programme. These can be found at http://www.casp-uk.net/#!checklists/cb36. You should access the one related to qualitative research. (Please note: these questions have been updated and are worded slightly differently to those used in the research.) Please select any article cited in this book that uses a qualitative approach and use the questions to rate it. You might like to start off by considering:

- Question 1 'Was there a clear statement of the research aims?'
- Question 6 'Has the relationship between the researcher and the participants been adequately considered?'
- Question 9 'Is there a clear statement of the findings?'

Remember that some of the research examples are participatory so you need to think about the researcher/participant relationship and about who should have access to the findings.

Activity 2

The authors suggested asking the key stakeholders. Who do you view as the 'key stakeholders' in inclusive education? (Hint: you may find it helpful to think about this at classroom, school and system levels and consider whether the answers are consistent.)

What are the possible roles of 'buddying'?

We have considered the views of children with different resources and their peers. This section examines a structured way in which to encourage them to work together. Buddying systems are where two individuals work together so they can support and monitor each other. There are multiple examples of educational settings providing 'buddies' to incoming or vulnerable individuals. They have also been used as part of the curriculum provision (e.g. in relation to literacy http://www.literacytrust.org.uk/assets/0000/7718/Pupil_to_pupil_buddying_top_tips.pdf). There have also been initiatives based on buddying beyond the formal education system. 'Best Buddies' is an international organization which is 'dedicated to establishing a global volunteer movement that creates opportunities for one-to-one friendships, integrated employment and leadership development for people with intellectual and developmental disabilities (IDD)' (http://www.bestbuddies.org).

The next example of research is concerned with buddying partnerships to access the views of young children. It returns us to the theme of participation considered in Chapter 3, since it is concerned with all children regardless of age having a right to have their views heard. It also links back to Lundy's analysis of the UNCRC in terms of the right of children to have their views given due weight, insofar as they would be contributing 'towards the creation of an information DVD that would help teachers and parents understand the factors that influence children's engagement with reading' (Levy and Thompson, 2015, 137). It also links to Article 5 of UNCRC related to appropriate direction and guidance. Reference is made in the UNCRC to adults providing this but in this instance the support is from older peers.

The focus in the account of the research is on the methodology employed, not the substantive findings.

Example of research: Creating buddying partnerships

Boys' engagement with and achievement in reading has been a matter of ongoing debate. Levy and Thompson's research was concerned with understanding '5- and 6-year-old boys' attitudes towards reading, including factors that promote their engagement with reading and factors that put them off' (2015, 141).

A secondary school was contacted to identify twelve boys with 'core' abilities in English. Three feeder primary schools were contacted and each was asked to identify four pupils with 'core' ability in literacy. Dyads were then formed where the possible older partner had attended the current school of the younger pupil. The research activity is set out in Table 7.2.

Table 7.2 Research activities

Research event	Location	Participants	Purpose of event
Meeting with 11- and 12-year-olds	Secondary school	All 11- and 12-year-old boys (with teachers)	Explain project to 11- and 12-year-olds. Invite suggestions for activities to include at Introductory Event and in the buddy sessions. Gain consent from these boys.
Introductory event	Secondary school	All boys (with teachers and some parents)	Introduce children to each other and establish pairs. Range of activities (e.g. treasure hunt, dressing up) to help the children to get to know each other. Gain consent from 5- and 6-year-old boys.
First buddy session	Three primary schools	Four dyads in each session (with teachers)	Develop relationship within each pair: 5 and 6-year-olds learn to use (flip) cameras. All children gain background information about each other. Plan the DVD.
Second buddy session	Three primary schools	Four dyads in each session (with teachers)	Focus on film-making using flip cameras.
Celebration event	University research centre	All boys (with teachers, parents, university staff and students)	Completed DVD shown to all children, teachers and attending parents.

Source: Based on Levy and Thompson, 2015, 142

The authors suggested that, based on the activities and their observations, 'it became increasingly evident that this participatory technique depended on the relationship that was built between the young and older children' (2015, 143). They structured their discussion of this around three themes:

- shared understandings;
- creating comfortable environments;
- communication strategies.

Reflections on the research

This is a useful example of how the approaches, in this case buddying, can be applied in novel ways.

Activity 1

In previous examples of research, several research tools have been illustrated. Levy and Thompson cite Waller and Bitou, who asserted that there 'may be an assumption that the tools themselves somehow automatically enable participation. The key message from the literature is that it is the research design and relationships that confer real participation and engagement' (Waller and Bitou, 2011, 12).

We have also noted that participatory research tends to take more time than traditional approaches. Think about the balance between the benefits of participatory approaches and the resources involved in implementing it. (You may wish to refer to Table 7.2 and the purpose of the five research events.)

Activity 2

In your view, do you think that using research buddies aligns with the principles of inclusive research? Can you make links to any of the Articles in the UNCRC? (Hint: revisit Chapter 3 on Children's Participation.)

Chapter activities

The following activities are designed to help reflect back on some of the key concerns over the chapter as a whole.

Activity 1

Look through the chapter and its use of the concept of a 'school culture'.

1 What does the chapter say about the nature of such cultures and their relationships to inclusion?

2 How does the chapter's analysis relate to your own experiences and ideas about school culture and inclusion?

3 What can you take from the review of this aspect of educational theory and life in terms of how adults can contribute to such cultures?

Activity 2

The chapter quotes Thomas's assertion that there are 'new models of learning that stress the centrality of community, with an emphasis on meaning, narrative, and apprenticeship' (2013, 486).

1 Look through the chapter and try and identify examples of 'community' in relation to each of the following, or of interaction between the three elements:
   - meaning;
   - narrative;
   - apprenticeship.

2 What are the strengths and limitations of understanding 'community' through the lens of the three areas Thomas suggests?

Summary

This chapter has:

- reiterated that across countries, there are variations in the education systems and the evolution of inclusion;
- suggested that the insights of ex-pupils are valuable;
- associated inclusion with school culture and children's sense of belonging;
- reflected on how all pupils have views on inclusive education;
- illustrated that, in the context of research, productive relationships can exist between pupils.

Further reading

Nind, M., S. Benjamin, K. Sheehy, J. Collins and K. Hall (2004).
    'Methodological Challenges in Researching Inclusive School Cultures'.
    Educational Review 56 (3): 259–70.
This article is concerned with 'the challenges of who decides that a school is inclusive and worthy of attention in an inclusion study; how we look for and recognize inclusive school cultures; how much we do and should change things that we find; and how to put children and their experiences at the centre of our research' (2004, 259).

Sutton, L. and Joseph Rowntree Foundation (2007). *A Child's-eye View of
    Social Difference.* York: Joseph Rowntree Foundation.
This report explored children's own views, using their terms, of social differences. The study was conducted with forty-two children aged between eight and thirteen. Of these, nine were from a disadvantaged housing estate and twenty-three attended a fee-paying independent school.

A participatory approach was used, which enabled the children to lead the research focus. The report compared the similarities and differences between the findings from the two groups and included a section on education. See http://www.jrf.org.uk/publications/childs-eye-view-social-difference.

Woolley, H., M. Armitage, J. C. Bishop, M. Curtis and J. Ginsborg (2005).
    Inclusion of Disabled Children in Primary School Playgrounds. London:
    National Children's Bureau.
Relatively little attention has been paid to the social space in schools known as 'the playground'. This research was based in six primary schools in Yorkshire. The data came from small focus-group discussions with the children and a mapping exercise alongside observations of the playground and interviews with the teacher. There is a summary of the research at: http://www.jrf.org.uk/sites/files/jrf/0016.pdf which also gives details of the full report.

Research details

Barriers and aids to inclusion

This is based on data gathered in Spain from young people as they reflected on their earlier experiences of education.

Moriña Díez, A. (2010). 'School Memories of Young People with Disabilities:

an Analysis of Barriers and Aids to Inclusion'. *Disability & Society* 25 (2): 163–75.

Disaffected learners and school musical culture

This article explored data gathered in Spain, and considered why some adolescents 'fail in all other subjects but can be engaged in music learning'.

Rusinek, G. (2008). 'Disaffected Learners and School Musical Culture: An Opportunity for Inclusion'. *Research Studies in Music Education* 30 (1): 9–23.

Is disaffection another way of having a voice?

This research invited us to reframe our understanding of disaffection towards seeing it as a way in which children are trying to communicate messages to us.

Hartas, D. (2011). 'Young People's Participation: Is Disaffection Another Way of Having a Voice?' *Educational Psychology in Practice* 27 (2): 103–15.

To feel belonged

This Australian research explored how children understand well-being, and identified the commonalities and differences with other published approaches.

Foley, K. R., S. Girdler, A. M. Blackmore, M. O'Donnell, R. Glauert, H. Leonard and G. Llewellyn (2012). 'To Feel Belonged: The Voices of Children and Youth with Disabilities on the Meaning of Wellbeing'. *Child Indicators Research* 5 (2): 375–91.

Typically-developing students' views and experiences of inclusive education

To be inclusive we need to hear all voices, including those who are perceived to be developing in line with expectations. Whilst many of the articles have drawn on labelled groups or all children, this is focused on the group identified as 'typically-developing'.

Bates, H., A. McCafferty, E. Quayle and K. McKenzie (2014). 'Review: Typically-developing Students' Views and Experiences of Inclusive Education'. *Disability and Rehabilitation* 37 (21): 1929–39.

Creating buddying partnerships

Buddying is a relatively common approach which is seen as having benefits both for the buddied and the buddy. In the examples, buddying is used within the context of research. It links to the ideas developed in Chapter 3 on inclusive research by looking at a supportive approach with benefits to both children.

Levy, R. and P. Thompson (2015). 'Creating "Buddy Partnerships" with 5- and 11-year-old Boys: A Methodological Approach to Conducting Participatory Research with Young Children'. *Journal of Early Childhood Research* 13 (2): 137–49.

8

Themes across Inclusive Education, Participation and Inclusive Research

Introduction and key questions

The material within this book has been neatly divided into chapters and sections, each with a heading and sub-headings that indicate their content. It may therefore be possible to read this book by selectively dipping into an individual chapter or section. However, in a sense this misses the point, for two reasons. One of these is a matter of principle, and the other is a matter of pragmatism.

The text is about (inclusive) education and pupils' perspectives. The perspectives of individual pupils are formed through their linked experiences; specific views are part of an individual's whole experience, and are not compartmentalized. McCoy and Banks asserted the need to simultaneously examine 'the role of academic and social relations in shaping the engagement of children with SEN' (2012, 81). Their article was entitled 'Simply Academic? Why Children with Special Educational Needs Don't Like School'. The data they used came from 'the first wave of *Growing Up in Ireland,* the national longitudinal study of children in Ireland involving 8578 children' (2012, 85). The representativeness is relatively high, since this equates to one in seven of the nine-year-old children in Ireland. The study 'draws on multiple perspectives, particularly the voice of the child' (2012, 85). McCoy and Banks concluded that 'this paper represents an important advance in our understanding of how children with SEN fare in mainstream settings and how both academic engagement and social/peer relations play a central role in children's school experiences' (2012, 94).

This quotation makes reference to placement and to academic and social facts. The article also makes reference to enjoyment, engagement, friendship, particular curriculum subjects and homework. In other words, it encapsulates many of the ideas in this book and explores some of the relationships between the factors.

Articles such as this act as reminders that children's experience is holistic and not linked exclusively to placement, pedagogical and social factors. This book has divided those topics into separate chapters with limited explicit cross-referencing. To gain a rounded understanding, it is necessary to read beyond the artificially constructed boundaries of the chapters and sections.

In terms of the pragmatic considerations, there have been judgements about which research to identify and select, decisions about which to prioritize as examples of research and which to include as further reading, and choices about where in the text to locate a selected example. In terms of the placement of the examples of research, many could have been summarized slightly differently and thereby made relevant to a different chapter or section. There was intention behind each of the placement decisions, which were in part about developing some coherent themes across this book. The point of this chapter is to help make more visible some of the interconnections that exist. This is done by responding to the following questions:

- What were the challenges in selecting examples of research for inclusion in this book?

- Does stereotyping happen uni-directionally?
- How do children understand 'fairness'?
- Are the methods of data collection needed for working with children different from those used for working with adults?
- Can research be disseminated in more inclusive ways?
- How can schools benefit from the insights of (all) children?
- In what ways can inclusive research and inclusive education, as presented in this book, be linked?

What were the challenges in selecting examples of research for inclusion in this book?

We noted that a consensus about the definition of the term 'inclusive education' has proved elusive. In a similar way, different authors have used the terms 'pupil voice' and 'pupil participation' but have not consistently explained either the choice of terminology or the precise definition. There may be several reasons for these definitional challenges:

- Thinking in these areas is evolving and an ongoing process of refining the definitions is a natural (and positive) process.
- Researchers come from different disciplines, each of which has its own genre. So educationalists are likely to define things in a way that differs from that of lawyers; their purposes and need for specificity are not identical.
- In the case of inclusive education, the focus of attention is not consistent across the definitions. There have been examples where the focus is on children with SEN, in others the attention is on other groups that may be marginalized, and some considered all children.

Activity

1 Different frameworks for understanding which population(s) the term 'inclusion' refers to have been presented (e.g. in Chapter 2 Ainscow's overview of the use of the term in English policy; Cigman's model in Chapter 5). Review these frameworks.

2 Can you map some of the examples of research onto the frameworks?

The challenges of developing a review of existing materials by rigorously applying a set of predetermined criteria is illustrated in the next example of research. In this case, the term 'inclusive education' was used in the 'narrow sense' – restricted to provision for children with disabilities or in need of support. In an article entitled 'Conceptual diversities and empirical shortcomings – a critical analysis of research on inclusive education', Göransson and Nilholm (2014) critically analysed the published research related to inclusive education.

Example of research: A critical analysis of research linked to inclusive education

Göransson and Nilholm argued that whilst the definitional problems of inclusion have been recognized, 'the consequences of this state of affairs have not been analyzed fully' (2014, 265). Their research addressed three questions:

- What definitions of inclusive education are used in research about inclusion?
- What can be learned, conceptually and empirically, about inclusive education from prior reviews?
- Given a strict definition of inclusion, what results emerge from the empirical studies regarding factors that promote inclusion?

With regard to the definition of inclusive education, their analysis suggests that there are 'four qualitative categories of definitions':

A   Placement definition – inclusion as placement of pupils with disabilities/in need of special support in general education classrooms;

B   Specified individualised definition – inclusion as meeting the social/academic needs of pupils with disabilities/pupils in need of special support;

C   General individualised definition – inclusion as meeting the social/academic needs of all pupils;

D   Community definition – inclusion as creation of communities with specific characteristics (which could vary between proposals).

(2014, 268)

They argue that 'categories relate hierarchically to each other in the sense that category D presupposes categories C, B and A, and category C presupposes categories B and A, and so on (2014, 268). They provided examples to illustrate how they were interpreting these categories. This helped to provide an answer to their first research question (What definitions of inclusive education are used in research about inclusion?).

They then searched for relevant examples of research to answer the next two research questions. Their initial step was to review pre-existing reviews and they report on two of them. They then searched the electronic database potentially using four criteria:

> Eligible studies had (1) a research design covering a process over time; (2) indicators of inclusion encompassing both social and academic effects; (3) the indicators for inclusion studied for all or a representative sample of pupils with a separate report of data from children with disabilities/in need of extra support; and (4) data showing that the system studied (school or classrooms) became more inclusive as a consequence of the change.
>
> (2014, 272)

Initially the researchers identified 1,087 potential studies, from which they chose 105 which potentially met their criteria (2014, 273). The material had all been published between 2004 and 2014. Of these, twenty-five were selected for more detailed reading, with five of those rejected since they did not include empirical data. This resulted in just twenty articles remaining. They analysed these in terms of the four criteria identified above. They commented that they 'did not find any studies that met the four criteria' (2014, 273).

In their discussion, they raise a number of concerns two of which were as follows:

> we are quite uneasy with the lack of empirical evidence concerning how communities are to be established, especially in contrast to the abundance of advice about how one should proceed in order to make classrooms into communities.
>
> (2014, 276)

> We would like to coin the term 'tumble-weed referencing' for cases where evidence in referenced studies is weak or non-existent. 'Tumble-weed referencing' is very common in research about inclusive education. This follows from the fact that there is hardly any reliable evidence as regards the factors

that make schools and classrooms more inclusive, yet research is referenced as if such connections have been established.

(2014, 276)

With regards to the definition of inclusive education, they accept the need for plurality but also the need for clarity.

It should be obvious that we are not comfortable with the status of the field. There is a definite need for clarity regarding what is meant by inclusive education, both in studies of inclusive education and in reviews of the field. This does not mean that we advocate a single, common definition; rather, we maintain that the operative definition – whatever that might be in the given context – ought to be clear.

(2014, 276)

In looking for research linked to their Category C, they noted: 'Because we only found one study that reliably and validly identified interventions that make educational environments more inclusive according to definition C, we have not discussed the possibility of generalising across studies' (2014, 277).

Reflections on the research
Their research was limited to children with disabilities or in need of support. It does, however, illustrate some of the challenges in working with published research.

Activity 1
In Chapter 5, you were introduced to another analysis of definitions of inclusion which used two categories (radical, moderate). This chapter categorizes the definitions as A, B, C and D.

1 Compare the two categorizations and look for any similarities.
2 Consider why researchers have produced different definitions.

Activity 2
Göransson and Nilholm comment that 'we did not find any study that met the four criteria' (2014, 273).

1 What is your reaction to the finding in the above study that there were no examples that met the four criteria?
2 This book used a wider literature (i.e. not restricted to special educational needs). Apply their criteria to one or more of the examples of research.

(In the Further Reading section of this chapter, there is an artlicle linked to this Research Example.)

Interpretation of the term 'inclusive education' can extend beyond SEN/ disabilities. It was therefore possible to draw on a wider range of sources in this book. That didn't remove the problems identified above, since researchers have either used varied definitions of 'inclusion/inclusive education', or have failed to define the terms. For the purposes of this book, a relatively pragmatic approach has been adopted to the identification of the literature and the selection of the examples of research:

- The presence of the term 'inclusion' or 'inclusive education' fairness was a selection criteria. Not all the articles were explicit about the definitions of their terminology.
- Given the evolving nature of inclusion/inclusive education and the interest in and emphasis on pupil participation, the balance was towards recently published material.
- Preference was given to articles which, where appropriate, involved children in the research process, although the nature and extent of that involvement varied. It was judged appropriate to use some research that didn't include children. For example, international comparisons of access to education need a different approach.

The acceptance of varied definitions of the terminology does leave the selection open to the criticism that some of the materials don't represent inclusion as understood by a particular reader. Positions about this can be strongly held and emotive. Indeed, Chapter 1 on inclusive education has noted that some find the terms 'inclusion' and 'inclusive education' so unhelpful that they view them as barriers, and they have argued for a different approach.

Furthermore, rigour comes in many forms, and is not simply a process of adherence to a particular definition. That could result in a dichotomization, i.e. 'this fits a definition; this doesn't fit'. Binaries such as that are problematic since they oversimplify the issues and appear to promise that objective judgements are possible. The section in this chapter on stereotypes may help you to think about some of the complexities in having a single criterion.

It is also important to be clear about the purpose of the cited research. It is rarely offered as a blueprint; the three Cs (complexity, contested and contextual) preclude this. Rather, the examples are intended to be provocations; invitations to reflect on issues. The adoption of 'loose' definitions of the terms has allowed for a wide range of perspectives to be included in order to trigger reflection.

Another form of rigour can be to ensure that there is a breadth within the examples. The selection of the material can be designed to ensure that, for example, it illustrates a range of positions, that the research is based on different groupings (including the group of 'all') and embraces diversity in research methodology.

Activity

Select a chapter and analyse the focus of the examples of the research in terms of the geographical location, the pupils involved and the methodology. Is there diversity?

Reflection on what has been provided is only part of the equation. Some of the examples of research have made specific reference to values, whether they are held by the researched or the researchers. However, you, the reader, will have brought your own experiences, values and ideas to this book. Through reading this book, you should have expanded your thinking about the issues. A personal anecdote may help to illustrate this point. As a child, I had the book *The Water-Babies* (Kingsley, 1893) read to me. I then progressed to reading it for myself, and then as an adult I reread it. At that point, what had seemed to be just a 'good story' was transformed. I saw the messages about child exploitation and the cheapness of their lives, the prejudice against particular groups, including Irish and Jewish people, and the role of repentance and penitence. The book hadn't changed; it was the copy I was originally given. It was me who had changed.

Similarly, rereading educational material published many years ago enables it to take on new layers of meaning. Revisiting the original texts by authors such as Bernstein, Bruner and Vygotsky can feel like reading them for the first time. Increasingly, there is evidence of researchers positioning in the sense of knowing something of their backgrounds, their wider interests and their evolving thinking. This was evident in the interviews with researchers (Shier, Ryan, Leat et al. and Foley). The importance of the researchers' backgrounds is illustrated in the next two examples of research. One illustrates that the authors regard their biographies as significant, and the other that prior experiences can result in 'non-traditional' perspectives.

Example of research: The role of biographies

In the book, *Doing Inclusive Education Research* (Allan and Slee, 2008), the second chapter is entitled 'Researching the Researchers'. It opens with the following comment:

> As researchers designing a project, we bring our own personal and intellectual histories. Research is never disinterested or objective. We receive and interpret the world in ways that are shaped by our own individual biography and, naturally enough, have strong views about what a better world would look like and about the role of inclusive education, as each of us understands it, in contributing to that better world.
>
> (2008, 11)

The subsequent section of their book is entitled 'Unpacking our own bags'. It sets the context for unpacking 'Julie's case' and 'Roger's portmanteau'. These are brief accounts of 'the assumptions that they brought to the research' (2008, 12). They are explicitly asserting that research is not value-free.

Activity 1

The quote above asserts that research is 'never objective'. What is your reaction to that view? (Hint: Avoid restricting your thinking about research to the gathering and analysis of data. It also includes processes such designing the questions and dissemination.)

The next researcher, Southwell, illustrates how his biography led him to propose an alternative analysis of a phenomenon. Southwell entitled his article 'Truants on Truancy – a Badness or a Valuable Indicator of Unmet Special Educational Needs?' (2006, 91). He stated that 'Policy and practice to date … tended to be united in locating responsibility for truancy with truants and their families' (2006, 91). He further argued that 'truancy might be more advantageously understood in relation to unmet educational needs. In such an understanding, truancy becomes a valuable indicator rather than an evil or badness' (2006, 91).

Southwell was himself a persistent truant from school and he (along with others) reframed the issues, moving the 'blame' from the truants and their families to defects in schools and policies. He doesn't restrict this approach to the situation of those who have personal experience of truanting: 'Researchers adopt a truantist perspective when their approach is informed by an adopted understanding of truancy as a self-actuated exclusion imposed by defective schools that have failed to meet the special educational needs of truants. Researchers achieve a truantist perspective when truant participants openly and fully include them within it' (2006, 95).

Activity 2

The quotation above refers to the disposition of the researcher and the trust engendered between the researcher and the researched. Are these principles that could be applied more widely? If so, what are the implications for (inclusive) research?

Whilst both of these examples involve adult researchers, they are reminders that the position of the researchers (and the research questions they ask) are not neutral. This book has illustrated that children have topics they would like to research, have ideas about how to conduct the research, have the capacity to be involved in the process (including by contributing to the analysis) and can be involved in research dissemination.

This section has made reference to researchers, those being researched and the readers of research – and to some of the interactions between these people. To pursue this further, our attention will now shift to another recurring theme in this book – that of stereotyping. Is it simply that we associate particular groups with a stereotype, or is something more complex occurring?

Does stereotyping happen uni-directionally?

My anecdote about fiction made reference to prejudice against particular groups, i.e. Irish people and Jewish people. Other examples of stereotyping have been illustrated in this book, including the habit of making links between characteristics and character (Chapter 2), or of viewing children as being passive and without rights. We thus need to think carefully about how we stereotype others. The presence of stereotyping is a constant challenge in work related to inclusion. If a group of children with (name of some shared feature) is selected, then the emphasis is on the homogeneity within the group without a fuller recognition of the heterogeneity within the group. A crude example which illustrates this point is that some research might compare and contrast 'girls' and 'boys'. However, there is diversity within each of those groups. Also, in many instances, there is overlap between the groups. As illustrated above, binary positions are problematic.

Researchers have dealt with this complexity in different ways. Whilst some of the examples of research have referred to particular groups, other research has included all children, thus avoiding any 'them/not them' distinctions. The quote from Southwell in the previous section nudges us to remember that stereotyping is not a unilateral process. We stereotype and are stereotyped. In the article "'If you were the researcher what would you research?": Understanding Children's Perspective on Educational Research in Mongolia and Zambia', the children's initial associations with the term 'researchers' were 'scientific research' and 'white coats' (Morgan and Sengedorj, 2015, 208). How we view others and how they view us involves sensitive and complex interrelations. As a way to consider the issues, the insights of Chimamanda Ngozi Adichie may be useful as she speaks about 'the danger of a single story'.

Example of research: *The Danger of a Single Story*

Chimamanda Ngozi Adichie, the author, was born in Nigeria and initially lived on a university campus. At the age of nineteen, she moved to the USA to study. In this lecture, entitled *The Danger of a Single Story*, she reflects on her life and education in an engaging and insightful manner. You can view it at: http://www.ted.com/talks/chimamanda_adichie_the_danger_of_a_single_story?language=en.

Activity 1
Adichie says, 'Show a people as one thing, and only one thing, and that is what they become'. What are the implications of this for the ways in which we view children and those with different resources? And what could be the implications for how they view researchers?

Activity 2
Having watched this material, return to Chapter 2 (on inclusive education), which makes reference to sub-Saharan Africa. Return also to Chapter 6 (on developing an inclusive curriculum informed

by children's perceptions), which refers to books and resources that represent diversity. Consider these in the light of Adichie's early literacy activities (the blue-eyed children eating apples) and her current ambitions for children's access to literature. How do we avoid what she termed the 'flattening of experience'?

This resource demonstrates how various aspects of an individual's life can be seen as interlinked. That is consistent with the assertion that inclusive education is both about experiences during educational activities and about having a potential impact on society. The longer-term ambitions are about having fairer, more inclusive societies. The concept of 'fairness' and children's understanding of it is another recurrent theme in this book. Reference to 'unfairness' was made by a participant in the research undertaken by Burke and Grosvenor cited in Chapter 1.

How do children understand 'fairness'?

A variety of terms have been used in the preceding chapters, such as 'to be belonged', 'included' and 'participation'. All of these are linked to inclusion. There is a question about whether or not children would understand this term. This is similar to the dilemma faced by other researchers. In Chapter 7, the researchers who studied children's understandings of well-being (Foley et al., 2012) did not use that term, but instead used a term that they hoped would be more meaningful to children. This dilemma also resonates with the two pieces of research cited earlier in this book: *The School I'd Like: Children and Young People's Reflections on an Education for the 21st Century*' (Burke and Grosvenor, 2003) and 'Today's Learning Object is to have a Party: Playing Research with Students in a Secondary School Special Needs Unit' (Greenstein, 2014).

In the next example of research, Gorard explored how children understand 'fairness' and some of the complexities involved. Given the emphasis on inclusion, equality, equity and allocation of resources, this international research is included to provide another lens through which to view the issues.

Example of research: Experiencing fairness at school

This study involved 13,000 pupils in five countries: French-speaking Belgium, the Czech Republic, England, France and Italy. Gorard's article opens with a discussion of fairness and some of the complexities involved. This resonates with our earlier discussion about inclusion since he asserts that any 'single formulation will tend to lead to injustice in some situations' (2012, 128). Gorard poses the rhetorical question, 'Should schools and teachers discriminate between pupils?' and responds, 'We probably would not want schools to use more funds to educate boys than girls, or offer different curriculum subjects to different ethnic groups. But we might want schools to use more funds for pupils with learning difficulties, or to respect the right of each pupil to gain a qualification in their first language' (2012, 128). This exemplifies some of the complexities involved and, drawing on earlier research, Gorard sets out six principles of fairness and applies them to various educational activities. There isn't an assumption that all the principles will apply to any particular area.

Table 8.1 Some principles of justice and the areas in which they might be applied

Principles	Domains or settings		
	School procedures	Classroom interactions	Final outcome
Recognize merit			*
Equal opportunities	*		
Equal outcome	*		*
Respect individual		*	
Fair procedures		*	*
Appropriate treatment	*		

Source: Based on Gorard, 2012, 129, Table 1

In the article, Gorard drew on earlier research to assert that 'low achievers and pupils from socially disadvantaged backgrounds feel more injustice from their teachers than other pupils' (2012, 129), and that 'The judgements on justice in schools expressed by the least able pupils are sometimes more severe that those expressed by others, either because they *were* more often the victims of school injustice, or because they tended to emphasise external causal attributions' (2012, 129).

The data for this article involved a survey which took place in 2006/07 and involved children with an average age of fourteen. The participants came from five countries: Belgium (n=1608), Czech Republic (n=1,512), England (n=2,836), France (n=3,626) and Italy (n=2,992). The data was gathered through a questionnaire. Where appropriate, reasonable adjustments were made, such as having 'the questions read to the pupil and the answer written for them [the pupil], and some took part as if it were a structured interview' (2012, 130).

Table 8.2 Percentage agreeing with statements about how schools should be run

	Belgium	Czech Republic	England	France	Italy
All pupils should be treated with equal respect.	94	92	84	93	94
Teachers should treat pupils' opinions with respect even if they disagree.	94	87	87	93	86
Teachers should take care not to humiliate pupils.	90	92	80	91	90
Teachers should continue explaining until all understand.	88	82	81	84	85
Pupils' marks should reflect the quality of their work.	81	91	71	81	84
Teachers should praise deserving pupils.	81	80	87	82	72
Pupils' marks should reflect their efforts.	73	73	69	77	72
Teachers should treat hard-working pupils the best.	20	10	27	22	27

Source: Based on Gorard, 2012, 134, Table 8

In the first section of the findings, Gorard reports the data under the headings:

- The treatment of individual pupils by the teachers;
- The treatment of all pupils by the teachers;
- The interaction of pupils with other pupils.

He then moves on to write about 'Views of justice in schools'. The percentage of children agreeing with each of eight statements is provided.

Gorard comments that 'It is, according to these respondents, fair for pupils struggling through no fault of their own to be given extra attention … It is also fair for teachers to allocate marks and praise differentially in proportion to talent and effort. Respect does not have to be deserved, in this logic, but a reward does' (2012, 134).

In addition to this type of question, the questionnaire included some vignettes as a way in which to 'understand more about the conflicting criteria of justice in play when making decisions about equity' (2012, 134). The example provided was about how a teacher should respond to a girl who has difficulty in reading and is therefore struggling to keep up with the class. The respondents were offered a three-way choice between the teacher spending more time with this pupil, the pupil working harder to keep up with the rest of the class and the pupil being taught in another class. Gorard provided the data for each country.

The final part of the article identified and discussed some of the themes linked to 'Implications for equity and the preparation of teachers' (2012, 135). This section opens with the comment that:

> despite the different school systems and countries involved in this study, the views of the pupils are very similar on many issues … Their [the pupils] views on how schools **should** be run shows that children distinguish between the universal aspects of fairness, such as respect for pupils by teachers, and the discriminatory ones, such as merited reward and punishment. They generally (over 90%) want all pupils treated with equal respect, and for teachers to take care not to humiliate them, even though this is not what they reported experiencing.
>
> (2012, 135; emphasis in original)

Reflections on the research
Gorard makes a link between pupils' views of fairness and teacher education. Indeed the theme of teacher education/development has been referred to in several of the chapters of this book (e.g. Chapters 1 and 2).

Activity 1
Review the findings in Table 8.2 and consider how you would respond to the questions. Do this either by remembering your own schooling or with reference to your current educational setting. What does this tell you about how you understand justice/equity/fairness? (If you have access to a current pupil of a similar age (fourteen), you could try the questionnaire with them.)

Activity 2
Gorard comments that 'Perhaps the major difference between countries is that pupils in the more comprehensive school system at age 14 of England are less tolerant of extra help given to a struggling pupil. This may be because they are more likely to encounter diversity of talent and motivation than pupils in heavily selected and tracked systems elsewhere' (2012, 136).

How do you reconcile this finding and the comments about it with the movement towards more inclusive education? (Hint: be wary of reducing inclusion to simply the location of the education.)

The above research illustrates a particular methodology (questionnaire including vignettes) that might just as easily have been used with adults as with children. (Indeed, vignettes were used in the report by the World Bank cited in Chapter 2.) Throughout this book, varied forms of research (including examples that involved images, drama, poetry, focus groups, interviews and narratives) have been used. A question that this raises is whether inclusive research (or even research that is gathering data from children) requires data-gathering approaches that are distinct and different from those used with adults. That is the focus of the next section.

Are the methods of data collection needed for working with children different from those used for working with adults?

It is reasonable to ask whether there are different methods needed for research conducted with children. This also links to how we see children, a topic considered in Part I of this book. Are they so different from adults that we need other ways to collect data? Or are they similar enough that we can use the same approaches, albeit in a more nuanced manner? Can the category 'children' be viewed as a homogenous group so that methods appropriate to one child are appropriate for all? You may remember Shier's comments on this in Chapter 3.

One way to develop a response to the question about research methods is to review the examples of research presented in this book and consider whether the methods *could* be used with adults and whether there is evidence that they *have* been used. Another approach is to consider whether there are examples of research methods used with adults (particularly those with different resources) that have later been adapted for use with children.

Activity

Select one chapter of this book and locate all the examples of research. For the purposes of this activity don't consider the findings but focus on the research methods. Complete the following activities:

1 Compile a list of how the data was collected.
2 Where possible, list how it was analysed
3 Note any information about dissemination (excluding the journal article).

Is anything you have identified exclusive to either adults or children?

An obvious answer to this general question about whether some approaches can be used with children and adults is 'yes'; methods such as interviews and observations fall into this classification although the levels of support for the participants need to be matched to the participants' resources. This was a point made by Foley in Chapter 7. There are also examples where a data-collection method designed for groups of adults with particular resources has informed research with children. The following qualitative research example was undertaken to explore children's multicultural awareness.

Some researchers assume that there are realities that can be known, whilst others assume 'that there are multiple realities that are constructed by social actors' (Elton-Chalcraft, 2011, 187). The first approach can be labelled a realist perspective whilst the second is constructivist.

Example of research: Jelly beans

Elton-Chalcraft viewed children's attitudes and knowledge as socially constructed. She therefore needed to design a research approach that would allow her to access those views. She provided two quotations to illustrate that the children understood her aims: Manpreet, a British Asian Sikh girl, said 'So you want to find out what we think – like we are a computer with information and you click on it'. Similarly Mahvesh, a British Asian Muslim girl from one of the pilot multiethnic schools, said 'We are like dictionaries, Miss, you can look things up in us' (2011, 188). The second of these quotations was used in all subsequent data-gathering activities to clarify Elton-Chalcraft's focus.

She worked with the children to design a prompt sheet to use in the research. This became known as the 'Bean Schedule' since for each question the children placed jelly beans to 'pictorially represent how much they felt they knew about a particular culture' (2011, 196). The convention was that:

3 beans = a lot
2 beans = a reasonable amount
1 bean = a little
0 beans = nothing

She links this to Participatory Rural Appraisal (PRA) as reported by O'Kane (2000), noting that 'PRA was originally used amongst illiterate farmers where the researcher measured their understanding of a concept by asking them to put some beans in a jar' (2011, 196).

Reflections on the research

PRA is associated with the work of Freire and with activist adult education approaches. It builds on Rapid Rural Appraisal by adding some radical activist perspectives. The additional concepts are:

- empowerment;
- respect;
- localization;
- inclusiveness.

Activity 1

Elton-Chalcraft argued that 'if rich data are to be gathered, the researcher's ontological and epistemological standpoint, their choice of research paradigm and their strategies for data collection all have to be carefully considered' (2011, 200).

1 How do you understand the terms 'ontological' and 'episte-mological'?
2 What are the links between your views and inclusive research?

Activity 2

Elton-Chalcraft did not include the children in the analysis stage 'for several reasons' (2011, 199). She mentioned time commitment and access to software. Additionally she commented that through working in all four schools she was able to see the bigger picture. Can you think of any ways in which she could have created the circumstances within which children could have been involved in the analysis?

Activity 3

PRA has recently been renamed as Participatory Learning and Action (PLA). In your view, what does the change of name signify? (Hint: you may find it useful to return to the work of Lundy in Chapter 3 and this website http://idp-key-resources.org/documents/0000/d04267/000.pdf.)

An aspect of 'action' is the focus of the next section. Undertaking research should have built into it a consideration of how it can be disseminated and how it might have impact. These are an integral part of the research process. You may remember that in the interview Shier said 'Before I start developing a research project, I've already thought about the potential impact'. The next section looks at impact in terms of both accessible dissemination and that specifically focused on those who work (or are training to work) in the education sector.

Can research be disseminated in more inclusive ways?

Predominantly, the examples of research included in this book have relied on traditional forms of research dissemination, i.e. books and journal articles. However, it has also highlighted some other ways in which the materials are shared, including the use of social media. Whilst these may appear to be opportunistic examples, they are part of a wider movement towards making research findings accessible and engaging for a wide range of audiences. For research to have greater impact, it needs to include (but also extend beyond) other academics. Even in terms of academia, there is a need to be outward-looking. In Chapter 4 (on inclusive research), reference was made to Slee, who authored the first editorial of the *International Journal of Inclusive Education*, entitled 'Supporting an International, Interdisciplinary Research Conversation' (1997). This book has emphasized the international aspects of inclusion, but with some reference to other disciplines. The next example is drawn from the Social Care area but has a wider relevance. It was selected for the breadth and innovativeness of the ideas it conveys.

Example of research: Social Care Research Impact website

This website 'arose out of activities from the Social Care Evidence in Practice Project (http://socialcareresearchimpact.org.uk/category/website), funded by the London School of Economics and Political Science's Higher Education Innovation Fund 5. It was 'designed to inspire your thinking and practice in creating impact in the field of social care research', or (more emotively), 'to revolutionise the way in which knowledge was exchanged in social care, particularly between researchers and professionals'. Specifically, it aims to help researchers:

- understand and debate what impact is;
- plan and strategize the impact and research relationship;
- consider methods and approaches to increasing impact;
- record [their] own impact activity.

The website (http://socialcareresearchimpact.org.uk/what-is-impact) refers to:

- political impact;
- economic impact;
- social impact;
- organizational impact;
- technological impact;
- legal impact;
- ecological impact;
- academic impact.

Part of the website (http://socialcareresearchimpact.org.uk/the-sceip-project-and-six-lessons-to-date) identifies the top six lessons that its authors have learnt:

- planning is important – avoid treating knowledge exchange (KE) as something that 'gets tagged on after a research project has been fully planned out';
- research doesn't end with KE;
- knowledge exchange needs time and resources;
- you should know your audience and target knowledge exchange methods to them;
- innovative knowledge exchange methods and traditional methods are not mutually exclusive;
- evaluating is important.

Activity 1
Part of their website is entitled 'Tools and Methods'. Visit this area and identify which approaches have been exemplified in this book. Look for additional ideas.

Activity 2
Can you recall any dissemination of research, regardless of the topic, that has been both effective and inclusive? If not, what does that tell you? If yes, what made it effective and inclusive?

Activity 3
As we noted earlier, Slee (1997) suggested that we should, as researchers, be 'outward looking'. This example of research was developed in relation to Social Care.

1 Do you agree that it has a wider relevance?
2 What would be the implications for how you and other researchers proceed?

It is necessary, however, to distinguish between making all the stages of research accessible and the messages about achieving a balance between the stakeholders. For example, Chapter 3 (on Childen's Participation) noted concerns about taking into account the views of parents and those of children. Would giving attention to one have a negative impact on the other group of stakeholders? Is that an unintended consequence of how research is designed?

Some examples of research report on a virtuous link between parents and children rather than highlighting potential tensions. The access – or rather the lack of access – to education for Roma children was highlighted in Chapter 2. Flecha and Soler reported on a longitudinal study undertaken in Spain. They reported on an approach that involved the whole community, stating that 'the case discussed in this article shows that when schools and communities dream together the school they want for their children, stereo-typed folk assumptions are broken down and then educational possibilities emerge' (2013, 464).

Much of the research cited in this book has privileged the data from children either by selecting articles in which all the participants were children or selecting the data from children when there was a more diverse group of participants. In other words, the approach was biased. This was intentional and a conscious effort to redress the balance away from teachers, parents and policies, on the basis that insights from children may have been undervalued.

Some of the cited research was selected to illustrate that teachers can benefit from the insights of children. Think back to the role of student researchers in the example of research by Leat and Reid (2012). There are articles that also highlight the need for reciprocity; of both being listened to and listening. This theme is neatly encapsulated in the title of an article from the USA: 'If they'll listen to us about life, we'll listen to them about school: seeing city students' ideas about "quality" teachers' (Marquez-Zenkov et al., 2007).

If we accept that children have views which don't replace, but rather complement and enhance, those of others, that leaves the question of the function of pupil voice in general and its contribution to inclusive education. The next section explores these issues.

How can schools benefit from the insights of (all) children?

Chapter 3 outlined that participation can vary in degree rather than be absent/present. It also provided a link to information about school councils, which are '[d]emocratically elected groups of pupils who represent their peers and enable pupils to become partners in their own education, making a positive contribution to the school environment and ethos' (www.school-councils.org). Whitty and Wisby (2007) researched the role of school councils and also critiqued pupil voice.

They argued that there are four main drivers of pupil voice:

- children's rights;
- active citizenship;
- school improvement;
- personalization.

All of these have been evident in this book and have been presented in a positive manner. Whitty and Wisby did, however, raise some concerns, examples of which include the following:

- They suggested that we need to be as critical of pupil voice as we have been of parent voice, which is regarded as often 'classed', 'raced' and 'gendered' (2007, 313). Their research 'revealed a significant "excluded middle" within schools – with high achieving and disaffected pupils drawn into pupil voice activities, whether out of their own initiative or through encouragement by school staff and these other pupils being allowed to remain outside such provision' (2007, 314). This links back to the ideas behind *The Danger of a Single Story* in terms of why some pupils were encouraged and others were not.
- They also questioned how far pupils were 'being allowed a voice other than to legitimise the policies of the Government or school leaders' (2007, 314). Pupil voice has the potential to challenge the status quo (again, think back to the work of Leat and Reid [2012]). They stated that 'where there is no such potential for challenge there is a real danger that school councils will produce a cohort of young people convinced that democracy is tokenistic and sham' (2007, 314).
- They also posed the question 'Is pupil voice then largely about making

pupils responsible for the success of their school? And, if so, on whose terms?' (2007, 315)

This summary provides a flavour of their findings and was included to provide a critique of something that is often treated as inherently good. It is not intended to deny the potential of pupil voice but rather as a restatement of the need to approach all initiatives from a critical perspective.

This example may challenge some of the stereotypes that exist. This comment relates to who is involved in school councils. It is suggested that two groups of pupils are present albeit their backgrounds are rather different but they also referred to a group that rarely receives attention, the 'excluded middle'. This is a group that has received little explicit attention in this book.

In what ways can inclusive research and inclusive education, as presented in this book, be linked?

If attention now turns to inclusive education and inclusive research, it would allow us to reconsider the potential links. That was the theme of a recent paper by Nind (2014b) entitled 'Inclusive research and inclusive education: why connecting them makes sense for teachers' and learners' democratic development of education'. She poses several questions, including:

- What do inclusive research and inclusive education have in common?
- Where have the moves towards inclusive (participatory and emancipatory) research happened and why?
- How viable are the claims to the moral superiority of inclusive research?
- What kinds and quality of knowledge does inclusive research produce?

Activity 1

Reflect on the contents of this book.

1 in the accounts of 'inclusive (participatory and emancipatory) research' have there been any claims to moral superiority?
2 If there has been a claim, was it justified?

Part I of this book was planned to give you a sense of the areas of commonality between inclusive education and inclusive research. The latter is linked to emancipatory and participatory research, and predominantly the examples of research have foregrounded the view of children. This section argues that there are four ways in which inclusive education and inclusive research can be linked.

There is strong encouragement for teaching to be evidence-based, which raises the question of what constitutes evidence. This book has illustrated a wide range of research approaches, but has not included randomized controlled trials. Some (though not all) would suggest that these are the 'gold standard'. However, given the nuanced, complex and contextually based nature of inclusive education, there is scope for other forms of research. Therefore one link between inclusive research and inclusive education is that the former enriches and extends the ways in which we can understand the latter. Learning about inclusive research extends the repertoire of approaches available to researchers. They can consider why, when and how it would be appropriate.

A second link is the extent to which the findings can inform inclusive education in terms of policy and practice. There has been consistent encouragement for you to critically reflect on each example of research, with the aspiration that you will reflect on both the processes and the findings – this aspect was evident in Chapters 5, 6 and 7. Additionally, the insights provided open up further aspects for further research. The messages from children about their physical environment (e.g. Chapter 5) drew on all the senses, and whilst there is published research around light and sound, the issue of smell is rarely mentioned. This could be an area for further research.

From the perspective of those involved in the research, there is a further potential benefit. The case has been made that citizens should be able to understand research, and this book has illustrated a number of instances where being included in the process has had an educational dimension. For example, revisit the examples of those with learning difficulties being involved in data analysis (Chapter 4) or the children from Nicaragua influencing policy (Chapter 3).The boundary between education and research is blurred in the sense that engagement in research has an educational dimension which can benefit all learners.

A fourth potential use involves a variation on inclusive research. The origins of inclusive research are associated with learning difficulties. The 'research involves people who may otherwise be seen as subjects for the research as instigators of ideas, research designers, interviewers, data analysts, authors, disseminators and users' (Walmsley and Johnson, 2003, 10). That description does not need to be restricted to those with learning difficulties. This chapter has already illustrated how some potentially marginalized adults can be included in research (Elton-Chalcraft, 2011) and the value of a community-based approach (Flecha and Soler, 2013).

The families linked to those involved in inclusive education could fit the description rather than being seen as the passive recipients of services or as 'warrior' parents fighting for their own children. As a parent, Truss wrote of her experiences of 'accessing help and support for her son, Peter' (2008, 376). She goes well beyond a personal account of her experiences to an analysis from a parental perspective of the SEN system, which she sees as including at least three distinct domains: educational, legal and medical. Her child concurrently occupies spaces as a 'pupil', a 'case' and a 'patient' (2008, 365). She also makes reference to the 'emotional domain' (2008, 375). Her concluding comment is that 'Achieving "whole systems" change is an arduous process involving multiple interventions at all levels, it can only succeed if the rights and need of children with disabilities are placed at the centre of the political agenda' (2008, 376). She was occupying a space that was markedly different from that of a passive respondent to research designed by a researcher.

Black-Hawkins and Amrhein (2014) also made a link between inclusive research and a group of adults, in this case student teachers.

Example of research: Researching inclusively in inclusive education?

Black-Hawkins and Amrhein's research involved student teachers in German and England. They adapted the principles set out by Walmsley and Johnson to inclusive research in initial teacher education.

Table 8.3 Inclusive research in initial teacher education (adapted from Walmsley and Johnson, 2003, 64, using authors' highlighting)

Researching with people with learning disabilities	Researching with student teachers
The research problem must be one that is owned (though not necessarily initiated) by disabled people.	The research problem must be one that is owned (though not necessarily initiated) by *student teachers*.

Researching with people with learning disabilities	Researching with student teachers
It should further the interests of disabled people; non-disabled researchers should be on the side of people with learning difficulties.	It should further the interests of *student teachers*; teacher educators should be on the side of student teachers.
It should be collaborative – people with learning disabilities should be involved in the process of doing the research.	It should be collaborative – *student teachers* should be involved in the process of doing the research.
People with learning disabilities should be able to exert some control over process and outcomes.	*Student teachers* should be able to exert some control over process and outcomes.
The research question, process and reports must be accessible to people with learning disabilities.	The research question, process and reports must be accessible to *student teachers*.

Source: Based on Black-Hawkins and Amrhein, 2014, 361

In their final reflections, the authors suggest the importance

> *of aligning the values that underpin our understanding of inclusive education with those that inform our methodical decisions and approaches. Maintaining the integrity of our work, as both researchers and teacher educators, was also a way of modelling inclusive values and practices in our teaching and learning with student teachers.*

(2014, 370)

Reflections on the research

Activity 1
Using Table 8.3 as a model, can you apply the principles of inclusive research as articulated by Walmsley and Johnson to any other groups?

Chapter activities

The following activities have been designed to help reflect on some of the key concerns over the chapter as a whole.

Activity 1
This chapter cannot highlight all of the themes that pervade this

book, and that was never the intention. Rather, it was provided to illustrate that a holistic approach is appropriate and to illustrate how you can track themes.

1 Review this book and reflect on the themes that were identified in this chapter and the extent to which they were evident to you.
2 Consider whether there were other recurrent themes that could have been identified.

Activity 2
This book has drawn on a wide range of sources from different disciplines, from different locations and written at different times.

1 Inclusion has been portrayed as being a worldwide, interdisciplinary concern. Review the examples of research in terms of:
    • the country or countries where it was undertaken;
    • the discipline of the researchers.
2 The journals cited include: *Disability and Rehabilitation, International Journal of Inclusive Education, European Journal of Special Needs Education* and *British Journal of Special Education.* What might the titles indicate about the values of the journals?

Activity 3
The terminology used by policy-makers, researcher, practitioners and children is contentious. You will remember that in Chapter 3 Shier critiqued the use of the term 'child'. Review the research examples for the terms used by the authors for children and reflect on the terms. What would be your preferred term and why?

Summary

This chapter has:

• encouraged you to examine themes across the chapter;
• considered the quality of research in relation to inclusive education and some of the challenges involved;
• drawn attention to the influence of individuals' biographies in the arena of research;
• presented another perspective on stereotyping;
• considered the nature of inclusive research.

Further reading

Gorard, S. and B. H. See (2011). 'How can we Enhance Enjoyment of Secondary school? The Student View'. *British Educational Research Journal* 37 (4): 671–90.
Some the research cited in this book has conveyed the sense of 'fun' for young people and the importance of play. It is easy to read into those examples a sense of enjoyment, but there is also a perception that it declines (and is maybe less valued in secondary education). Enjoyment can be viewed as an outcome in its own right but also 'as a characteristic of students who want to achieve well, want to participate and progress further in education training, and are confident, responsible citizens' (2011, 672). All of these are consistent with inclusive education.

Haug, P. (2014). 'Empirical Shortcomings? A Comment on Kerstin Göransson and Claes Nilholm, "Conceptual Diversities and Empirical Shortcomings – a Critical Analysis of Research on Inclusive"'. *European Journal of Special Needs Education* 29 (3): 283–5.
A comment was published alongside the article by Göransson and Nilholm (2014), and this provides an example of how academics critique each other's work.

Kumpulainen, K., L. Lipponen, J. Hilppö and A. Mikkola (2014). 'Building on the Positive in Children's Lives: A Co-Participatory Study on the Social Construction of Children's Sense of Agency'. *Early Child Development and Care* 184 (2): 211–29.
This research involved children as 'co-researchers' and explains their roles. Furthmore, it comments on the links between co-participatory practices and children's sense of agency.

Susinos, T. and I. Haya (2014). 'Developing Student Voice and Participatory Pedagogy: A Case Study in a Spanish Primary School'. *Cambridge Journal of Education* 44 (3): 385–99.
This innovative project reported on both an initiative linked to student voice and a more participatory pedagogic model.

Woolner, P., J. Clark, E. Hall, L. Tiplady, U. Thomas and K. Wall (2010). 'Pictures are Necessary but not Sufficient: Using a Range of Visual Methods to Engage Users about School Design'. *Learning Environments Research : An International Journal* 13 (1): 1–22.
In this book there has been a bias towards visual methods of data collection and to a lesser extent analysis and dissemination involving visual aspects. This article reports on using a range of visual approaches.

Research details

A critical analysis of research linked to inclusive education

This review applied strict criteria to the research associated with the inclusion of children with disabilities or in need of support. It raised questions about the availability of high quality examples.

Göransson, K. and C. Nilholm (2014). 'Conceptual Diversities and Empirical Shortcomings – a Critical Analysis of Research on Inclusive Education'. *European Journal of Special Needs Education* 29 (3): 265–80.

The role of biographies

Uniquely, two examples of research were presented in this section, each of which helped to illustrate that the biographies of each researcher were seen by them as important.

Allan, J. and R. Slee (2008) *Doing inclusive Education Research*. Rotterdam: Sense Publishers.
Southwell, N. (2006). 'Truants on Truancy – a Badness or a Valuable Indicator of Unmet Special Educational Needs?' *British Journal of Special Education* 33 (2): 91–7.

The Danger of a Single Story

This was a lecture given by Chimamanda Ngozi Adichie, who is the author of a number of books including *Purple Hibiscus* and *Half of a Yellow Sun*. She reflected on her route into reading, her education and her ambitions associated with reading.

Adichie, C. (2009). 'The Danger of a Single Story'. Available online: http://www.ted.com/talks/chimamanda_adichie_the_danger_of_a_single_story?language=en (accessed 14 July 2015).

Experiencing fairness at school

This was an international survey covering five countries, which suggested that the 'children's growing sense of fairness could be influenced by individual interaction with the teachers and the nature of the school system' (2012, 127).

Gorard, S. (2012). 'Experiencing Fairness at School: An International Study'. *International Journal of Educational Research 53*: 127–37.

Jelly beans

Elton-Chalcraft researched children's multicultural awareness. She needed to clarify with the children that her interests were in *their* views and not what their parents or teachers knew or what the books told them (2011, 190). She worked with a group of children to develop a prompt sheet which was reported in the text. However, the article has a wider significance in terms of the adult–child relationship and ethical issues.

Elton-Chalcraft, S. (2011). '"We are like dictionaries, Miss, you can look things up in us": Evaluating Child-centred Research Methods'. *Education 3–13* 39 (2): 187–202.

Social Care impact is an interactive website that addresses issues of impact and dissemination. Particular attention is given to innovative approaches, including the use of social media.

Personal Social Service Research and NIHR School for Social Care Research. (n.d.). *Social Care Research Impact.* Available online: http://socialcareresearchimpact.org.uk (accessed 5 August 2015).

9
Conclusion

Introduction and key questions

How can we summarize the main arguments and themes in this book?

First, from the outset you were encouraged to adopt a critical stance and to avoid superficiality and prejudice. There are multiple words and concepts that seem attractive and which have a 'feel-good' factor. For example, we have used terms such as inclusion, well-being and fair. However, we need to ensure that there is clarity about what the terms mean and how others are using them.

Second, we have been involved with three major themes, namely inclusive education, children's participation and inclusive/participatory research. Whilst a recurrent issue has been establishing the meaning of these terms, what is not in doubt is that there are links between them. The relationship is dynamic, fluid and complex. How inclusive education is conceptualized varies across countries and settings and over time. Although there has been promotion of children's participation for decades, progress is patchy. Inclusive education is an emerging field.

Third, we have seen how these themes are relevant in very different circumstances, whether that is the location, the focus of the research, the methodology adopted, the backgrounds of the researcher and the participants or the timeframe. The selection of the examples of research was designed to demonstrate the relevance of the issues to diverse contexts, issues, scales and participants.

Fourth, the book has illustrated that progress towards inclusive education, children's participation and inclusive/participatory research is inconsistent and often patchy. Additionally, there may be incomplete alignment between aspirations, policies, practices and lived experiences. Alongside this, we have acknowledged some of the barriers and opportunities that exist.

Fifth, despite the challenges, the tone of the book has been optimistic. By rejecting restrictive models, it is possible to avoid limiting opportunities for others. For example, children have long been viewed as dependent and in need of protection, whereas childhood has now been reconceptualized to recognize children as having views and agency. Similarly, people with disabilities were often infantilized or restricted by a view that the difficulties only resided within them, and that they alone needed to be 'fixed'. The focus needs to be more encompassing so that we reflect on the context and our own contribution to those difficulties. We have seen how blame culture can emerge so that truanting is perceived as 'bad' behaviour by the pupils rather than a comment on current provision.

Finally, what has been demonstrated is that children, all children, have views and a right to be heard. The UNCRC is universal and non-negotiable.

Having summarized the main themes, we will now present three challenging questions, designed to support you in the process of synthesizing policy, theory, research and practices. They are:

- Did engaging with this text help you to develop and become more academically literate?
- Can children's perspectives help us to rethink inclusive education?
- What can we learn from inclusive/participatory research into inclusive education?

Did engaging with this text help you to develop and become more academically literate?

This may seem a rather odd question to ask, particularly if you think books are simply about the substantive material. The point has been made that different readers gain distinctive insights from reading the same material. The differences can be attributed to factors such as prior knowledge, motivations for reading the material and levels of attention to the detail. Think back to the discussion in Chapter 8 and the video by Chimamanda entitled *The Danger of a Single Story*

Reading a book – *really* reading a book – influences the reader. It may introduce new perspectives, it may challenge preconceptions or it might strengthen the evidence for a particular viewpoint. Those changes are facilitated by adopting a critical stance. To guide that process, the introduction to this book ended with some questions. These were:

- The book is based on some values associated with inclusive education, children as active agents and the linking of policy, research and practice. Are these values evident to you? How might they have influenced the selection of themes and materials?
- Research and scholarly writing are produced for various purposes. Within the limits of this book, only some examples have been selected. In your view, are some sources more convincing than others? If so, why?
- In your view, did the selection of material result in any gaps in coverage?
- It has been noted that inclusive education is complex and contentious. Can you identify instances where cited writers disagree with each other or offer alternative perspectives? (How did you deal with these instances?) How do you understand the reasons for these disagreements or alternatives?
- Inclusive education and understandings of childhood are both evolving fields. How does the content link to your experiences? Are you convinced by the argument that international and interdisciplinary research of these topics is relevant and important?

Hopefully, you reflected on these questions as you read the book. Now is a good time to revisit them so that they can help you to review the book in its entirety.

Can children's perspectives help us to rethink inclusive education?

Progress towards inclusive education may never be complete; it has been described as a journey. Yet progress has been variable, with some concerns that it has stalled, or – in the face of competing policy imperatives – been displaced from the agenda. It may be time for a rethink.

Early in the book, it was asserted that children have views and that these should be taken into account. Consistently, the book has presented education as something to be done *with* children, rather than *to* them. Children are not passive recipients of adult knowledge which they absorb and then regurgitate. With very few exceptions, adults and children construct learning together. Further, you have been invited to consider children as stakeholders in education. These are all examples of how we conceptualize various aspects and are all associated with values; your values, and those of society – including children.

Inclusive education is about pluralism, recognizing and celebrating diversity and avoiding stereotyping or other forms of thinking that limit opportunities. Children have views about education in general and about inclusion specifically. There have been examples of the views of individual children, groups of children and whole cohorts. All were able to express views.

If we combined the values of inclusive education and children's participation, there may be synergies that would benefit both. There is ample evidence that children, when given the opportunity, can be involved in innovative ways – whether by suggesting research questions, by being researchers or buddies for researchers, or by being designers or disseminators of research. There have been examples of all of these roles and others. Children have much to offer in rethinking inclusive education and acknowledging what is important to them.

What can we learn from inclusive/ participatory research into inclusive education?

Part of the answer to this question appeared in the previous section, in the sense that there are lessons to be learnt about inclusive education itself. But there are other opportunities for learning. The book has provided a discussion of the emerging field of inclusive research, and has considered multiple examples of published research and some interviews with researchers. Whilst the fields are relatively new, they are international, and it has been possible to demonstrate the links between inclusive education and research that takes into account the views of children from countries with diverse circumstances and priorities.

The book has promoted the view that children being involved in researching education is a manifestation of inclusion. Such involvement can challenge the traditional power balances between researchers (adults) and the researched (children). Where children are treated as more than objects of research, engagement in research can be a learning opportunity in its own right. However, neither inclusive education nor research of this type can be considered as simple, universally accepted or rigid.

Attempts have been made to explore some of the links and values of these ideas. For example, Allan and Slee 'wanted to find a way of opening up some of the controversies and counterpoints that characterised research on inclusive education' (2008, 7). Their approach was to research the researchers. They tried 'to get inside the research process and explore how decisions were made, for example about the questions to be addressed in the research, who was to be included, how sense was to be made of the data, writing and the impact of the work' (2008, 7).

This book may also have made a modest contribution to your inclusive thinking by drawing your attention to research that was undertaken in diverse settings, using a range of research methodologies with a variety of participants, and that was analysed and disseminated in both traditional and innovative ways. There has been some reference to how research findings have had an impact, although that is often absent from written reports of completed research. There has also been a message about the benefits to children of engaging in research. Engaging in research is an educative process in its own right. Whilst the emphasis has been on children benefitting from research into inclusive education both through their enhanced understandings of this concept and through being researchers, those ideas also apply to you, the reader. You have read and thought about research undertaken by others and hopefully opportunities will arise for you to undertake research. There may be ideas in the examples of research that stimulate ideas – a very practical benefit of this book. However, it may be that it influences you in how you understand research and the relationship between the researcher and the researched. Allan and Slee offered some 'tentative propositions about undertaking inclusive education research – inclusively' (2008, 97). These are summarized below.

Doing inclusive education research inclusively

In the final chapter of their book, Allan and Slee considered both the challenges and benefits of inclusive education research. They describe their portrayal as 'characterised by tensions, counterpoints and controversies, with hidden dangers for those entering it …' and noted that it 'might lead to speculation on why anyone would want to do it' (2008, 97). They also pointed to a unity across researchers in this area, in the sense of 'a collective conviction amongst the researchers, that they want to make a positive difference' (2008, 97). These comments are followed by 'some tentative propositions about undertaking inclusive education research – inclusively' (2008, 97). These propositions are summarized below and more fully developed on pages 97–102 of Allan and Slee's work.

- *Itchy questions: deciding what to do.* You must really (really) want to do the research.
- *Making choices. Remember the choices are yours to make.*
- *Position yourself.* Be prepared to scrutinize your interests, motives and desires.
- *Ideology: smelling your own sweat.* Inclusive education research is never ideology-free.
- *Enabling sense-making.* Trouble your data and expect it to trouble you.
- *Writing and doing justice.* Expect to struggle with writing but also allow your writing to help with sense-making. Try, if possible, to enjoy the struggle.

- *Making an impact.* Remember, it's 'only' inclusive education research; don't expect too much.

Their final paragraph urges that researchers should be 'double-handed' and explain this through an example: 'in preparing a research proposal, students could provide a clear account of the theoretical perspectives they plan to adopt to analyse their findings, whilst also preparing to be open to alternative perspectives as the research unfolds' (2008, 102).

Activity 1

This book contains four interviews with researchers (Shier in Chapter 3, Ryan in Chapter 5, Leat et al. in Chapter 6 and Foley in Chapter 7). Reread those interviews and look for links to the 'itchy questions' above. These questions may help you but they are only examples.

1 Did any of the researchers 'smell their own sweat' (i.e. make a clear statement about their ideology)?
2 Were the motivations of the researchers explicit either in the articles or in the interviews?
3 Did any of the researchers acknowledge that they made choices?

This book has illustrated the 'tensions, controversies and counterpoints' that Allan and Slee referred to. It should also have provided reassurance that any uncertainties that you feel are shared by fellow researchers, whatever their level of experience.

Chapter activity

Activity

Think back to Chapter 4 on inclusive research, and specifically this example of research:
Morgan, J. and Sengedorj, T. (2015). '"If you were the Researcher what would you Research?": Understanding Children's Perspectives on Educational Research in Mongolia and Zambia'. *International Journal of Research & Method in Education* 38: 200–18.

In the light of your understanding after reading this book, answer the modified version of the questions by those researchers to facilitate discussion. The modification is that 'inclusion/inclusive education' has been used to replace 'school/schooling'.

- What do you understand by the term 'researcher'?
- If you were the researcher, what would you research about education and inclusive education?
- How would you research these questions?
- What do we need to think about to keep children safe and comfortable when they are answering the questions?
- Who should carry out the research? (e.g. children alone, children/adults as co-researchers or adults alone)

There are no right and wrong answers but you need to be able to say, to yourself or others, why you answered as you did.

Summary

This chapter has:

- asked you to reflect critically on your reading of the book, using the questions introduced at the end of Chapter 1;
- asked you to consider the links between inclusive education and children's participation;
- suggested links between inclusive education and inclusive research;
- prompted you to think about your own research agenda.

The book closes with a comment from Freire which is applicable to adults and children alike:

'One cannot expect positive results from any educational or political action program which fails to respect the particular view of the world held by the people. Such a program constitutes cultural invasion, good intentions notwithstanding' (1970, 84).

Further reading

Allan, J. and R. Slee (2008). *Doing Inclusive Education Research*. Rotterdam: Sense Publishers.
Whilst there are other books linking inclusive education and inclusive research, this book makes a special contribution. It accepts that both of these concepts are contentious and fraught with challenges. The authors identified a number of key researchers in the field and gathered data from them. By researching the researchers, they provided a rich and fascinating account of the differences and similarities between them, including insights into their decision-making processes and ambitions.

References

Adderley, R. J., M. A. Hope, G. C. Hughes, L. Jones, K. Messiou and P. A. Shaw (2015). 'Exploring Inclusive Practices in Primary Schools: Focusing on Children's Voices'. *European Journal of Special Needs Education* 30 (1): 106–21.

Adichie, C. (2009). *The Danger of a Single Story*. Available online: http://www.ted.com/talks/chimamanda_adichie_the_danger_of_a_single_story?language=en (accessed 14 July 2015).

African Union (1990) *The African Charter of the Rights and Welfare of the Child*. Available from: http://pages.au.int/acerwc/documents/african-charter-rights-and-welfare-child-acrwc (accessed 18 March 2016).

Ainscow, M., A. Dyson and T. Booth (2006). *Improving Schools, Developing Inclusion*. London: Routledge.

Aldridge, J. and K. Ala'l (2013). 'Assessing Students' Views of School Climate: Developing and Validating the What's Happening in this School? (WHITS) Questionnaire'. *Improving Schools* 16 (1): 47–66.

Allan, J. and R. Slee (2008). *Doing Inclusive Education Research*. Rotterdam: Sense Publishers.

Armstrong, A. C., D. Armstrong and I. Spandagou (2010). *Inclusive Education: International Policy & Practice*. London: Sage.

Bates, H., A. McCafferty, E. Quayle and K. McKenzie (2014). 'Review: Typically-developing Students' Views and Experiences of Inclusive Education'. *Disability and Rehabilitation* 37 (21): 1929–39.

Bernstein, B. (1971). 'On the Classification and Framing of Educational Knowledge'. In M. Young (ed.), *Knowledge and Control: New Directions for the Sociology of Education*. London: Macmillan.

Bernstein, B. (1975). *Class, Codes and Control Vol. 3 Towards a Theory of Educational Transmission*. London; Boston: Routledge & Kegan Paul.

Bernstein, B. (2000). *Pedagogy, Symbolic Control and Identity*. London: Rowman & Littlefield.

Biehal, N., S. Ellison, C. Baker and I. Sinclair (2009). *Characteristics, Outcomes and Meanings of Three Types of Permanent Placement – Adoption by Strangers, Adoption by Carers and Long-term Foster Care, DCSF Research Brief, DCSF-RBX-09-11*. London: Department for Children, Schools and Families.

Black-Hawkins, K. and B. Amrhein (2014). 'Valuing Student Teachers' Perspectives: Researching Inclusively in Inclusive Reducation?' *International Journal of Research & Method in Education* 37 (4): 357–75.

Black-Hawkins, K., L. Florian and M. Rouse (2007). *Achievement and Inclusion in Schools*. Abingdon: Routledge.

Board of Education Consultative Committee and Hadow, W. H. (1923). *Report of the Consultative Committee on Differentiation of the Curriculum for Boys and Girls Respectively in Secondary Schools*. London: HMSO.

Booth, T. and M. Ainscow (2011). *Index for Inclusion: Developing, Learning and Participation in Schools* (3rd edn). Bristol: Centre for Studies on Inclusive Education.

Booth, T., M. Ainscow and Centre for Studies on Inclusive Education (2002). *Index for Inclusion: Developing Learning and Participation in Schools*. Bristol: Centre for Studies on Inclusive Education.

British Educational Research Assocation (2011). 'Ethical Guidelines for Educational Research'. Available online: https://www.bera.ac.uk/wp-content/uploads/2014/02/BERA-Ethical-Guidelines-2011.pdf?noredirect=1 (accessed 5 April 2016).

CESESMA (2012) 'Learning to Live without Violence'. Available online: http://www.harryshier.net/docs/CESESMA-Learn_to_live_without_violence.pdf (accessed 20 February 2016).

Changing Faces (2016) 'Face Equality on Film Campaign'. Available online: https://www.changingfaces.org.uk/Face-Equality/face-equality-on-film (accessed 20 February 2016).

Children's Rights Alliance for England (2009). 'Beyond Article 12: The Local Implementation of the UN Convention on the Rights of the Child'. Available online: http://www.crae.org.uk/publications-resources/beyond-article-12-the-local-implementation-of-the-un-convention-on-the-rights-of-the-child (accessed 2 June 2015).

Cigman, R. (2007). *Included or Excluded?: The Challenge of the Mainstream for Some SEN Children*. London: Routledge.

Cobbett, M., C. McLaughlin and S. Kiragu (2013). 'Creating "Participatory Spaces": Involving Children in Planning Sex Education Lessons in Kenya, Ghana and Swaziland'. *Sex Education* 13: S70–83.

Cooper, P. and B. Jacobs (2011). *From Inclusion to Engagement: Helping Students Engage with Schooling through Policy and Practice*. Chichester: Wiley-Blackwell.

Costa, A. L. and B. Kallick (2000). *Discovering & Exploring Habits of Mind*. Alexandria, VA: Association for Supervision and Curriculum Development.

Cross, A. B., S. Hall, M. Hulme, J. Lewin and S. McKinney (2009). 'Pupil Participation in Scottish Schools: Final Report'. Available online: http://eprints.gla.ac.uk/49601/1/id49601.pdf (accessed 13 March 2016).

D'Alessio, S. and A. Watkins (2009). 'International Comparisons of Inclusive Policy and Practice: Are We Talking about the Same Thing?' *Research in Comparative and International Education* 4 (3): 233–49.

Dawson, E. (2014). 'Equity in Informal Science Education: Developing an Access and Equity Framework for Science Museums and Science Centres'. *Studies in Science Education* 50 (2): 209–47.

Delors, J. (1996). *Learning: The Treasure Within: Report to UNESCO of the International Commission on Education for the Twenty-first Century*. Paris: UNESCO.

Department for Education (2013). 'National Curriculum in England: Framework for Key Stages 1 to 4'. Available online: https://www.gov.uk/government/publications/national-curriculum-in-england-framework-for-key-stages-1-to-4/the-national-curriculum-in-england-framework-for-key-stages-1-to-4 (accessed 18 March 2016).

Department for Education and Skills (2001). *Inclusive Schooling: Children with Special Educational Needs*. London: DfES.

Duffell, N. (2000). *The Making of Them: The British Attitude to Children and the Boarding School System*. London: Lone Arrow.

Dyson, A. (2001). 'Special Needs in the Twenty-first Century: Where we have Been and Where we are Going'. *British Journal of Special Education* 28 (1): 24–9.

Education Scotland: Curriculum Review Group (2004). 'A Curriculum for Excellence'. Available online: http://www.educationscotland.gov.uk/learningandteaching/thecurriculum/whatiscurriculumforexcellence/thepurposeofthecurriculum/index.asp(accessed 24 June 2015).

Edwards, R., P. Armstrong and N. Miller (2001). 'Include Me Out: Critical Readings of Social Exclusion, Social Inclusion and Lifelong Learning'. *International Journal of Lifelong Education* 20 (5): 417–28.

Electoral Commission (2014) 'Scottish Independence Referendum Report on the Referendum Held on 18 September 2014'. Available online: http://www.electoralcommission.org.uk/__data/assets/pdf_file/0010/179812/Scottish-independence-referendum-report (accessed 18 March 2016).

Elton-Chalcraft, S. (2011). '"We are like Dictionaries, Miss, you can look things up in us": Evaluating Child-centred Research Methods'. *Education 3–13* 39 (2): 187–202.

Epstein, S. E. and J. Lipschultz (2012). 'Getting Personal? Student Talk about Racism'. *Race, Ethnicity and Education* 15 (3): 379–404.

European Agency for Development in Special Needs Education (2003). *Key Principles for Special Needs Education: Recommendations for Policy Makers*. Middelfart, Denmark: European Agency for Development in Special Needs Education.

European Agency for Development in Special Needs Education (2009). *Key Principles for Promoting Quality in Inclusive Education: Recommendations for Policy Makers*. Odense, Denmark: European Agency for Development in Special Needs Education.

European Agency for Development in Special Needs Education (2011). *Participation in Inclusive Education: A Framework for Developing Indicators*. Odense, Denmark: European Agency for Development in Special Needs Education.

European Agency for Development in Special Needs Education (2012). *Teacher Education for Inclusion: Profile of Inclusive Teachers*. Odense, Denmark: European Agency for Development in Special Needs Education.

Flecha, R. and M. Soler (2013). 'Turning Difficulties into Possibilities: Engaging Roma Families and Students in School through Dialogic Learning'. *Cambridge Journal of Education* 43 (4): 451–65.

Flechtner, S. (2014). 'Aspiration Traps: When Poverty Stifles Hope'. Available online: http://www.worldbank.org/content/dam/Worldbank/document/Poverty%20documents/inequality-in-focus-january2014-final.pdf (accessed 28 February 2016).

Flutter, J. and J. Rudduck (2004). *Consulting Pupils: What's in it for Schools?* London: RoutledgeFalmer.

Foley, K. R., S. Girdler, A. M. Blackmore, M. O'Donnell, R. Glauert, H. Leonard and G. Llewellyn (2012). 'To Feel Belonged: The Voices of Children and Youth with Disabilities on the Meaning of Wellbeing'. *Child Indicators Research* 5 (2): 375–91.

Freire, P. (1970). *Pedagogy of the Oppressed*. New York: Herder and Herder.

Freire, P. (1982) 'Creating Alternative Research Methods. Learning to do it by Doing it'. In B. Hall, A. Gillette and R. Tandon (eds), *Creating Knowledge: A Monopoly*. New Delhi: Society for Participatory Research in Asia, 29–37.

Göransson, K. and C. Nilholm (2014). 'Conceptual Diversities and Empirical Shortcomings – a Critical Analysis of Research on Inclusive Education'. *European Journal of Special Needs Education* 29 (3): 265–80.

Gorard, S. (2012). 'Experiencing Fairness at School: An International Study'. *International Journal of Educational Research* 53: 127–37.

Gorard, S. and B. H. See (2011). 'How can We Enhance Enjoyment of Secondary School? The Student View'. *British Educational Research Journal* 37 (4): 671–90.

Greenstein, A. (2014). 'Today's Learning Objective is to have a Party: Playing Research with Students in a Secondary School Special Needs Unit'. *Journal of Research in Special Educational Needs* 14 (2): 71–81.

Griffiths, E. (2007). '"They're gonna think we're the dumb lot because we go to the special school": A Teacher Research Study of how Mainstream and Special School Pupils View Each Other'. *Research in Education* (78): 78–87.

Gyimah, E. K., D. Sugden and S. Pearson (2008). 'An Investigation into the Emotional Reactions to Inclusion of Ghanaian Mainstream Teachers'. *Support for Learning* 23 (2): 71–9.

Hanko, G. (2003). 'Towards an Inclusive School Culture – but What Happened to Elton's "Affective Curriculum"?' *British Journal of Special Education* 30 (3): 125–31.

Hart, R. A. (1992). *Children's Participation: From Tokenism to Citizenship.* Florence: UNICEF International Child Development Centre.

Hartas, D. (2011). 'Young People's Participation: Is Disaffection Another Way of Having a Voice?' *Educational Psychology in Practice* 27 (2): 103–15.

Haug, P. (2014). 'Empirical Shortcomings? A Comment on Kerstin Göransson and Claes Nilholm, "Conceptual Diversities and Empirical Shortcomings – a Critical Analysis of Research on Inclusive"'. *European Journal of Special Needs Education* 29 (3): 283–5.

Hemingway, J. and F. Armstrong (2012). 'Space, Place and Inclusive Learning'. *International Journal of Inclusive Education* 16 (5–6): 479–83.

Hickling-Hudson, A. (2000). '"Post Marxist" Discourse and the Rethinking of Third World Education Reform'. In A. Welch (ed.), *Third World Education: Quality and Equality.* New York: Garland, 177–201.

Hodkinson, A. and P. Vickerman (2009). *Key Issues in Special Educational Needs and Inclusion.* London: Sage.

Howgego, C., S. Miles and J. Myers (2014). 'Inclusive Learning: Children with Disabilities and Difficulties in Learning'. Available online: http://www. heart-resources.org/wp-content/uploads/2014/09/Inclusive-Learning-Topic-Guide.pdf (accessed 5 April 2016).

Inclusion BC (2016) 'Our Vision for 2015'. Available online: http://www. inclusionbc.org/our-priority-areas/inclusive-education (accessed 20 April 2016).

Jones, P. (2009). *Rethinking Childhood: Attitudes in Contemporary Society.* London: Continuum.

Kellett, M. (2005). *How to develop children as researchers: A step-by-step guide to teaching the research process.* London: Paul Chapman.

Kellett, M. (2010). *Rethinking Children and Research: Attitudes in Contemporary Society.* London: Continuum.

Kesby, M. (2005). 'Retheorizing Empowerment-through-Participation as a Performance in Space: Beyond Tyranny to Transformation'. *Signs* 30 (4): 2037–66.

Kesby, M. (2007). 'Methodological Insights on and from Children's Geographies'. *Children's Geographies* 5 (3): 193–205.

Kingsley, C. (1893). *The Water-Babies: A Fairy Tale for a Land Baby.* New York: Frederick A. Stokes Co.

Koller, D. and V. San Juan (2015). 'Play-based Interview Methods for Exploring Young Children's Perspectives on Inclusion'. *International Journal of Qualitative Studies in Education* 28 (5): 610–31.

Kramer, J. M., J. C. Kramer, E. García-Iriarte and J. Hammel (2011). 'Following through to the End: The Use of Inclusive Strategies to Analyse and Interpret Data in Participatory Action Research with Individuals with Intellectual Disabilities'. *Journal of Applied Research in Intellectual Disabilities* 24 (3): 263–73.

Kumpulainen, K., L. Lipponen, J. Hilppö and A. Mikkola (2014). 'Building on the Positive in Children's Lives: A Co-participatory Study on the Social Construction of Children's Sense of Agency'. *Early Child Development and Care* 184 (2): 211–29.

Lansdown, G. (2005). *The Evolving Capacities of the Child*. Florence: UNICEF Innocenti Research Centre.

Leat, D. and A. Reid (2012). 'Exploring the Role of Student Researchers in the Process of Curriculum Development'. *Curriculum Journal* 23 (2): 189–205.

Leeson, C. (2013). 'Asking Difficult Questions: Exploring Research Methods with Children on Painful Issues'. *International Journal of Research & Method in Education* 37 (2): 206–22.

Levin, B. (2000). 'Putting Students at the Centre in Education Reform'. *Journal of Educational Change* 1 (2): 155–72.

Levy, R. and P. Thompson (2015). 'Creating "Buddy Partnerships" with 5- and 11-year-old Boys: A Methodological Approach to Conducting Participatory Research with Young Children'. *Journal of Early Childhood Research* 13 (2): 137–49.

Lewis, A. (2010). 'Silence in the Context of "Child Voice"'. *Children & Society* 24 (1): 14–23.

Lewis, A. and B. Norwich (2005). *Special Teaching for Special Children? Pedagogies for Inclusion*. Maidenhead: Open University Press.

Llewellyn, G. (2012). 'Indicators of Health and Well-being for Children and Young People with Disabilities: Mapping the Terrain and Proposing a Human Rights Approach'. Available online: http://www.aracy.org.au/publications-resources/command/download_file/id/105/filename/Indicators_of_Health_and_Well-being_for_Children_and_Young_people_with_disabilities_-_literature_review.pdf (accessed 18 March 2016).

Lundy, L. (2007). '"Voice" is not Enough: Conceptualising Article 12 of the United Nations Convention on the Rights of the Child'. *British Educational Research Journal* 33 (6): 927–42.

Lyle, S. (2014). 'Embracing the UNCRC in Wales (UK): Policy, Pedagogy and Prejudices'. *Educational Studies* 40 (2): 215–32.

Marquez-Zenkov, K., J. Harmon, P. van Lier and M. Marquez-Zenkov (2007). '"If they'll listen to us about life, we'll listen to them about school": Seeing

City Students' Ideas about "Quality" Teachers'. *Educational Action Research* 15 (3): 403–15.

McConachie, H., A. F. Colver, R. J. Forsyth, S. N. Jarvis and K. N. Parkinson (2006). 'Participation of Disabled Children: How should it be Characterised and Measured?' *Disability & Rehabilitation* 28 (18): 1157–64.

McCoy, S. and J. Banks (2012). 'Simply Academic? Why Children with Special Educational Needs Don't Like School'. *European Journal of Special Needs Education* 27 (1): 81–97.

McInerney, P. and J. Smyth (2014). '"I want to get a piece of paper that says I can do stuff": Youth Narratives of Educational Opportunities and Constraints in Low Socio-economic Neighbourhoods'. *Ethnography and Education* 9 (3): 239–52.

McIntyre, D. (2004). 'Important Questions about Consultation'. In M. Arnot, D. McIntyre, D. Pedder and D. Reay (eds), *Consultation in the Classroom: Developng Dialogue about Teaching and Learning*. Cambridge: Pearson, 3–6.

McLaughlin, C. and S. Swartz (2011). 'Can we Use Young People's Knowledge to Develop Teachers and HIV-related Education?' *Prospects: Quarterly Review of Comparative Education* 41 (3): 429–44.

McLeod, A. (2007). 'Whose Agenda? Issues of Power and Relationship when Listening to Looked-after Young People'. *Child & Family Social Work* 12 (3): 278–86.

McQuillan, P. J. (2005). 'Possibilities and Pitfalls: A Comparative Analysis of Student Empowerment'. *American Educational Research Journal* 42 (4): 639–70.

Messiou, K. (2006). 'Conversations with Children: Making Sense of Marginalization in Primary School Settings'. *European Journal of Special Needs Education* 21 (1): 39–54.

Messiou, K. (2012). *Confronting Marginalisation in Education: A Framework for Promoting Inclusion*. London: Routledge.

Miles, S. and I. Kaplan (2005). 'Using Images to Promote Reflection: An Action Research Study in Zambia and Tanzania'. *Journal of Research in Special Educational Needs* 5 (2): 77–83.

Ministry of Gender, Labour and Social Development and UNICEF (2008). 'National Child Participation Guide for Uganda'. Available online: http://en.kindernothilfe.org/multimedia/KNH/Downloads/Fremdsprache_+Englisch/Child+Participation+Guide+Uganda+Final.pdf (accessed 15 June 2015).

Mintz, J. (2014). *Professional Uncertainty, Knowledge, and Relationship in the Classroom: A Psychosocial Perspective*. London: Routledge.

Mittler, P. (2008). 'Planning for the 2040s: Everybody's Business'. *British Journal of Special Education* 35 (1): 3–10.

Moll, L. C., C. Amanti, D. Neff and N. Gonzalez (1992). 'Funds of Knowledge for Teaching: Using a Qualitative Approach to Connect Homes and Classrooms'. *Theory into Practice 31* (2): 132–41.

Morgan, J. and T. Sengedorj (2015). '"If you were the researcher what would you research?": Understanding Children's Perspectives on Educational Research in Mongolia and Zambia'. *International Journal of Research & Method in Education* 38 (2): 200–18.

Moriña Díez, A. (2010). 'School Memories of Young People with Disabilities: An Analysis of Barriers and Aids to Inclusion'. *Disability & Society* 25 (2): 163–75.

Morrison, T. (1987). *Beloved: A Novel.* New York: Knopf.

Nind, M. (2011). 'Inclusive Education Research'. *Research Intelligence* 115: 18.

Nind, M. (2014a). *What is Inclusive Research?* London: Bloomsbury.

Nind, M. (2014b). 'Inclusive Research and Inclusive Education: Why Connecting them Makes Sense for Teachers' and Learners' Democratic Development of Education'. *Cambridge Journal of Education* 44 (4): 525–40.

Nind, M., S. Benjamin, K. Sheehy, J. Collins and K. Hall (2004). 'Methodological Challenges in Researching Inclusive School Cultures'. *Educational Review* 56 (3): 259–70.

Nind, M., G. Boorman and G. Clarke (2012). 'Creating Spaces to Belong: Listening to the Voice of Girls with Behavioural, Emotional and Social Difficulties through Digital Visual and Narrative Methods'. *International Journal of Inclusive Education* 16 (7): 643–56.

Nind, M. and H. Vinha (2012). 'Doing Research Inclusively, Doing Research Well?' Available online: https://www.southampton.ac.uk/assets/imported/transforms/content-block/UsefulDownloads_Download/97706C004C4F4E68A8B54DB90EE0977D/full_report_doing_research.pdf (accessed 7 April 2016).

O'Boyle, A. (2013). 'Valuing the Talk of Young People: Are We Nearly There Yet?' *London Review of Education* 11: 127–39.

O'Kane, C. (2000). 'The Development of Participatory Techniques: Facilitating Children's Views about Decisions which Affect Them'. In P. Christensen and A. James (eds), *Research with Children: Perspectives and Practices.* London: Falmer Press, 136–59.

OfSTED (2000). *Evaluating Educational Inclusion: Guidance for Inspectors and School.* London: OfSTED

OfSTED (2011). 'Schools and Parents'. Available online: https://www.gov.uk/government/uploads/system/uploads/attachment_data/file/413696/Schools_and_parents.pdf (accessed 7 April 2016).

Organisation for Economic Co-operation and Development (2012). 'Equity and Quality in Education Supporting Disadvantaged Students and Schools'. Available online: /z-wcorg/ database Available from http://public.

eblib.com/choice/publicfullrecord.aspx?p=873379 (accessed 18 March 2016).

Participation Works Partnership Network for England (n.d.). 'Partnership Works'. Available online: http://www.participationworks.org.uk (accessed 20 February 2016).

Pearce, G. and R. P. Bailey (2011). 'Football Pitches and Barbie Dolls: Young Children's Perceptions of their School Playground'. *Early Child Development and Care* 181 (10): 1361–79.

People First of Canada (n.d.). 'Some History'. Available online: http://www.peoplefirstofcanada.ca/about-us/history (accessed 18 March 2016).

Pinter, A. and S. Zandian (2015). '"I thought it would be tiny little one phrase that we said, in a huge big pile of papers": Children's Reflections on their Involvement in Participatory Research'. *Qualitative Research* 15 (2): 235–50.

Rich, J. (1968). *Interviewing Children and Adolescents*. London: Macmillan.

Rix, J., M. Nind, K. Sheehy, K. Simmons, J. Parry and R. Kumrai (eds) (2010). *Equality, Participation and Inclusion 2: Diverse Contexts*. London: Routledge.

Rix, J., M. Nind, K. Sheehy, K. Simmons and C. Walsh (eds) (2010b). *Equality, Participation and Inclusion 1: Diverse Perspectives*. London: Routledge.

Rojas, S., T. Susinos and A. Calvo (2013). '"Giving Voice" in Research Processes: An Inclusive Methodology for Researching into Social Exclusion in Spain'. *International Journal of Inclusive Education* 17 (2): 156–73.

Rose, R. and M. Shevlin (2004). 'Encouraging Voices: Listening to Young People who have been Marginalised'. *Support for Learning* 19 (4): 155–61.

Rudduck, J. and J. Flutter (2000). Pupil Participation and Pupil Perspective: 'Carving a New Order of Experience'. *Cambridge Journal of Education 30* (1): 75-89.

Rudduck, J. and D. McIntyre (2007). *Improving Learning through Consulting Pupils*. London: Routledge.

Rusinek, G. (2008). 'Disaffected Learners and School Musical Culture: An Opportunity for Inclusion'. *Research Studies in Music Education* 30 (1): 9–23.

Ryan, D. (2009). '"Inclusion is more than a place": Exploring Pupil Views and Voice in Belfast Schools through Visual Narrative'. *British Journal of Special Education* 36 (2): 77–84.

Save the Children (2003). *Missing Out on Education: Children and Young People Speak Out*. London: Save the Children.

Save the Children (2005). 'Practice Standards in Children's Participation'. Available online: http://www.savethechildren.org.uk/resources/online-library/practice-standards-children%E2%80%99s-participation (accessed 20 February 2016).

Save the Children (n.d). 'Monitoring, Evaluation, Accountability and Learning'. Available online: http://www.open.edu/openlearnworks/course/view.php?id=1641 (accessed 20 February 2016).

Scottish Executive (2004) 'A Curriculum for Excellence'. Available online: http://www.gov.scot/Resource/Doc/26800/0023690.pdf (accessed 7 April 2016).

Segal, S. S. (1967). *No Child is Ineducable; Special Education – Provision and Trends*. Oxford and New York: Pergamon Press.

Sensoy, Ö. (2011). 'Picturing Oppression: Seventh Graders Photo Essays on Racism, Classism, and Sexism'. *International Journal of Qualitative Studies in Education* 24 (3): 323–42.

Shaw, C., L. Brady and C. Davey (2011). 'Guidelines for Research with Children and Young People'. Available online: http://www.nfer.ac.uk/schools/developing-young-researchers/NCBguidelines.pdf (accessed 5 April 2016).

Shier, H. (2001). 'Pathways to Participation: Openings, Opportunities and Obligations'. *Children & Society* 15 (2): 107–17.

Shier, H. (2007). 'The Tao of Development'. Available online: http://www.harryshier.net/docs/Harry_Shier-Tao_of_development.pdf (accessed 20 February 2016).

Shier, H. (2010). 'Children as Public Actors: Navigating the Tensions'. *Children & Society* 24 (1): 24–37.

Shier, H. (ed.) (2012). *Learning to Live without Violence: Transformative Research by Children and Young People*. Preston: University of Central Lancashire and CESESMAc.

Shier, H. (2015). 'Children as Researchers in Nicaragua: Children's Consultancy to Transformative Research'. *Global Studies of Childhood* 5 (2): 206–19.

Shier, H., M. H. Méndez, M. Centeno, I. Arróliga and M. González (2014). 'How Children and Young People influence Policy-makers: Lessons from Nicaragua'. *Children & Society* 28 (1): 1–14.

Singal, N., R. Jeffery, A. Jain and N. Sood (2011). 'The Enabling Role of Education in the Lives of Young People with Disabilities in India: Achieved and Desired Outcomes'. *International Journal of Inclusive Education* 15 (10): 1205–18.

Singal, N. and M. Swann (2011). 'Children's Perceptions of Themselves as Learner Inside and Outside School'. *Research Papers in Education* 26 (4): 469–84.

Slee, R. (1997). 'Supporting an International, Interdisciplinary Research Conversation'. *International Journal of Inclusive Education* 1 (1): i –iv.

Slee, R. (2011). *The Irregular School: Exclusion, Schooling and Inclusive Education*. London and New York: Routledge.

Slee, R. (2013). 'How do we make Inclusive Education Happen when Exclusion is a Political Predisposition?' *International Journal of Inclusive Education* 17 (8): 895–907.

Smit, S. (2012). 'Pupils as Co-researchers'. Available online: https://www.youtube.com/watch?v=L8p8fLBx54I (accessed 6 April 2016).

Smith, E. (2005). *Analysing Underachievement in Schools*. London: Continuum.

Southwell, N. (2006). 'Truants on Truancy – a Badness or a Valuable Indicator of Unmet Special Educational Needs?' *British Journal of Special Education* 33 (2): 91–7.

Sriprakash, A. (2010). 'Child-centred Education and the Promise of Democratic Learning: Pedagogic Messages in Rural Indian Primary Schools'. *International Journal of Educational Development* 30 (3): 297–304.

Stevenson, M. (2014). 'Participatory Data Analysis Alongside Co-researchers who have Down Syndrome'. *Journal of Applied Research in Intellectual Disabilities* 27 (1): 23–33.

Sumida Huaman. E. and L. A. Valdiviezo, L. A. (January 2014). 'Indigenous Knowledge and Education from the Quechua Community to School: Beyond the Formal/non-formal Dichotomy'. *International Journal of Qualitative Studies in Education* 27 (1): 65–87.

Susinos, T. and I. Haya (2014). 'Developing Student Voice and Participatory Pedagogy: A Case Study in a Spanish Primary School'. *Cambridge Journal of Education* 44 (3): 385–99.

Sutton, L. and Joseph Rowntree Foundation (2007). *A Child's-eye View of Social Difference*. York: Joseph Rowntree Foundation.

Symonds, J. E. (2008). 'Pupil Researchers Generation X: Educating Pupils as Active Participants – an Investigation into Gathering Sensitive Information from Early Adolescents'. *Research in Education* 80 (1): 63–74.

Thomas, G. (2013). 'A Review of Thinking and Research about Inclusive Education Policy, with Suggestions for a new Kind of Inclusive Thinking'. *British Educational Research Journal* 39 (3): 473–90.

Topping, K. (2011). 'Primary-secondary Transition: Differences between Teachers' and Children's Perceptions'. *Improving Schools* 14 (3): 268–85.

Treseder, P. (1997). *Empowering Children & Young People: Training Manual*. London: Save the Children.

Truss, C. (2008). 'Peter's Story: Reconceptualising the UK SEN System'. *European Journal of Special Needs Education* 23 (4): 365–77.

UNESCO (1990). *Education for All*. Bangkok: UNESCO Principal Regional Office for Asia and the Pacific.

UNESCO (1994). *The Salamanca Statement and Framework for Action on Special Needs Education*. Paris: UNESCO.

UNESCO (2000). *The Dakar Framework for Action*. Paris: UNESCO.

UNESCO (2010). 'The Central Role of Education in the Millennium Goals'. Available online: http://www.unesco.org/new/fileadmin/MULTIMEDIA/HQ/ED/ED_new/images/education_for_all_international_coordination_new/PDF/analyticalnote.pdf (accessed 18 March 2016).

UNESCO (2012). 'World Atlas of Gender Equality in Education'. Available online: http://www.uis.unesco.org/Education/Documents/unesco-world-atlas-gender-education-2012.pdf (accessed 6 April 2016).

UNESCO (2013). 'Revisiting Learning: The Treasure Within. Assessing the Influence of the 1996 Delors Report'. Available online: http://unesdoc.unesco.org/images/0022/002200/220050e.pdf (accessed 22 February 2016).

UNESCO (2014). *Inclusion from the Start: Guidelines on Inclusive Early Childhood Care and Education for Roma Children*. Paris: UNESCO.

UNESCO (2015). *Education for All 2000–2015: Achievements and Challenges*. Paris: UNESCO.

UNESCO (n.d.). 'Different Meanings of Curriculum'. Available online: http://www.unesco.org/new/en/education/themes/strengthening-education-systems/quality-framework/technical-notes/different-meaning-of-curriculum (accessed 18 March 2016).

UNICEF (2007). *Child Poverty in Perspective: An Overview of Child Well-Being in Rich Countries: A Comprehensive Assessment of the Lives and Well-Being of Children and Adolescents in the Economically Advanced Nations*. Florence: UNICEF Innocenti Research Centre.

UNICEF (2011). *The State of the World's Children 2011: Adolescence – An Age of Opportunity*. New York: UNICEF.

UNICEF (2012). *The Right of Children with Disabilities to Education: A Rights-based Approach to Inclusive Education*. Geneva: UNICEF Regional Office for Central and Eastern Europe and the Commonwealth of Independent States (CEECIS).

UNICEF (2013). *Child Well Being in Rich Countries: A Comparative Overview*. Florence: UNICEF Office of Research – Innocenti.

United Nations (1989). 'Convention on the Right of the Child'. Available online: http://www.unicef.org.uk/Documents/Publication-pdfs/UNCRC_PRESS200910web.pdf (accessed 2 June 2016).

United Nations (2006). 'Convention on the Rights of Persons with Disabilities'. Available online: http://www.un.org/disabilities/convention/conventionfull.shtml (accessed 2 April 2016).

United Nations (2012). 'Secretary-General's Message on International Youth Day'. Available online: http://www.un.org/en/events/youthday/2012/sg.shtml (accessed 7 April 2016).

Urwick, J. and J. Elliott (2010). 'International Orthodoxy versus National Realities: Inclusive Schooling and the Education of Children with Disabilities in Lesotho'. *Comparative Education* 46 (2): 137–50.

Wagner, T. (2006). *Road Map for Arts Education; Building Creative Capacities for the 21st Century*. Paris: UNESCO.

Waller, T. and A. Bitou (2011). 'Research with Children: Three Challenges for Participatory Research in Early Childhood'. *European Early Childhood Education Research Journal* 19 (1): 5–20.

Walmsley, J. and K. Johnson (2003). *Inclusive Research with People with Learning Disabilities Past, Present, and Futures*. London: Jessica Kingsley Publishers.

Welsh Government (2011). 'Pupil Participation: Good Practice Guide'. Available online: http://www.pupilvoicewales.org.uk/uploads/publications/540.pdf (accessed 7 April 2016).

West, P., H. Sweeting and R. Young (2010) 'Transition Matters: Pupils' Experiences of the Primary–Secondary School Transition in the West of Scotland and Consequences for Well-being and Attainment'. *Research Papers in Education* 25 (1): 21–50.

Whitty, G. and E. Wisby (2007). *Real Decision Making?: School Councils in Action*. Nottingham: Department for Children, Schools and Families.

Wickenden, M. (2011). '"Talk to me as a teenager": Experiences of Friendship for Disabled Teenagers who have Little or No Speech'. *Childhoods Today* 5 (1): 1–35.

Wickenden, M. and G. Kembhavi-Tam (2014). 'Ask us too! Doing Participatory Research with Disabled Children in the Global South'. *Childhood* 21 (3): 400–17.

Woolley, H. (2013). 'Now being Social: The Barrier of Designing Outdoor Play Spaces for Disabled Children'. *Children and Society* 27 (6): 448–58.

Woolley, H., M. Armitage, J. C. Bishop, M. Curtis and J. Ginsborg (2005). *Inclusion of Disabled Children in Primary School Playgrounds*. London: National Children''s Bureau.

Woolner, P., J. Clark, E. Hall, L. Tiplady, U. Thomas and K. Wall (2010). 'Pictures are Necessary but not Sufficient: Using a Range of Visual Methods to Engage Users about School Design'. *Learning Environments Research: An International Journal* 13 (1): 1–22.

Woolner, P., E. Hall, K. Wall and D. Dennison (2007). 'Getting together to Improve the School Environment: User Consultation, Participatory Design and Student Voice'. *Improving Schools* 10 (3): 233-48.

World Bank (2006). *Equity and Development*. Washington, DC: World Bank Institute.

World Bank (2014). 'Proposed Guidance Framework for Development of Curriculum and Teaching Materials to Avoid Prejudice on Vulnerable Children Groups'. Available online: http://www-wds.worldbank.org/external/default/WDSContentServer/WDSP/IB/2014/11/24/000456286_20141124171732/Rendered/PDF/E46770EA0v20P10disclosed0110140140.pdf (accessed 24 March 2016).

World Bank (2015) 'Girls' Education'. Available online: http://www.worldbank.org/en/topic/education/brief/girls-education (accessed 28 February 2016).

YouGov (2012). 'Goodies and Baddie's. Available online: https://yougov.co.uk/

news/2012/04/16/do-bad-teeth-equal-bad-character (accessed 20 February 2016).

Yousafzai, M. and C. Lamb (2013). *I am Malala: The Girl Who Stood Up for Education and Was Shot by the Taliban*. London: Weidenfeld & Nicolson.

Index